WORK
MAKES ME
NERVOUS

WORK MAKES ME NERVOUS

OVERCOME ANXIETY *and* BUILD *the* CONFIDENCE *to* SUCCEED

JONATHAN BERENT L.C.S.W. / **AMY LEMLEY**

WILEY

JOHN WILEY & SONS, INC.

Published by John Wiley & Sons, Inc., Hoboken, New Jersey.
Published simultaneously in Canada.

For general information on our other products and services or for technical support, please contact our Customer Care Department within the United States at (800) 762-2974, outside the United States at (317) 572-3993 or fax (317) 572-4002.

Wiley also publishes its books in a variety of electronic formats. Some content that appears in print may not be available in electronic books. For more information about Wiley products, visit our web site at www.wiley.com.

ISBN 978-0-470-58805-5 (cloth); ISBN 978-0-470-88216-0 (ebk);
ISBN 978-0-470-88217-7 (ebk); ISBN 9780-470-88218-4 (ebk)

Printed in the United States of America.

10 9 8 7 6 5 4 3 2 1

For Barbara, Momo, and the creative pursuit of family
—Jonathan Berent

For Robert Emery and Mary Shemo, with gratitude
—Amy Lemley

CONTENTS

PREFACE

The Truth from Two Perspectives

Destiny. Kismet. Beshert. Throughout the world's cultures, there are words to describe the notion of fate—something that was simply meant to be. Our chance meeting on a community basketball court 20 years ago led to our writing this book together—one of us a psychotherapist and one of us a person who suffers from anxiety and avoidance. These two perspectives combine in a unique way to present the full spectrum of affliction and recovery. That is our commitment to this project—and our commitment to our readers.

—Jonathan Berent, L.C.S.W., and Amy Lemley

Ten Thousand Voices

In 1976, fresh out of graduate school in psychology, I was working as a youth counselor in a community center. An associate of mine had an idea: Establish a socialization program for teenagers with learning disabilities. A socialization program? Learning disabilities? I had no idea what she was talking about. Nevertheless, we embarked on this endeavor. I would interview applicants prior to their starting the program. A high percentage of the teenagers would not come to the group after the initial interview. What was this about? This was fate introducing me to social anxiety a long time before the term gained widespread attention. Shortly after I held this position, I started my own psychotherapy practice. From the beginning, I was working with stress-related disorders and biofeedback. This evolved into the specialty of social anxiety and performance anxiety and related issues.

Since 1977, I have treated approximately 10,000 people of all ages in individual, group, and family therapy. My clients with workplace anxiety have included C-suite executives, middle managers, and entry-level employees, bankers, salespeople, engineers, entrepreneurs, teachers, principals, professors, performers, scientists, artists, athletes—and more. As for results, I have seen it all, from a total cure to the problem being permanent and everything in between. I have served as a stress management consultant to numerous corporations and organizations including NBC, United Federation of Teachers, Technicon Science Center, Bloomingdale's, and Bankers Trust. I have worked with special needs groups also and have established a number of socialization programs for them. In addition, in 1988, I was feeling compelled to educate the community about the little-known problem of social anxiety and I embarked on a public relations campaign. Since that time, I have done more than 1,500 radio and television shows, from *Oprah* to *Opie & Anthony*. I have experienced my own dramatic learning curve with performance issues—on the front line.

My work as a psychotherapist began on a different kind of front line. I started graduate school in clinical social work in 1973. All the classes were conducted in a circle discussion group. I was new to the field of psychotherapy and experienced substantial intimidation. I worried about what I would say in class. What would the others think of me? This was not an anxiety disorder, however, but a lack of confidence.

Internships are an integral part of the graduate educational experience. My first placement was rather benign, a community center. For my second, I asked for, and received, placement as a counselor in a correctional institution. At this time in my life, I was somewhat naïve—some of my primary motivators were exploration and creativity. Later in this book, you will learn about this aspect of the personality as the "natural child mind state," which can be a wonderful, inspiring, and freeing part of yourself when correctly balanced with the other mind states you will learn about.

I had no idea what I was getting into. I found myself working in a halfway house in the Bronx, New York. My clientele consisted of adolescents who had committed serious crimes. There were 12 kids in this halfway house—50 percent of whom were there for homicide. All the residents were black or Hispanic.

I was able to develop a few relationships with clients because there was a basketball court across the street. It was a pretty wild scene, playing in this drug-infested playground. There was a pool table in the basement of the house, around which we had some interesting conversations. I recall one 16-year-old saying matter-of-factly, "I feel sorry for that woman"—"that woman" being the victim he had shot in the head and killed. At one point, one of the clients went AWOL and returned with a gun, intending to kill the resident social worker. It was then that my university took me out of this placement. I finished my internship in an elementary school in Brooklyn.

The halfway house internship was a tremendous learning opportunity for me—a multimillion-dollar educational experience, in my view—because nothing that I would ever do professionally could be as scary. I do remember feeling some anxiety at night at home, sometimes saying to myself, "I can't believe I have to go there tomorrow!" In addition to learning that rehabilitation with this clientele was a near impossibility, I also learned that anxiety is a relative phenomenon. The more I dealt with it, the easier it became to deal with. This was true for me, and I could see that it was true for others as well. At some point I began to realize, almost unconsciously, that my professional destiny was to work with anxiety.

What dramatic irony that I met Amy Lemley—a gifted writer with anxiety and avoidant personality! We wrote our first book together in 1992: *Beyond Shyness: How to Conquer Social Anxieties*. Almost 20 years later, we are working together again on a topic about which both of us are experts, though from different perspectives.

I met Amy in 1988 in East Hampton, New York. Her then-boyfriend, who also happened to be a writer, and I were involved in a regular basketball game. He introduced me to Amy, who was working as a freelance journalist and editor, and soon we were collaborating on our first book. Amy is a seasoned professional with 26 years of experience in all facets of writing—books, magazine and newspaper articles, plus columns, newsletters, Web sites, and marketing and advertising. Most people who know her do not realize that she has suffered from a little understood but extremely pervasive, almost epidemic, problem called avoidant personality disorder. This problem is caused by anxiety. Although she still confronts her natural tendency to avoid situations that might make her anxious, Amy has recovered from her addiction to avoidance (yes, addiction—more on this later in the book).

Very little is written about the avoidant personality. But in this book, as I discuss anxiety and avoidance from a clinical perspective, Amy tells her own story—the good, the bad, and the ugly along with the triumphs that have made her a success. She summarizes her experiences in the following section of this Preface. I see Amy as a role model for those who say what she says: "Work makes me nervous."

—Jonathan Berent, L.C.S.W.
East Hampton, New York

A Life in Hiding

I have spent most of my life feeling like a fraud. If people really knew me, I believed, they would think so little of me that I would face rejection constantly. My public persona has almost always been that of an outgoing, vivacious, engaging, and confident person. But I hid a terrible secret: I was anxious, avoidant, selfish, and passive-aggressive. This was true even in childhood. Here's how a first grader practices avoidance: At age seven, I was already using a sixth-grade English textbook and loved doing my "language arts" homework each day; but I avoided doing my math workbook for months, hiding my lack of ability (and therefore interest) in that subject. When my parents found out, they kept me home for two days and made me complete months of work to catch up. I managed to do it—and that may have been the first deadline rush I'd ever encountered;

I had gotten away with something—avoiding my assignment, denying to myself that it mattered, and coming through in the nick of time with a selfish attitude of "I'll do it my way and you're gonna like it."

Much later in life, I continued with a pattern of last-minute work, missed deadlines, and a tendency to arrive late or screen my phone calls. As one friend says, sometimes my "screen just went dark," and I fell out of communication in a way that cost me freelance assignments and friendships. Avoidance is no way to live—despite the many justifications an avoidant person will offer.

As you can imagine, it is a big, big (BIG!) deal for a person with anxiety around the issues of work and socializing to state those things so plainly. But when I committed to co-writing this book, I promised to share the whole truth about my work-related anxiety, even though that truth is not always pretty. I have worked Jonathan Berent's program since we met and started collaborating in 1989, and my journey away from avoidance is the journey you will now undertake. In sharing my struggles—my losses from and triumphs over workplace anxiety—I intend to serve as your fellow traveler, your trusted ally, and, at times, your role model for fighting the time-wasting, esteem-robbing, job-risking problem of the avoidance-to-anxiety-to-avoidance-to-anxiety game. And it is a game: Somewhere along the way, without even knowing it, you and I came up with this game of stimulus, response, and retreat. There are short-term prizes—avoiding that which makes us nervous provides relief from physical symptoms such as blushing, sweating, heart palpitations, and a break from the obsessive self-doubt that preoccupies us. If we hide out, if we avoid, then we can escape our own destructive thought patterns: "They can tell I'm nervous." "I shouldn't have said that." "I am not qualified/welcome/intelligent/respected/valued."

The short-term prizes come with harsh penalties, however—penalties that rob us of time, energy, relationships, income, self-expression, fulfillment, and even health. I suspect it's possible that this kind of negative stress could take years off our lives—it certainly feels like it when I have symptoms resembling a heart attack or pinched nerve. It certainly feels like it when someone's gastrointestinal problems are so intense that he seeks medical help. It definitely feels like it when a full-blown panic attack spurs thoughts of "I'm going to die!"

Those are the things workplace anxiety sufferers have in common. Our stories may be diverse—but all of us have the same fear of being noticeably nervous. Despite that often crippling anxiety, many anxiety sufferers achieve great things professionally. Throughout the writing of this book, I was astonished at how many times Jonathan told me about clients whose salaries were in the six figures—managers, vice presidents, C-suite overachievers. Yet these men and women had anxiety problems so severe that their jobs were in jeopardy. Of course, there are others who have stayed in lower-paying, lower-stress jobs to avoid the situations that make them nervous; perhaps the skill or talent was there, but the fear of scrutiny was too great.

There are, of course, a great many of us, myself included, who fall somewhere in between. I have made my living as a writer for 26 years. I am the co-author of six (now seven) books. I have been the editor-in-chief of newsletters and magazines. I have had my own weekly newspaper column. My work has appeared in *Newsweek* and *Reader's Digest*. Yet when my anxiety/avoidance takes hold, I feel incompetent, disrespected—not taken seriously (and that may well be an accurate assessment of how people are feeling about me in that moment, given how anxiety sometimes causes me to behave).

My reaction to anxiety is to retreat, to "go to ground" like a hunted animal. As my friend told me, my screen goes dark. The truth is, even during times of low stress, it is my default to avoid. I avoid communicating in person or on the phone. I seriously considered recording a voice mail greeting instructing people to e-mail rather than leave a message.

Still, I have had a successful career despite these challenges. When I "tune in" (a prompt you will recognize throughout this book), I am able to engage Jonathan's training to halt anxiety in its tracks. I am able to stop my negative "internal script" (that loop tape in my head that repeats an endless litany of cautions, admonishments, and insults). I am able to focus on, even welcome, the flow of adrenaline that comes from any deadline, arrives before any presentation, shows up before any performance. I remind myself that not all stress is bad stress. A starter pistol is not designed to kill. It's a signal to do what you do best, to do what you were born to do, to give it your all because you said you would. When I come from that place, my life is rich, fulfilling, joyful, and free. It is my heartfelt wish that this book gives you the same richness, fulfillment, joy, and freedom.

—Amy Lemley
Charlottesville, Virginia

WORK MAKES ME NERVOUS

CHAPTER 1

The Real Story of Anxiety at Work

"I love brainstorming! Nothing energizes me more than being in a roomful of people calling out ideas—even silly ones."

"If I don't understand something, I ask. There are no stupid questions. Other people are probably wondering the same thing."

"I prefer to do business face to face. The personal touch is always better."

Yeah, *right*. Sure, there may be millions of people in millions of workplaces out there who would agree with these statements. But not you. Not if work makes you nervous. Brainstorming sessions may cause you to snap shut like a clam, hoping no one will ask you to even give an opinion on someone *else's* idea, let alone offer one of your own. Asking a question—any question—is too great a risk to take: Surely everyone else knows the answer, or somebody else would be asking. As for doing business face-to-face—well, e-mail, instant messaging, and texting have made that kind of personal contact a thing of the past (and are far more appealing to workplace anxiety sufferers than speaker phones, teleconferencing, and webcams). Recent surveys show that text-messaging is most people's primary—and preferred—way of communicating. Unfortunately, these technological "advances" only enable avoidant behavior—and suck the life out of social skills development for those who are most at risk of workplace and social anxiety. Meeting face-to-face is not just old-fashioned; if you are nervous at work, it feels nothing short of dangerous. What if they see you blush bright red the minute somebody says your name? What if they notice your excessive sweating as you try to explain your concept? What if your mind goes blank and you can't even *think* of a concept?

So many "What Ifs." Here's another one: What if you could live the rest of your life and career free of these fears? Free of these symptoms? Free to express yourself fully and be as successful as you can be?

You can. You will. Here's how: Take this book on as your personal coaching system. Commit to spending 21 days working through it the first time, and refer to it regularly as part of your maintaining a healthy lifestyle. Do that, and you will conquer your nervousness at work. I have developed this program during 30 years of working with literally thousands of people at all levels of career success. These clients have included:

- New college grads whose fear of going blank at job interviews was keeping them from entering the job market.

- Seasoned executives with six- or seven-figure incomes, who were ready to give up rather than speak at regional trade shows and have the world see that they blush, twitch, stammer, stutter, mumble, or sweat profusely.

- Non-native speakers of English stunned into selective mutism out of fear that their accents are too thick or they might misuse an English word.

- IT geniuses who refused lucrative promotions if they required interaction with the public because doing so caused them facial tics, muscle twitching, or nausea.

I have thousands of stories about people who were cured, those whose problems turned out to be permanent, and those who fell somewhere in the middle. You can learn from them all. Of course, to protect these people's privacy, all names and identifying details have been changed. But the stories are true. Throughout this book, you will meet people who suffered silently, believing they had a permanent character flaw, men and women who actually considered having *surgery* to cut the facial nerves that cause blushing and sweating! And these people triumphed over the workplace anxiety that had made them miserable, scared, even sick, for years and years. Tom is a good example.

To hear Tom talk about his struggle and his triumph, visit www.socialanxiety.com and select "Tom: Senior Executive of Billion-Dollar Company—Public Speaking Anxiety Resolved." Tom's 10-minute audio interview is part of a library of 40 interviews with real clients. Other audio interview subjects will be identified throughout this book.

By the time Tom had reached his mid-40s, he was the picture of success: This happily married father of two was a vice president of a large engineering development company. Those who knew him respected him for his past careers, first in the military police and later as a semi-pro football player. But his game face had long since disappeared.

His first panic attack occurred during a very important meeting with his fellow members of the senior management team. By then, Tom was a seasoned executive and felt completely confident about the presentation he had taken a week to prepare. Laptop at the ready, PowerPoint slides prepared, he ran through his report in his mind while the other managers took their turns. He stood to make his presentation, and it went according to plan. Then the unthinkable happened.

"Tom, where do Steve's figures fit into your survey results?"

In that moment, Tom's mind went blank. He had no answer. His presentation—and his entire focus for the weeks leading up to it—had centered on one and only one way of thinking. Now, his boss was asking him to think outside the box. Tom could not rely on the script he had prepared. His singular focus had made his thinking too rigid. Tom had a panic attack—his first one ever—and that single incident caused him to develop extreme anxiety at work. This was far more than a loss of confidence; it was a traumatic event that Tom will never forget.

"I found myself unable to even talk," he recalls. "I was so sure everyone was looking at me and thinking, 'What's wrong with this guy?' But I couldn't help it; I got up and walked out. I thought it was the end of the world." It was a twenty-first-century executive's version of "fight or flight." And Tom chose flight. He became obsessed by what happened and did whatever he could to avoid attending meetings. Yet he discussed it with no one. Ashamed of his problem, he says he "tried everything," turning to the Internet to read articles with names like "Top 10 Ways to Beat Stage Fright" and "Become a Better Public Speaker." But nothing worked. "There was something inside me," he says. "I decided I had been born with it. There was nothing to do."

Born with it. Nothing to do. Those beliefs are all too common among people who suffer from anxiety related to work. When Tom came to me, however, I let him know there was hope. More than hope: There was a cure.

A Life-Changing Journey

As you begin your own journey to recovery from workplace anxiety, it is important to know the four essential steps you must take.

1. **Clarify your motivation.** Consider why you want to change. Preserving your job? Finding a new one? Improving your health?
2. **Diagnose your particular anxiety symptoms and use them to create a map for change.** We will guide you through numerous exercises that train you to recognize your own symptoms and stressors and create a proactive recovery plan.
3. **Develop a High Performance Mind.** A High Performance Mind requires understanding the "mind states" that make up

the personality—then balancing those mind states to achieve synergy. Whereas anxiety sufferers are *reactive*, high performers are *proactive*. When I explained this to Tom, his football lingo came back to him, and he said, "That's it! I've been playing defense. You're saying I should be quarterbacking!" Play offense, not defense!

4. **Master the Five-Step Adrenaline Control Technique.** Based on scientific principles of biofeedback, you will learn to surf the wave of adrenaline rather than be pulled down by its undertow. In time, with practice, you will be able to use self-regulation techniques to interrupt your anxiety response within seconds.

Your training—which requires attention, precision, and repetition—will free you to use that flow of adrenaline energy to become active, productive, and expressive at work. Tom is one of thousands who have done so. His transformation led to a dramatic improvement in self-esteem and a healthy, happy, and high performance lifestyle. He was promoted to a senior position and is now among his company's most motivating leaders.

Your Most Valuable Asset

Tom was smart. He recognized his most valuable asset. Do you know what your most valuable asset is? Think for a moment. Seriously, think carefully right now. Do you have the answer? It's not your bank account or 401(k). It's not your car or your home. It's not even your career. Your most valuable asset is time. Time is finite. Time is not elastic. Time does not stretch. You can borrow money; you cannot borrow time. Spending your precious time to complete this self-guided program will be one of the best investments you ever make. Imagine how much extra time you'll gain when you won't have to spend minutes, hours, days, and nights obsessing over your workplace stressors. Your health will improve, and you will be able to make the most of every workday.

Having picked up this book, you have demonstrated your potential as an astute investor in time. Spend time now to *gain* time later. If you spend—that is, *waste*—time suffering from anxiety, that negative investment tends to grow, leading to more and more anxiety.

Invest your most valuable asset wisely—and expect great returns!

Cold Hands, Warm Hands

Before almost every public appearance I've ever made, an amazing phenomenon has occurred. About 10 to 15 minutes before each presentation, my anticipatory energy manifests itself by making my hands cold. This was true when I started seeking publicity for my social anxiety therapy programs back in 1988, and it is true 20 years later. I am a confident, experienced speaker. Yet I still get cold hands!

That may surprise you. But let me explain. Our peripheral blood flow is affected by the body's natural fight-or-flight response: In get-ready-for-action mode, less blood flows to the hands, so they feel either cold, cool, or sweaty. The hands of a relaxed body are dry and warm. These processes are called "vasoconstriction" (cold, cool, or sweaty hands) and "vasodilation" (warm, dry hands). Varying degrees of stress and relaxation occur from person to person and from moment to moment, and the hand's skin temperature varies up to 25 degrees Fahrenheit in any one day, sometimes within minutes. Skin temperature is not the same as body temperature, which is considered normal at 98.6 degrees Fahrenheit. A hand temperature of about 90 degrees or higher represents relaxation. Here is a table showing precise skin temperature measurements and what they indicate.

Hand Temperature	Degree of Relaxation or Stress
Above 95°F/35C	Deeply relaxed
90°F to 95°F/32°C to 35°C	Quietly relaxed
84°F to 90°F/29°C to 32°C	Mild calm
79°F to 84°F/26°C to 29°C	Moderate stress
Below 79°F/26°C	High tension

So what do my cold hands mean? They mean that my adrenaline is flowing. My blood vessels are constricted. I am gearing up to perform.

This is good stress for me—a positive example of the fight-or-flight response. Nothing to be scared of. But those same cold hands could represent the beginning of a panic episode to a person who does not understand performance physiology.

Becoming aware of hand temperature lets you gauge your stress level. Your challenge at this point is to begin to differentiate between positive and negative stress and how they relate to your hand temperature. You will learn that "stress" and "anxiety" are not dirty words but important phenomena that require a practical understanding.

Often in my clinical work I integrate *biofeedback* with therapy. The term has a simple meaning: "bio" refers to body processes and "feedback" refers to the collection of objective information reporting about those processes. As I mentioned, I use high-tech biofeedback machines at my office. But there are other effective ways to receive biofeedback—ways you can employ every day, such as using a cuff to check your blood pressure, getting on a scale to weigh yourself, and even looking in the mirror!

The basic idea is this: Measure where you are, learn to recognize what is happening, and master steps to control it. Taking an objective measurement allows you to condition yourself. First, you observe: "My hands are cold." Then, you ask questions: "What am I thinking? What am I feeling?" The essence of biofeedback is to pair, associate, or connect your internal (proprioceptive) sensations as they relate to objective feedback—the more you are able to do so, the more effective the technique becomes. And the more confident you will be.

Skin temperature measurement is one biofeedback mode. I have used hand-warming training to help people resolve panic and anxiety attacks, migraine headaches, and many other stress-related disorders. I have been a proponent of hand-warming since early in my career, when I witnessed how the technique helped stop hemorrhaging in an adult with diabetic retinopathy. Picture it: This man learned to recognize his body's stress signals—in this case, bleeding from his eyes—and engage in a quick technique *that actually stopped his eyes from bleeding!* Powerful stuff. And it's yours to learn.

Hand-warming is an internal process, and ambient temperature has only a slight influence. Rubbing your hands together or putting them in warm water is not going to work. As you learn, be aware that sometimes, when a person consciously increases skin temperature, it can cause a tingling sensation as the hands warm. That's a good sign!

The Physiology of Performance

Most people's adrenaline flow increases before a performance—which can be anything from a conversation to a full-scale speech in front of an audience of hundreds or thousands. How a person handles that adrenaline is the only difference between feeling anxiety and "going with the flow."

For me, the adrenaline flow means, "Ready! Set! Go!" I don't interpret the feelings as negative—trouble swallowing on a few high-stress occasions, cold hands, and so on. They're not scary, but just a reminder to focus and remember that adrenaline is my friend.

To promote my message that people can live happier, more productive lives by freeing themselves from anxiety, I have appeared on more than 1,500 radio and television shows in the last 20 years or so. I *love* doing shows that reach a large audience because of what I can teach and the great public relations and marketing opportunities they give me. I still feel stress. The difference is, I have trained my body and mind to kick into control mode using the techniques that I will teach you. It's almost automatic, and it takes only seconds. Once, I was beginning a three-minute live segment on Fox television. The producer was in the process of counting down "5 . . . 4 . . . 3 . . . 2 . . . 1 . . . and Live!" On the number four I had difficulty swallowing due to stress (not a good thing to have when you are about to speak to an audience). But by the number one and the exciting call of "Live!" I was ready to go, having utilized the same Five-Step Adrenaline Control Technique you will learn.

On another occasion, I was waiting by the phone for famed "shock jock" Howard Stern to call and interview me live for a radio show about "involuntary virginity." (The perfect subject for Howard, don't you think?) This was a big deal for me—and I had told about 1,000 people I would be on. As I waited, I felt a lot of anticipatory energy and the same swallowing challenge I had right before the Fox interview. I used my technique, and used it, and used it . . . But alas,

Howard blew me off for "the biggest rubber band ball in the world" and a hermaphrodite. My call never came. Such is the nature of show biz!

These two experiences characterize the *physiology of performance*. When you understand it, and learn to control it, the result will be high performance and more potential for confidence and success. When you do not understand the physiology of performance, there is more of a chance that adrenaline will control you instead of you controlling the adrenaline.

Why discuss public speaking? Because public speaking is most people's number one fear (ahead of even death!). It is also—according to self-made multibillionaire Warren Buffett—"the number one business skill." At its most essential, the definition in my program is that public speaking occurs any time you are the only one talking. In this context, public speaking means speaking in or to a group—and a group is defined as more than one person. Public speaking is therefore not limited to making a speech or presentation. It also means speaking spontaneously around the conference table or in another meeting, participating in a conference call, standing up to ask a question during a presentation, and even informal chatting around the water cooler. Think of it as "speaking up." Public speaking is not the only workplace stressor that makes people nervous, but its broad definition encompasses many of the specific anxiety triggers in the workplace. Addressing nervousness at work is critical because, as one business reporter put it, "In today's workplace, there is no room for the shy."

Nor is there room for nervousness on the job market. If professional, comfortable interaction and a certain level of confidence are absent, job interviews are liable to go poorly. Networking opportunities are left unexplored. Instead, many people who are nervous at work hope in vain that a job search Web site will hand-deliver their resumes to dream employers—or in a lot of cases these days, to any employer at all. But sitting in front of the computer—avoiding true human interaction—will not land you a job. A very small percentage of hiring occurs through advertisements. To excel, you have to sell yourself, make connections, ask for favors, follow up, and keep following up, all of which are almost impossible to do while sitting at home by yourself in front of a computer screen.

Of course, anxiety about speaking up is not the only thing that makes people nervous at work. Ask 50 people (and we did; see the sidebar) and they may well give you 50 different answers for "What makes you nervous at work?"

We began writing this book just before the economy collapsed in 2008. As job losses soared into the hundreds of thousands, I heard from more and more people whose anxiety was through the roof because of a perceived lack of job security. It's a reasonable thing to fear—even people without an anxiety problem feel anxious about the circumstances. But it is reality, and coping with it can mean the difference between keeping your job and being among those who are laid off and not merely reassigned. According to *New York Newsday*, "Losing your job is painful, but worrying about losing the job you have may be even more harmful to your health. Researchers at the University of Michigan concluded that 'chronically high job insecurity is more strongly linked with health declines than actual job loss or unemployment.' The study also found that job security is more strongly linked with health declines than actual job loss or unemployment."

---

50 Workplace Anxiety Triggers . . . What Are Yours?

"Speaking up during a meeting"

"Answering my phone without knowing who's calling"

"Learning new skills"

"Introducing a guest speaker"

"Making a presentation"

"Giving a speech to an audience of strangers"

"Giving a speech to an audience that includes people I know"

"Being interviewed for a job"

"Making the follow-up phone call about a job interview"

"Technology"

"Making small talk"

"When my boss asks to meet with me"

"Having to talk during a conference call"

"Being seen on a webcam"

"Knowing I'm going to miss a deadline and not saying anything"

"Using a microphone"

"Meeting with people outside my division"

"When other people get credit for my work"

"Attending company social events"

"Traveling with colleagues"

"Forgetting something"

"Asking a question"

"When someone asks me a question"

"Making an appointment then realizing I am double-booked"

"Interacting with colleagues of the opposite sex"

"Doing team projects"

"Giving feedback to my employees"

"Asking for help within earshot of my supervisor"

"Seeing people who know I interviewed for a job I didn't get"

"Arriving late"

"Being dressed too casually or too formally"

"That my co-workers will find out I'm gay"

"Covering the receptionist's duties during lunch break"

"Team-building exercises"

"Passing the company president in the hallway"

"Introducing myself"

"When something happens that makes me think my talents aren't valued"

"When I fail to meet a project goal"

(continued)

"Remembering people's names"

"People I don't like but have to ask for something"

"Eating with my colleagues—I'm afraid I'll look like a slob"

"When colleagues discuss personal subjects such as religion or politics"

"Writing—e-mails, memos, reports, anything!"

"Using the public restroom when others are in there"

"Delegating tasks to other people"

"Being singled out in a crowd"

"Suggesting a solution and having someone explain why it's wrong"

"Being in situations where I have to sign my name or write anything in front of people"

"Being attracted to a fellow employee"

"Giving my opinion without knowing what other people think"

In 1988, 10 years into my clinical practice, I hired my first public relations firm. I did so out of the desire to provide community education about social anxiety and the related issues with which I was working. The timing obviously was right. Three months into the public relations effort, I was booked on *The Oprah Winfrey Show*. Oprah was relatively new to the TV airwaves at the time, but it was already a very big deal to appear on her show. From 1988 to now, I have done well over 1,500 television and radio shows and countless newspaper and magazine interviews and given many lectures. I have experienced the good, the bad, and the ugly of working the media. Public speaking has very much been a key to my career success. I have *learned* to be productive with the art and science of public speaking and high performance at work. As I've described, I use the same adrenaline-channeling techniques as I will teach you. And they work. They work for me, and they work for thousands of other people whose anxiety once crippled them.

Affordable Biofeedback Learning Aids

You can learn our all-important hand-warming technique using only the instructions provided in this book—provided you follow them precisely and complete the exercises, all of which are presented as part of a developmental program.

If you are interested in accelerating your learning curve, you might consider obtaining a feedback device. Used in conjunction with this program, these devices are quite effective. There are a lot of temperature machines that provide specific feedback you can use as you practice and master the quieting response technique. These devices range in price from a few dollars to a few hundred.

My personal favorite—the one I recommend to all my clients—is a credit-card-size biofeedback card. It's handy, economical, and accurate. We wanted to include the card in this book, but that proved problematic (for example, it could too easily become lost in transit). So I am offering it to you for $1 (my cost) plus shipping and handling. Simply visit www.socialanxiety.com and click on *Send My Biocard*.

If you decide to obtain the Biocard from me, you will want to use it many times throughout each day. After substantial experimentation, you should become so proficient at knowing your skin temperature that you will know the stress level the card would show without actually having to put your thumb on it. If you choose to purchase a temperature machine (these are inexpensive), your objective is the same: to become adept at knowing what the temperature reading will be without actually putting your hand on it. Obviously, this will take some practice. But the developmental process will increase your awareness of internal cues dramatically—and that is true whether you purchase a device of some kind or not. I often play a game with people where I try to guess the temperature of their hands, and then put them on a temp machine to measure my accuracy. I'm pretty good at it because I've had more than 30 years of practice doing it.

Biofeedback Lesson Number One: Awareness

It's just about impossible to have a panic attack when hands are dry and warm! *And increasing your hand temperature three to four degrees is enough to stop a panic attack in its tracks.* Developing awareness of hand temperature is the first step in learning to control it. Your training begins now. Here is what I want you to do:

1. **TUNE IN:** Become aware of the temperature of your hands at different times during the day.
2. Develop a general awareness of hand temperature. Are your hands warm or cold? Sweaty or dry?
3. When your hands are cold, cool, or sweaty—indicators of stress—identify your thoughts and your emotions. Become aware of your energy. Do you believe it is good or bad? What is your reasoning?
4. When your hands are warm and dry—indicators of emotional relaxation—identify your thoughts and feelings. Again, become aware of your energy.

The Many Faces of Workplace Anxiety

Here are some typical examples of people who suffered social and performance anxiety in the workplace:

By his mid-40s, Roger held an important position in banking, working with hedge funds. Making a seven-figure salary, Roger was the go-to guy in his department when it came to public speaking. Only his wife and I knew that his obsessive worry regarding public speaking was so debilitating that he was considering changing careers.

Jim, age 25, recently married, was highly intelligent, a good athlete, and a social butterfly. He was preparing to take the reins of his family-owned business. But he dreaded the idea of being in charge and having to appear front and center because he knew he blushed. At one point, Jim considered getting an operation to sever his nerves because of fear of blushing.

Carol, an ovarian cancer survivor who had almost died, once said to me very genuinely, "Jonathan, I'd rather be back in chemotherapy than speak in front of a group."

Lauren graduated from an Ivy League school with a 4.0 average and was holding a $95,000-a-year job by the age of 28. She shocked her family, though, when she quit abruptly because of burnout caused by the anxiety that her excessive perfectionism was causing.

Alice, a 48-year-old human resources associate director earning $55,000, never said a word during weekly staff meetings because she suffered from selective mutism—in other situations, she could quietly hold her own. But in these meetings, she was silent.

Jerry, an accomplished Army flight surgeon, experienced heart palpitations and racing thoughts whenever he had to make "rounds" or give presentations to his peers—he never told anyone about the problem, and instead tried unsuccessfully to treat his problem with prescription medications.

Kevin was a lawyer who had once dreamed of running for public office. He abandoned that dream after he began feeling extremely nervous in court. He even had to leave courtroom proceedings due to his sweating attacks.

Maureen was a psychology intern at a children's hospital. Four months into her internship, she realized that she had never introduced herself to the doctor in the office adjacent to hers. At first she had merely been too busy getting settled into the program, but as the weeks became months, she felt more and more awkward when she walked by his open office or saw him around the hospital. Yet she couldn't work up the courage to remedy the situation before it grew even more uncomfortable for her.

Bill, age 55, a senior vice president in a national advertising firm, traveled nationally on a weekly basis to meet clients and division executives. As top dog in those meetings, it fell to him to lead the meetings. He was fine in discussions, but whenever the spotlight was on him to speak for several minutes while everyone else listened, his anxiety would take over. Bill developed an elaborate technique for avoiding these monologue situations: For example, he would be introducing a new vice president to a regional staff. That introduction should take 10 to 12 minutes to complete. But Bill would manage only 20 *seconds* before figuring out a way to take the spotlight off himself and turn the monologue into a dialogue. He was very skilled at doing so, and this went on for 30 years—becoming a kind of "tic" that Bill was known for. The toll it took was exhausting: Bill lived on high alert—in a constant state of apprehension that he would be asked to speak. Sadly, he became alcohol-dependent because of this anxiety—he would always have a drink right before one of these meetings no matter what time of day it was.

Sherry, age 20, a hair colorist intern, was stuck in her career due to her panic during consultations. Despite excellent training in a leading cosmetology program, she was terrified of producing a result that her client wouldn't like. Having the client tell her that she could just do whatever she thought would look good only heightened the anxiety.

Corey, age 24, a gifted musician, dropped out of music school because of his performance anxiety. By himself, he played and composed music and astounded his professors. But he simply couldn't replicate those performances onstage because his stage fright shut him down.

Phyllis, a vice president in an accounting firm, was let go after a 20-year career because of the changing culture in her bank and management's perception of her unproductive poor social skills—even though she was an excellent manager. Phyllis, too, was a selective mute, and barely spoke to her colleagues, even informally.

One out of eight individuals suffers from social anxiety, yet the medical and psychotherapy communities have not been productive in their response to this problem. The primary reason for this is that people who experience this problem are so controlled by fear of feeling embarrassed, ashamed, and humiliated that they do not seek help. This is not the type of problem a person shares with a friend over a cup of coffee. Most suffer in silence. In most cases, it's an invisible problem. The last thing that perfectionists are going to do is to let anyone know they aren't perfect!

Celebrities Suffer, Too

Sometimes the problem comes out of the closet. Pro football player Ricky Williams, a Heismann Trophy winner, had social anxiety. The press at one time thought it was quite weird when he would not take his helmet off during interviews. This was to protect himself—not physically, but emotionally. Zack Greinke, an all-star pitcher for the Kansas City Royals, lost 17 games in 2005. Greinke's struggles reportedly deepened his depression and bouts of social anxiety, distancing him from his fellow players. Although Greinke does not talk publicly about social anxiety, others have made comments about what he was going through. Dayton Moore, the Kansas City general manager, said, "I can't speak to this because I've never experienced it, but I can only imagine how difficult it must have been to recognize his condition and evaluate it honestly and do something about it. He's been able to take all of those experiences and combine them and that's why he is where he is today."

Numerous performers have identified themselves as having performance anxiety—commonly called stage fright. Superstar Beyoncé describes her last moments backstage as fraught with fear: "I get so terrified before I go onstage. My secret is no eye contact. I find that if I don't look directly at people and just concentrate completely on the singing and dance moves, then I can get through." A star since childhood, Donny Osmond admitted to a serious panic attack onstage in 1994 during which he was unable to sing and feared he would black out; the attacks continued to plague him, and he began to fear going out in public because he thought fans would make fun of him. The legendary Barbra Streisand did not perform for 27 years after an embarrassing concert during which she couldn't remember the lyrics to some of the songs she was singing.

Sir Laurence Olivier, regarded as one of the greatest actors of all time, confided in his memoir that he suffered social phobia for five years after he began to fear he would be too tired to remember his lines on stage. When actress Kim Basinger stood onstage to accept an Academy Award, she was unable to speak—even though she had practiced a speech to give if she won. Basinger apparently suffered anxiety as a child also, becoming mute when she was asked to read in class (a poorly understood disorder called selective mutism).

Highly respected NPR talk show host Diane Rehm's distinctive voice is the result of a neurological disorder called spasmodic dysphonia. According to a *Washington Post* interview with Rehm, there are surprising psychological side effects—stage fright, shortness of breath, excruciating self-doubt. "It's not the anxiety that originates the problem," she says. "The anxiety follows. But the anxiety feeds the fear and the fear feeds the anxiety, and caught in the cycle is the voice." In her 1999 memoir, *Finding My Voice*, Rehm discusses her lifetime struggle with self-esteem: "I couldn't overcome the constant self-criticism I heaped on myself. It was as though there was a voice inside telling me that no matter what I did or how others might praise me, there was no truth to what they were saying."

Tony-nominated actress Cherry Jones describes feeling "nearly paralyzed by a profound case of stage fright" because she was following in the footsteps of a play's previous star and feared she couldn't equal her talent. Nicole Kidman says she never feels worthy of the acting roles she is offered: "Every time I star in a film, I think I cannot act. I've tried to pull out of almost every one I've done because of sheer terror."

Many performers, however, learn to ride the wave of adrenaline, using it for energy. Actress Alison Lohman, for example, seems to have borrowed a page from our book—recognizing that the adrenaline some people experience as anxiety can come in handy. "It's those nerves that bring you to a higher level and make you more hyper-aware," she explains. "It makes your performance better."

Drugs and Anxiety

Prescription drugs and alternative treatments have their place in the treatment of anxiety. I want to make this clear: I am not opposed to using those treatments as part of an overall treatment plan; in fact, I embrace their use because they can be so effective *when used the right way*. But most of the time, working through my program is enough (we discuss the appropriate use of medications in a later chapter). I do contend that there is a right way and a wrong way to apply them. Aggressive marketing has made it harder for patients and their doctors to determine the best way to integrate prescription drugs into an overall treatment program. Viewers who see advertisements promising a drug will eliminate anxiety believe there's a quick fix—and do not stop to consider whether that fix is short-term or long-term.

During the last decade, pharmaceutical companies have embarked on a mega campaign to sell their goods. This is a multibillion-dollar industry, and much of their campaign has been aimed at social anxiety. The good thing about this media phenomenon has been that for the first time many individuals understand that they are not alone in what they have. But the negative is that many people are left with the belief that they have a "medical disorder"— a physically rooted problem that can be resolved only via medicine. Nothing is further from the truth. I am not opposed to medication, but I am opposed to its misuse. Later in the book, we will discuss this issue in detail.

Heavy advertising of prescription medications for depression, anxiety, and bipolar disorder led first to patients' clamoring for prescriptions. More recently these media campaigns have faced opposition, which has had a negative effect on the serious but treatable problem of anxiety. For example, on one radio show where I was a guest, the well-known host attacked my "cause" from the get-go: "I don't believe there's anything called social anxiety. It's just something that the pharmaceutical companies made up." My response to this was, "I guess there's a chance I've been hallucinating for the last 30 years." I hope the listeners got the point: The host was being provocative, but not productive. Anxiety is real. And it can be treated. The bottom line is that there is a tremendous amount of confusion in our society about social anxiety. This book will help to resolve it.

Selective Mutism

We all remember that one kid who always sat in the back of the classroom. The teacher never called on him, and he never raised his hand. He talked to no one. You and your classmates got used to him, and the kid became all but invisible.

There is a clinical term for that behavior: "selective mutism." A person—and it is not always a child, though children are most often brought for treatment by their worried parents—simply does not talk (is "mute") in certain situations (hence the term "selective"). Parents occasionally seek treatment for their children's selective mutism. Unfortunately, only a very small percentage of parents decide to take that step. Far too often, the attitude among parents, teachers, and even school counselors is, "He'll grow out of it" or "She's just shy." Selective mutism is so insidious and complex that it can bring schools to their knees. The school psychologists and guidance counselors are not equipped to deal with it in most instances, nor are the teachers. If there is a precursor of social and performance anxiety at risk, this is the earliest indication.

It's not often that I use the term "mind-blowing," but I feel compelled to do it here. Selective mutism is a very specific form of social anxiety, awareness of which is just emerging. Here is what's mind-blowing: Ten in 1,000 children have some form of autism—thank goodness society is now being educated about this disability and the many therapeutic programs that are in place. But get this: Seven out of 1,000 children have selective mutism, and it is extremely difficult to find effective help anywhere in the world. This typifies the state of social anxiety in our society. We may hear the term "selective mutism," but many of the people using it do not know what it really means.

Most of the information available regarding selective mutism is about children, in whom it is often misdiagnosed as a speech disorder or autism. But on the contrary, it is a very specific social and performance anxiety–related self-censorship that affects people of all ages. For example, Alice, the human resources consultant, never said a word at Friday staff meetings. She believed she "had nothing to say of importance" and that what she might say would be "stupid." Choosing silence protected her from feeling the adrenaline that would flow if she took the risk. In essence, she was specifically censoring herself. This is a key component of selective mutism.

Would You Like to Cut Your Nerves?

Fear of being noticeably nervous is a major concern for workplace anxiety sufferers. Blushing and sweating are major causes of this fear. A medical procedure to treat these symptoms is becoming more and more popular. Called endoscopic thoracic sympathectomy, it severs the nerves that cause facial hyperhidrosis, a condition that includes excessive sweating and blushing. My client Jim sought this surgery but backed out at the last minute, opting for treatment with me instead; his success story is featured in www.socialanxiety.com's free one-hour teleseminar on blushing and performance anxiety. Jim was fully prepared to go through with this risky surgery, but changed his mind in the waiting room and left. He eventually resolved his problem via therapy with me.

I have no doubt that this surgical procedure has helped some people; however, the invasiveness of it shows the desperation and intense degree of embarrassment that many people experience by being noticeably nervous. Another client had this surgery before pursuing treatment with me. "It did resolve 50 percent of my sweating," he says, "but it left me feeling imbalanced internally." Of course it did. Just because no one can see you blushing or sweating does not mean that you are not experiencing that same uncomfortable adrenaline rush. Until you learn to ride that wave—to welcome adrenaline as the energy that will make your performance shine—you are doomed to suffer. Before you choose to go under the knife, I urge you to research your options completely.

How about injecting a little botulism into your body to prevent excessive sweating? That's right—Botox, the same popular injection used to freeze-frame facial wrinkles using botulinum toxin type A—is being used to reduce axillary hyperhidrosis, also known as excessive underarm sweat, a condition that affects up to one million people in the United States. Is it safe? The FDA approved its use for this purpose in 2004. Is it the best solution for someone whose anxiety causes him or her to sweat profusely? In some cases, it can be helpful. But I think the surgery is overused for this purpose and is not always the best option. I feel the same way about facial injections of Botox to prevent people's emotions from appearing on their faces during meetings and other anxiety-causing situations.

Whatever You Think, Think the Opposite

Whatever You Think, Think the Opposite. As the title of Paul Arden's book makes clear, sometimes "the opposite" is right. Paradoxical (opposite) thinking and behaviors will be important in your learning to control anxiety and stress and developing a High Performance Mind. It comes down to trust. Imagine that you are in training, and you must open your mind to coaching and do just as the coach says in the order he says to do it. This reminds me of the 1980s classic movie *The Karate Kid*: A young teen seeks training from an elderly sensai whose coaching begins with several weeks of chores around his property. The boy is about ready to quit when he's asked to wax the sensai's car. "Wax on," the sensai tells the kid, making a clockwise circle with his right hand. "Wax off," he then says, circling counterclockwise with his left. Eventually, the boy recognizes the method in his coach's madness: The gestures he embedded in his muscle memory became highly valuable moves in karate competition.

"Wax on, wax off." I know doing what the coach says can be challenging. I exercise regularly and diligently and am in good shape. I once hired a personal trainer to help me prevent basketball injuries. My trainer took me through a new routine that exercised muscles I usually did not work out. There were times that I dreaded going to a training session because of this challenge. But the payoff was great! I became stronger and more flexible. I gave up dreading and gave in to the coaching, and it worked. Such is the nature of this book. Much of the content may be the opposite of what you know or believe currently. *Invest strongly in this cross-training.*

Productive Therapy

I have often been asked, "What kind of therapy do you practice?" My answer often has been "a productive one." The therapy I practice integrates many different modalities, including analysis and deep emotional work, cognition, behavior, family dynamics, and physiology. It brings mind and body together in a way that allows me to teach a systematic self-regulation and relaxation incorporating simple but proven biofeedback methods. It presents biofeedback-based techniques along with diaphragmatic breathing, progressive relaxation, and imagery—which are the cornerstones of stress management and recovery from anxiety.

Time to Focus: The 10 Key Points for Using This Book

This program is highly systematic. You owe it to yourself to work it start to finish—ideally within 21 days the first time. You can reread passages as you wish. But proceed in order because the concepts, exercises, and techniques build on what has come before.

We highly recommend using a specific notebook, computer file, or handheld application to complete the exercises and chart your progress. *Please make your decision now and plan to use the same place for notes throughout the process.* Refer back to your notes as you progress. Here are 10 things to bear in mind as you transform yourself.

1. **Attach yourself to the new ideas and information in this book.** Attachment is critical for anxiety management and learning to take responsibility for your health.

2. **Get absolutely clear on your motivation for change.** Take a moment to picture yourself in a life not driven by anxiety. Describe that life in your notes:

   When I manage my anxiety, I will be able to

   _____

   _____

   _____

   When I have more confidence, I will be able to

   _____

   _____

   _____

   Your own comfort within the social hierarchy is important: You must accept that you contribute to others and have an impact on the world, that you can make a difference. Yet social anxiety could prevent you from having those two basic pleasures. You could continue to live the exact life you are living now. But doing so has costs. These could include the physical symptoms of stress, strained relationships with friends and family, declined raises and promotions, and even job loss. Imagine your work life continuing in the same direction. What does a typical day look like? What do you accomplish? How do you feel? Now complete the following:

If I do not manage my anxiety, I will

_____

If I do not develop more confidence, I will

_____

3. **Refer often to the Feelings List on page 30.** Become an expert at identifying your feelings and learn to correlate them to your skin temperature.

4. **Read and work this self-help program within 21 days (the first time).** Twenty-one is the number of days required to learn a new habit according to the science of psychocybernetics. Use that simple rule to maximize your learning curve. *Do not skip any exercises or skip ahead to other chapters or exercises.* Give yourself the gift of focus. Follow the program exactly as it's designed. Trust that it works.

5. **Be ready to think the opposite** of what you currently think. Paradoxical thinking will be an integral part of your self-help.

6. **Learn from those who have been successful**—and from those who have not. Embrace the stories and ideas in this book. Look for the common thread. Don't say, "But *I'm* not an executive/baseball player/librarian/whatever. . . ." Say, "How is that person like me? What can I learn here?" Treat these stories as if they are the secret to life. In some respects, they are. Don't get caught up in whether the person has the same historical or family experience as you do.

7. **Be as honest as possible** in Chapter 2 as you create your map for change.

8. **Be patient, diligent, and *precise*** as you learn the techniques in this book. The sequence in which you learn these exercises is part of the program's design. Make sure you follow each

exercise's instructions very carefully—for example, when I say to time your diaphragmatic inhale–exhale to 8 to 12 seconds, train yourself until that timing is automatic.

9. **Accept the High Performance Mind** concept as a powerful strategy for change.

10. **Harness the power of integrating Function + Actions + Thoughts + Emotions (F.A.T.E.)** using this program of physical, behavioral, cognitive, and emotional strategies.

Fight or Flight . . . or Focus?

Clearly, people today are subject to an increasing barrage of stressors, all of which cause distinct patterns of mental and physical arousal. At work, those stressors include speaking to groups, dealing with authority figures, dealing with conflict, problem solving, facing unexpected challenges, and more. The individual's adaptive reactions have been variously characterized as "emergency," "alarm," or "fight or flight." Whatever the label, the stress responses are virtually automatic. The initial response usually occurs within five or six seconds of the body's perception of a stressor threat. The body's response is characterized by a flow of adrenaline. It is adrenaline that either drives the symptoms of panic and anxiety or becomes a source of power. For example, if you are walking down the street and you see a grizzly bear, you are going to use the power of the adrenaline to either fight or flee. The reality is that everyone is susceptible to the fight-or-flight response. Adrenaline is in all of us.

According to stress-management expert Charles Stroebel, PhD, MD, "Healthy individuals exhibit a capacity to cope effectively with stressors, usually regaining balance from the fight-or-flight response within a relatively short time after the emergency response. This inherent quieting response allows their bodies to restore needed energy reserves, and prepare them for subsequent and inevitable arousal periods." On the other hand, people who are predisposed to, or actually suffering from anxiety, have "autonomic hypersensitivity," meaning their nervous system is overreactive and they recover their balance much more slowly. In his pioneering re-search in biofeedback-based stress management, Stroebel identified a phenomenon he calls the Quieting Response. Based on that concept, the system of biofeedback-based exercises in this book will help you use the energy of adrenaline productively and help you control what appears to be an automatic response. We begin your training with the Five-Step Adrenaline Control Technique.

The Five-Step Adrenaline Control Technique

Are you ready? The five things that you are about to learn will change your life.

1. **Start with realistic expectations: Your adrenaline will be present!** Fact of life: Adrenaline flows or surges whenever you are set to perform (to say something, answer a question, attend a meeting, participate in a conference call, and yes, to make a presentation or speech on stage). This is your fight-or-flight response. It is natural and you cannot stop it. Trying to stop it would be an unrealistic expectation and would only frustrate you and make you angry. Those are the emotions that drive the anxiety you feel when adrenaline flows. The truth is, you must welcome the adrenaline as fuel for success.

2. **Accept the adrenaline.** This is the hardest step. Say to yourself, "Adrenaline is my source of power." Believe me, I know that you and adrenaline have not gotten along very well in recent years. But it's time to patch things up.

   Think back to your last anxiety episode. What was your initial sensation or thought? How did you react? You got either frustrated or angry, which made the problem worse. That sequence of events is the *opposite* of what we mean when we talk about acceptance. When it comes to high performance, adrenaline may well be the best friend you ever had. When my hands get cold because of vasoconstriction, that is adrenaline flowing. It's the same adrenaline that *could* cause panic. But it doesn't have to. All it really means is "Ready! Set! Go!"

3. **Surf the adrenaline!** Imagine a surfer on a wave, harnessing its energy . . . going with it and in control! The wave represents adrenaline. Accept it. Don't fight it.

4. **Breathe deeply and fully**. Inhale . . . 1 . . . 2 . . . 3 . . . 4 and exhale 4 . . . 3 . . . 2 . . . 1 . . . . Time this inhale–exhale to between 8 and 12 seconds. Breathing is the basis of self-regulation, relaxation, and learning the Quieting Response. Breathing is life!

5. **Say to yourself, "My hands are warm."**

Realistic Expectations

Accept the adrenaline as power

Surf the wave of adrenaline

Breathe

Diaphragmatic Breathing

Our breath is the most valuable tool we have to control our nervous system and manage anxiety. How can we make this tool available to us on command? By taking control of our breathing apparatus. Basic breathing is automatic. We seldom pay attention to it, let alone use it as the effective yet instantly acceptable stress management tool it is.

Conscious diaphragmatic breathing not only can help you control anxiety and manage stress but also can facilitate high performance in any situation. For example, all highly trained athletes and stage performers use conscious breathing techniques to enhance their efforts. A friend of mine is a third-degree black belt who has been practicing martial arts for about 30 years. He demonstrated the power of breathing as he was going through certain intricate moves including cracking thick boards with his hands. Very impressive, very powerful! Despite the act's intensity, my friend remained cool and calm. He was extremely focused—obviously channeling his adrenaline into his concentration and physical challenge.

At the 2010 Winter Olympics, legendary American speed skater Apolo Ohno, who has won more winter medals than any other athlete, drew attention to himself by doing the same thing seconds before each race: yawning, taking a deep breath in, then exhaling. "It makes me feel better," he told Yahoo! Sports. "It gets the oxygen in and the nerves out." Are you convinced?

Breathing Basics

Here are the basics of breathing: First, you intake oxygen through your nose into your lungs. The air then travels through the trachea. Next the lungs expand the ribs, and the pectoralis minor muscles contract. Finally the diaphragm contracts and flattens. This exhaling process involves the diaphragm's relaxing and moving up. Then the lungs contract, and the intercostal and pectoralis minor muscles relax. Carbon dioxide is then forced out of the mouth and nose.

TUNE IN: Now, in a relaxed sitting position, place your hands just above your navel, facing each other, fingertips facing and touching. Underneath your rib cage is a dome-shaped diaphragm muscle. It moves up and down as you breathe in and out. As you breathe, you will feel your fingertips separate upon inhalation and exhalation. Draw the air in through your nose as slowly as possible. As you draw the oxygen into your diaphragm rhythmically and slowly, concentrate on the diaphragm muscle under the ribs and notice your hands; feel them moving back and forth as you inhale and exhale. After you inhale slowly through your nose, pace your exhale to a slow count of 4 . . . 3 . . . 2 . . . 1. *This is conscious breathing*. Train yourself to pace the inhale–exhale to between 8 and 12 seconds total.

TUNE IN: Slow down for a moment. Calmly put your dominant hand up to your cheek. Keep it there for several seconds. Feel the temperature. Really feel it. Warm, cold, cool, sweaty, dry? In the next chapter, you will complete an important series of exercises that require your focus and your honesty. What are your thoughts and feelings as you get ready?

About Tuning In: Your Feelings A to Z

You will be tuning in throughout the book. Being able to put your feelings into words is critical for *attachment*—a vital part of your recovery program. Use the following **Feelings List** as a starting point for identifying where you are emotionally. As you identify other feelings, consider adding them to the list. Refer to this list whenever you need help identifying your feelings or putting them into words.

Abandoned	Complacent	Empty
Affectionate	Confident	Enchanted
Afraid	Confused	Energetic
Amazed	Conspicuous	Enraged
Ambivalent	Content	Enthusiastic
Angry	Contrite	Envious
Annoyed	Courageous	Excited
Anxious	Crazy	Evil
Apathetic	Cruel	Exasperated
Apprehensive	Crushed	Exhausted
Arrogant	Deceitful	Fascinated
Astounded	Defeated	Fearful
Awed	Delighted	Flustered
Bad	Depressed	Foolish
Betrayed	Desirable	Frantic
Bitter	Desirous	Frightened
Blissful	Despairing	Frustrated
Bold	Desperate	Free
Bored	Destructive	Full
Brave	Determined	Furious
Burdened	Different	Glad
Calm	Discontented	Good
Capable	Disrespected	Grateful
Captivated	Disregarded	Gratified
Challenged	Distracted	Greedy
Cheated	Distraught	Grief-stricken
Cheerful	Disturbed	Guilty
Childish	Dominated	Gullible
Childlike	Dubious	Happy
Clever	Eager	Hateful
Combative	Ecstatic	Heavenly
Competitive	Embarrassed	Helpless

Honorable	Nice	Scared
Honored	Numb	Screwed up
Hostile	Nutty	Servile
Humiliated	Obnoxious	Settled
Hurt	Obsessed	Sexy
Hysterical	Odd	Shocked
Ignored	Oppositional	Silly
Immoral	Outraged	Skeptical
Immortal	Overwhelmed	Smug
Imposed upon	Pained	Sneaky
Impressed	Panicked	Snobbish
Infatuated	Paranoid	Solemn
Infuriated	Peaceful	Sorrowful
Insecure	Persecuted	Spiteful
Inspired	Petrified	Startled
Intimidated	Pitiful	Stingy
Invisible	Pitying	Strange
Irritable	Pleasant	Stunned
Irritated	Pleased	Stupid
Isolated	Powerful	Suffering
Kind	Precarious	Sure
Lazy	Pressured	Sympathetic
Lecherous	Pretty	Tearful
Left out	Protected	Tempted
Lonely	Proud	Tenacious
Lost	Quarrelsome	Tense
Loving	Refreshed	Tentative
Low	Rejected	Tenuous
Lustful	Relaxed	Terrible
Mad	Relieved	Terrified
Marginalized	Remorseful	Thankful
Mean	Resentful	Threatened
Melancholy	Restless	Thrilled
Miserable	Sad	Thwarted
Mortified	Safe	Tired
Naughty	Sated	Trapped
Nervous	Satisfied	Troubled

Ugly

Uncomfortable

Uneasy

Unprotected

Unsettled

Unsure

Violent

Vehement

Vengeful

Vivacious

Vulnerable

Weepy

Wicked

Wonderful

Worried

Zany

CHAPTER 2

Diagnose Yourself and Create Your Map for Change

Mike was a successful software sales representative, age 42, making around $80,000 a year. Although he hid it fairly well most of the time, Mike was extremely anxious whenever he had to communicate or negotiate with higher-ups at his company. Despite his success, he lacked self-confidence and was always worried that they could tell he was nervous. At the end of the day, Mike would find himself heading for one of his favorite bars or nightspots to unwind. Over time, he developed a drinking problem. He knew for a long time that something wasn't right, and he was sure he had a character flaw that couldn't be fixed. But it wasn't a character flaw. It was an anxiety challenge that led first to alcoholism and then to depression. Confused, ashamed, and afraid, he fell into an abyss of avoidance—at work, he did all he could to duck out of meetings, relying on e-mail as much as he could. It was a slippery slope: Mike's confusion and lack of awareness resulted in worsening anxiety, avoidant behavior, procrastination, excessive alcohol, and self-esteem problems. Only when his job was at risk did he seek help.

Anxiety accrues if it is allowed to grow—it's like putting money in the bank to develop interest, but in this case the "interest" is negative. Believing he had a character flaw allowed Mike to detach from his circumstances. Once in treatment, Mike identified his stressors and learned techniques for managing his anxiety fairly quickly. That gave him the confidence to tackle his drinking issues successfully. By awakening his awareness, Mike was able to create a realistic map for change based on the concrete and objective information he obtained from diagnostics.

Information is power. It is the basis of your map for change, anxiety control, higher performance, improved confidence, self-growth, and success. Establishing a destination and determining a route makes sense for physical journeys and for emotional ones too. In this chapter, we will "Mapquest" your journey from the shame, fear, and avoidance due to workplace anxiety into a life of more confidence and success.

The first step in constructing this map is to create your individual anxiety profile—the "You are here" of your map for change. Remember the F.A.T.E. concept from Chapter 1? Functions + Actions + Thoughts + Emotions. The four profiles later in this chapter—Mental Anxiety, Physical Anxiety, Avoidance, and Dependence—assess those variables, which make up the whole of who you are. Your map for change will show you the direction in which you have to travel to reach your goals.

These profiles are not meant to be absolute measurements; rather, they are a concrete way to measure relative change. Completing them the first time will provide your baseline or starting point. After establishing your baseline, you will retake the profiles every few months. You will actually be able to document your progress as you learn to manage your anxiety with objective results.

About the Awareness Technique

This program is designed for use with a biofeedback monitoring device: Your hands. (Other biofeedback devices, including our Biocard, can enhance your learning curve.) You will recall that cold or sweaty hands are the result of vasoconstriction and that they indicate stress.

You know that warm and dry hands are the result of vasodilation and indicate relaxation. The following are the three most important things for you to do regarding this awareness:

- Differentiate between good and bad stress (energy) when your hands are cold.
- Increase your awareness of internal sensations and thoughts that create warm hands.
- Correlate the temperature of your hands with your feelings. Return to the Feelings List at the end of Chapter 1 for guidance.

TUNE IN: What's the temperature of your hands now? How's your energy? How's your mood? What are your thoughts and feelings?

Attachment, Detachment, and Avoidance

Many people with anxiety learn detachment as a defense mechanism. They simply don't want to feel uncomfortable or anxious, so their mind disconnects. Why feel discomfort? Why feel anxiety? Why feel adrenaline? There is a logic in this thinking, but the "benefits" of it are only short term. In the long term, avoiding these feelings simply costs too much: too much time, too much money, too many relationships. Detaching from your feelings is destructive because it binds you to the anxiety and helps it grow. The more you detach, the more emotion is repressed and recycled. This leads to increasing anxiety, panic, obsessive worry, depression, and a myriad of stress-related physical problems that threaten your health—in addition to performance and productivity problems.

Detachment leads to avoidance. When you avoid something—a situation, a person, a problem, a challenge, or an interaction—because it creates anxiety or discomfort, the degree of avoidance will tell you a lot about the degree of your anxiety problem. When avoidance of a particular thing is present consistently because of anxiety, it is called a phobia. The more that detachment leads to avoidance, the more potential we have for what is called an avoidant personality. Common sense, logic, and objectivity will tell you that the person who avoids will not learn new skills, will not be productive, and will cause problems. Avoidance can become a deadly and insidious habit. It can be an addiction. Not only does it affect the avoidant person, but it affects the people on whom that person relies. In the workplace, an avoidant person may skip meetings, miss deadlines, avoid taking on new projects, or neglect to ask questions critical to doing a good job. Would you want to rely on a person with an avoidant personality?

Peter, age 50, a married father of two, was one of five partners in an electronics manufacturer. The challenging economy and some internal problems in his organization had led the business to the verge of collapse. A very smooth R&D director with superb social skills, Peter nonetheless had a substantial capacity for detachment. A typical example: He knew he had to reschedule a business meeting, and instead of taking action on the spot to make the two or three phone calls it would take to rearrange things, he procrastinated overnight. He described to me how his worry increased during the overnight span. "Why didn't you make the calls right away?" I asked him. In response, he described a sensation of his "brain being squeezed." That was his anxiety response; to avoid it, he detached from the feeling and what had caused it, resulting in avoidant and unproductive behavior.

TUNE IN: As you read about Peter's detachment response, what is your mood? What are you thinking? What emotions are you feeling? Return to the Feelings List in Chapter 1 if you need help describing them. Survey your body for a moment: How's your breathing? Is it even and rhythmic? Is it forced? Are you breathing from your lower stomach or your chest? Feel the muscles in your body. Do your muscles feel loose or are you aware of tightness?

In time, it became obvious that Peter and his four partners had a collective tendency to detach from communication with each other. Nobody wanted to address the big issues, let alone small ones such as rescheduling meetings. This dysfunctional communication practice was no small variable in the collapse of their business.

Hand Temperature and Attachment

You have learned that dry warm hands are the result of vasodilation of blood vessels and are equated with emotional relaxation. You know that cold, cool, or sweaty hands mean that you are not relaxed and are experiencing stress. Keep in mind that *not all stress is bad stress*. You can learn to differentiate between good and bad stress and develop an awareness of which internal sensations equate to dry warm hands. Think of the process of becoming aware of skin temperature as *a vehicle for positive attachment*—of tuning in. This does not mean that your goal is to always have warm hands. One purpose of this book is to train you to apply temperature measurement as a specific skill. You also want to develop your awareness of the meanings of changes in skin temperature. Ultimately, cold hands are your body's signal to you that your energy is percolating—and not always for negative reasons. When something is challenging my brain in a new way, or if my team is tied with the other one in the final minute of a basketball game—at those times, too, my hands feel cool. That will be true for you, too.

A few times each day I tune into the temperature of my hands. This awareness helps focus. It helps clarify feelings and the degrees of stress. As you make this program a way of life, developing skin temperature awareness will help train your mind for productive attachment.

TUNE IN: Right now, are your hands warm, cold, dry, sweaty? What is your mood? What are your thoughts? What emotions are present? How does your body feel? Return to the Feelings List for guidance.

Technology and Avoidance

Cell phones. Voice mail. E-mail. Instant messaging. Texting. GPS. All are components of the incredible evolution of technology in our society. Communications technology has created an extremely interactive world with a curious paradox. The same technology that enhances connectedness enables avoidant behavior and inhibits the learning and development of social skills. This represents a dramatic, and in our view, negative change in social etiquette and human interaction. We have all seen people sitting down to business lunches and immediately taking out their iPhones or BlackBerries to text, check or send e-mail, or grab a quick look at the news or the stock market—assembled for a particular purpose, yet not at all present in the moment. Even two people—couples out together—will sit there texting other people during what appear to be dates! Children, too, are susceptible to this trend: My coauthor, Amy Lemley, told me her 11-year-old nephew came home from a party to report that he felt left out because the other 10 kids were sitting there in silence texting each other. His concern was not that they weren't talking to him. Instead, he was upset to be the only one unable to text because he didn't have a cell phone of his own! People of all ages and socioeconomic levels hide behind their technology. I was at an important social event recently where one of our host's friends was actually pretending to talk on his cell phone to avoid interacting! I've known many people who never spontaneously answer the telephone. Sound familiar? Have you ever checked caller ID and decided not to answer the phone? Sent a flurry of e-mails back and forth when a face-to-face meeting would have been more efficient? IM'd a co-worker who was sitting right next to you? Overdependence on technology enables avoidance.

It also teaches detachment. Millions of people have become literally addicted to computer games and the Internet, spending hours and hours in front of a computer screen rather than interacting with real people. When a person spends an inordinate amount of time involved with this technology, the part of the brain where social skills abilities are located is underdeveloped. I have countless stories of patients whose dependence on technology, at the expense of direct interaction and communication, became extremely unhealthy. The losses are huge: jobs, marriages and other relationships, and *time*.

Knowing how best to communicate with colleagues and customers is an important work skill. Sure, you may prefer to e-mail, but what if a customer seldom responds to your e-mails? Jeanine, who coordinates media contacts for a political think tank, observes that the older research fellows actually have a secretary print out their e-mails rather than reading them themselves. "I'd much rather do most of our communicating via e-mail, both because I am nervous around them and because it's typically more efficient. But I have to bite the bullet and stop by their offices, or at least pick up the phone."

Social skills can atrophy just like muscles you don't use, making it that much harder to overcome anxiety issues related to interacting with colleagues or customers. Think of it this way: If you go to the gym and you're always working out your arms and chest but not your legs, the leg muscles will not develop as much as those that you focus on. So it is with social skills and communication. The more withered the social skills, the more potential exists for social and performance anxiety. It's one thing to screen certain telephone calls, it's quite another not to have the confidence to handle spontaneous and direct communication. It's easy to avoid—and easier than ever given today's communications technology. You never have to pick up that phone. You can reply to that e-mail later or not at all. You can screen everything.

"It's all about how you use it," writes John T. Cappacio in an August 24, 2009, *Forbes* article entitled "Loneliness Can Kill You." "If you use e-mail or Twitter to arrange social interactions, the technology becomes a social connector. If, however, you have 4,000 Facebook friends but never see any of them face to face, there's only a façade of being connected. It can make you lonelier." Emotional and social intelligence are vital for success (and confidence) at work—and you can only acquire that intelligence through experience.

Internet Addiction?

An overdependence on the Internet has had a huge negative impact on the work or academic performance of many of my clients. According to a September 4, 2009, Associated Press article, the following are signs of Internet addiction or over-dependence. Do any of these apply to you?

- Increasing amounts of time spent on Internet
- Failed attempts to control behavior
- Heightened euphoria while on Internet
- Craving more time on Internet; restless when not there
- Neglecting family or friends

(continued)

- Lying to others about use
- Interference with work or school
- Feeling guilty or ashamed of behavior
- Changes in sleep patterns
- Weight changes, headaches, eye fatigue, carpal tunnel syndrome
- Withdrawal from other activities

A Story of Avoidance

When I supervise my staff, I always implore them to identify problems and share them with me as quickly as possible so we have more potential to resolve them before they get out of hand. The avoidant person tends to let problems fester, which breeds an underlying anxiety. It also makes productivity impossible for the avoidant person's colleagues. Careers suffer and even end because of avoidance. When work makes you nervous, you may start to avoid the tasks that keep you employed, and you could find yourself without any work at all.

I'm very punctual. I'm very organized. I'm not obsessive about time, but I highly value it as my most precious resource, and my schedule reflects that. In my clinical practice, I operate on the six-minute rule. If a client doesn't show up or call, I will make one phone call to see if everything's okay. After that, I assume either something is wrong or the person is being avoidant. Obviously, since I am treating people for avoidance, we will address the behavior during our next therapy appointment and deal with it pronto. In my personal life, I have no tolerance for avoidant people whatsoever. I make matter-of-fact decisions. And I am not going to professionally or personally invest in another person's avoidant tendency.

Has your avoidance caused similar reactions in others? Have you lost assignments, jobs, relationships, or other important things in life? How can anyone rely on such a person? To invest in a relationship with an avoidant person, that person must have some really special characteristics. But each time avoidance occurs, those special characteristics grow less important as the frustration and anger overshadow them.

Which is why in my practice, given that I specialize in social and performance anxiety, I act as a quarterback coach. I never, never enable a person, never give the person permission to detach or avoid. That is why I am successful. It is why my patients are successful. Otherwise they would avoid and leave. They would not be able to handle the positive stress of what my therapy is about. I suggest that during the 21 days of working through my program, you refuse to give yourself any slack either; be your own coach. Do not whip out your phone or handheld when you are with other people. Do not e-mail when a phone call would be quicker and more appropriate. If at all possible, when the phone rings, answer it—no matter who it is. When you need to initiate a call—even if it is to report negative information such as the need to extend a deadline or change plans—make the call. Will this be uncomfortable for you? Probably. But do it anyway.

Give yourself credit for every little triumph in this area. Treat it as a huge success when you answer the phone or return a call. For you, it is. Above all, realize that your life is your laboratory. Try these things, see how they feel, pay attention to which workplace situations cause you the most anxiety, and then employ the techniques in this book again and again until you master them.

Amy is a successful writer who has worked in every facet of publishing—writing books, newspaper columns, magazine articles, newsletters, and Web sites.

Hers is a world of networking, interviews, deadlines, and communication. Yet Amy suffers from workplace anxiety that leads to avoidance. We wrote our first book together in 1993—*Beyond Shyness: How to Conquer Social Anxieties*. The process of writing that book helped her recognize the causes of what she had always assumed was shyness, and she learned the stress and anxiety management techniques that have worked for thousands of my patients.

She uses them to this day—and admits that although workplace anxiety still makes her struggle, it is possible to work through this program, achieve a High Performance Mind, and manage stress. She says:

My anxiety triggers stem from anger I feel when I believe I am being marginalized or unacknowledged. I also experience extreme anxiety if someone points out that I've failed to do something or have done something incorrectly. My symptoms are cold hands, racing pulse, a feeling like an electrical charge moving through my arms, heaviness in my chest, trouble breathing, and a "hamster wheel" of thoughts running through my head: "They think I'm stupid." "You can't do this." "The person you need to interview doesn't want to talk to you." "You messed up." "You're not good enough."

For 13 years, I was a freelance writer. Because I worked from home and had a variety of clients, I could breeze in and breeze out, do my thing and go on to the next project. But after many years with a great track record, I started messing up. My work was excellent, but it was late— which, if you think about it, means it was not excellent at all, at least not for the people whose schedules I compromised.

A friend asked me then what I wanted most in life. "To retire." She smiled wisely and asked me an unexpected question: "If you were to retire, what would that look like?" My list went something like this: I wouldn't have to manage my time, I wouldn't have to juggle several clients and projects at a time, I wouldn't have to handle invoicing and bookkeeping. Basically, I was saying that I wanted to avoid and detach. "Retirement" had nothing to do with enjoying the good life—it was all about avoiding my real life. In that moment, I realized that my fears were running the show. I had a great life, but I was wasting it, squandering my time, my vitality, my friendships, and my career opportunities rather than confronting the avoidance-anxiety-avoidance-anxiety hamster wheel. So that was the moment for me.

I have since participated in and managed both small and large products successfully. Jonathan's program instructs us how to "tune in" to where we are, to recognize in the moment—or even right before the moment—that we are going into default mode. I think of default mode as akin to that Microsoft Word default mode—remember it? With that dopey little paper clip who pops up and offers to help? That's our default: A dopey little paper clip who pops into our consciousness and says, "You can't do this. Feel how cold and clammy your hands are? Feel how your pulse is racing? Don't think about it. Distract yourself with something else. You can't survive the deadline pressure, so just ignore it."

For me, it's about looking good—appearing competent and capable. That leads me to agree to take on extra work and agree to unrealistic deadlines because I'm afraid of seeming incompetent, because I can't do it all. I avoid saying no. I avoid saying "I need more time." I detach, go out of communication, and infuriate the people I work with. The result is that I look incompetent—the exact thing I wanted to avoid!

It embarrasses me to admit it—but I promised the whole truth, so here it is—I became so nervous at work recently that I was afraid to ask a simple question for fear that my supervisor would overhear me and decide that my question was one more piece of evidence that I was underperforming or incompetent. To overcome this issue, I used mind states balance: I stopped listening to the critical inner script and consciously attached myself to my feelings. Helpless. Judged. Guilty. A victim. I let myself tune in to those things for a moment before calling on my objective inner voice to remind me that, to be productive, we need to know how to do things; to know how to do things, we need to ask questions; therefore, we need to ask questions in order to be productive. Simple, right? It seems that way now, but at the moment I was a deer in the headlights.

We all are capable of learning and growing. And I wish we weren't so afraid of reaching out to one another and revealing some of our fears. I have gotten braver about that, and it has helped. One recent example is how I managed the anxiety I had around making a presentation at work. I am a crackerjack marketing copywriter. I was assigned to present an hour-long how-to session to a group of five colleagues. Now, these are people I work with every day and genuinely like. Yet I was obsessing over this presentation as though my career depended on it. Then I got in touch with my fears: fear that I would babble on and on, fear that I would seem like an arrogant know-it-all, fear that I would lose my place in the presentation, fear that I would be too clumsy to manage the technology that would allow me to project my laptop screen onto the LCD panel.

At first I couldn't shake my anxiety. So here's what I did: I attached to it. I acknowledged to myself that I was nervous. I figured out why. And then I took a brave step. I spoke one-on-one with each of my colleagues and said, "Hey, this may seem weird, but I am nervous about my presentation on Friday." Each person asked why, and I was honest about it. Each person was kind and reassuring. A few days later, as we sat around the conference table, I felt comfortable, relaxed, and supported. It wasn't that I no longer thought I would mess up or seem like a know-it-all. It was that I had expressed and acknowledged those fears, to myself and to my audience, ahead of time. The stress was there, it was real, but it was not a bad thing. As the adrenaline inevitably arrived, I rode it like a wave, using its energy to deliver a lively, engaging hour that was effective, informative, and well received.

I am usually able to recognize the anxiety trap before I fall into it—thanks to the techniques Jonathan presents in this book. I return to the diagnostics from time to time to check in with myself and see how well I am managing. I look at places where I have been avoidant—unaccountable, unreliable, out of communication. I remind myself every day to do what I said I would do when I said I would do it—which is the key to managing my particular brand of workplace anxiety. I have a phrase for this: "Managing my integrity as a health practice." My advice as we move forward together in this book? Take it on as though your life is at stake. Because, in many ways, it is.

TUNE IN: Focus on your breathing now, inhaling through your nose and exhaling through either your nose or mouth. Spend 60 seconds on a series of rhythmic breathing: Inhale slowly 1 . . . 2 . . . 3 . . . 4 . . . Then exhale 4 . . . 3 . . . 2 . . . 1 . . . . Each inhale–exhale should take 8 to 12 seconds. Focus only on your breathing for the next 60 seconds.

Recognizing Your Own Detachment

Right now, turn to your notes and make a list of the kinds of thinking you have learned to detach from. Write down this list. What are the three primary things you do not want to think about but you know you *should* be thinking about? Now ask yourself, besides being able to avoid anxiety at the moment, what are the repercussions of your detachment? For example, do you solve the problems that are present? Do they impact your productivity? Do you resolve the emotional challenges?

These are the three primary issues I don't want to think about but should think about

1. _____

_____

2. _____

_____

3. _____

_____

What do I gain from avoiding and detaching from these issues?

1. _____

_____

2. _____

_____

3. _____

_____

What are the costs of avoiding and detaching from these issues?

4. _____

_____

5. _____

_____

6. _____

_____

Now make a list of the situations or people you are currently avoiding that you should not or don't want to be avoiding. Do you see the negative implications of your avoidance?

People or situations I am currently avoiding:

1. _____

_____

2. _____

_____

3. _____

_____

What do I gain from avoiding and detaching from these issues?

7. _____

_____

8. _____

_____

9. _____

_____

What are the costs of avoiding and detaching from these issues?

10. _____

_____

11. _____

_____

12. _____

_____

"You Are as Sick as Your Secrets"

That is a saying from the 12-step addiction programs—and avoidance can be an addiction. Your anxiety issues are private. But as Amy can tell you, carrying the burden of workplace anxiety can be as debilitating as a physical illness—and can cause symptoms of physical illness as well as actual ailments. Think of the physical as well as emotional stress you experience when you are holding this "terrible secret" inside and doing all you can to avoid having it come out. Detaching from it is a coping mechanism that allows you to suffer in silence, without expressing your fears and frustrations even to yourself. You don't have to tell anyone that work makes you nervous. But you do have to be honest with yourself. Don't waste time. To ensure maximum productivity as you work through this program, it is imperative that you be as honest as possible when you complete the next section, the Physical Anxiety Profile. You don't want to have any secrets here. You want to be as open and as honest with yourself as is possible. After all, who is evaluating? What point—other than denial or detachment—is there in lying to yourself?

Understanding physical symptoms is one of the most confusing issues for the anxiety sufferer. Often when people experience symptoms they conclude that something is medically wrong. And there may be—but look first to anxiety as the cause. More than 70 percent of physician visits are due to stress and anxiety. In order to take an absolutely conservative and objective approach when physical symptoms are present, please consult with your physician to rule out physical causes. For example if you have recurring headaches, you want to know whether the cause is muscle tension or vascular constriction, dynamics that can be resolved by anxiety management, or an organic problem such as a tumor. Some of the symptoms listed in the Physical Anxiety Profile in the next section can be caused by factors other than stress and anxiety, such as hypoglycemia (low blood sugar); however, the symptoms listed are the ones most common to stress and anxiety. Before you consider these symptoms, study the Frequency, Severity, and Career Interference listings, and choose an appropriate number to assign to each symptom in the three boxes under these headings.

Physical Anxiety Profile

What does your body do when you feel nervous or anxious?

To produce your own Physical Anxiety Profile as a baseline, study the rankings under the three headings in the table below. Then rate the frequency and severity of your own physical symptoms; place the appropriate number in the boxes to the left of each symptom. Then do the ranking of career interference—how much the symptom prevents you from succeeding at work. Add up the total score and record it in your notes. Later in the program, and perhaps for months or years to come, you may want to monitor your progress by comparing your current score to this baseline. You could even use your current notes as a long-term journal of your progress. As you complete these profiles, be spontaneous and trust your instincts. No perfectionism necessary!

Frequency

    1 = Never

    2 = Two times a month or less

3 = One or two times a week

4 = Three times a week but not daily

5 = One or more times daily

Severity

1 = No problem at all

2 = Minor discomfort; manageable

3 = Noticeably uncomfortable

4 = Severe

5 = Absolute panic out of control

Career interference

1 = not at all

2 = a little

3 = moderately

4 = significantly

5 = severe to the point of incapacity or phobia

Let's discuss career interference.

1 = Not at all. If you choose the Not at all rating, there's no issue; you're able to concentrate and continue doing what you're doing, whether it's speaking in front of a group, working with your supervisor, interacting spontaneously with your peers, or talking on a conference call. You are fine; you're not distracted by this symptom. You certainly don't try to leave the situation.

2 = A little. The symptom may occasionally cause you to lose your train of thought, falter, or hesitate during conversation. You are able to find ways to compensate, and your interaction is not inhibited to a noticeable extent. You continue to interact on a regular basis. The symptom does not cause avoidance of interacting or procrastination or rationalizing why you should not follow through.

3 = Moderately. The symptom occasionally keeps you from doing something that you would like to do or are required to do. You are uncomfortable enough to consider whether the discomfort of not avoiding would be worth the effort.

4 = Significantly. The symptom has caused you to develop the habit of avoiding the situations that cause it; whether by procrastination or passive participation. While you do not avoid all interaction, you stay out of it when you can and spend a lot of time negatively evaluating or worrying.

5 = Severe to the point of incapacity. This is where anxiety turns into panic and phobia, complete avoidance of the situation. You are so uncomfortable that you will do anything to avoid.

Physical Anxiety Profile

Symptom or behavior	Frequency	Severity	Work Interference
Poor eye contact			
Mind going blank			
Selective mutism (not talking due to fear)			
Shortness of breath			
Accelerated heartbeat			
Sweating			
Blushing			
Nausea			
Abdominal discomfort			
Choking			
Difficulty swallowing			
Depersonalization; feeling of detachment from yourself			
Tingling, numbness			
Drinking alcohol to control nervousness			
Dizziness			
Muscle weakness			
Diarrhea			
Constipation			
Heart palpitations			
Inability to talk			
Mind going blank			

(continued)

(Continued)

Symptom or behavior	Frequency	Severity	Work Interference
Flushes			
Chills			
Voice quivering or shaking			
Sweaty palms			
Cold hands			
Twitches, tics, spasms			
Stuttering			
Using substances to control tension			
Compulsive behavior			
Hyperventilation			
Indigestion			
Chest pain			
Insomnia			
Problems sleeping			
Headaches			
Difficulty with bowel movements			
Other			
Total score			

Mental Anxiety Profile

What thoughts recur when you are nervous or anxious?

Everything starts with a thought. Thinking is the basis of cognition, which is defined as the phenomenon of knowing. What you think determines what you feel. What you think determines your behavior. Thinking occurs at conscious and at unconscious levels. The more that you can be conscious of your thinking, the more productive you will be at managing anxiety and developing confidence. Rate the Frequency, Severity, and Career Interference (using the previous scales) for the thoughts listed in the following table. Write your answers in your notes.

Mental Anxiety Profile

Thought	Frequency	Severity	Work Interference
People will see I'm nervous.			
I'll have nothing to say.			
I will not know what to say.			
I'll say something that does not make sense.			
I don't trust myself.			
I'm going to blush.			
I'm going to sweat.			
People will see who I really am.			
People will not get to see who I really am.			
What will people think of me?			
Am I dressed okay?			
I might embarrass myself.			
I might humiliate myself.			
I'm going to panic and I'll have to leave.			
If they knew me they wouldn't like me.			
They will think I'm a fraud.			
They can see I don't belong.			
I'll screw up.			
Am I good enough?			
I'm ashamed.			
I'm going to lose control.			
I'll do the wrong thing.			
They will see I'm different.			
They are better than I.			
I don't look right.			
They can see my flaw.			
Other			
Total Score			

Avoidance Profile

Do you have an addiction to avoidance? Victor was a brilliant economist teaching at a major American university. In addition, he had successful business interests in Europe. He was the beneficiary of many grants and a much sought after researcher and consultant. Victor, a perfectionist, was obsessed with fear of being noticeably nervous during any presentation in front of his peers. Because of this obsession, Victor avoided presenting his work at professional symposiums and conferences. The result of this avoidance was frustration and anger, which turned into self-loathing despite his successes. His self-esteem was very much at risk because the truth of Victor's desire was that he *wanted* to be in front of the groups. He wanted the accolades!

As discussed in Chapter 1, the philosophy and strategy for high performance and productivity are based on being proactive. This is the process of quarterbacking—playing offense, not defense. Defensive positioning is the opposite of being proactive. This is where avoidant thinking and behaviors come in to play. Amy's story clarifies this. She described how her avoidant thinking and behavior became a lifestyle and an ingrained personality trait that she, like so many people, believed was a permanent flaw. Avoidance occurs to different degrees. It can become an *addiction*. Again, using the same numbers as before to rate Frequency, Severity, and Work Interference, complete the following profile to determine your degree of avoidance.

Avoidance Profile

Statement	Frequency	Severity	Work Interference
I avoid talking about myself.			
I avoid speaking in front of groups.			
I avoid speaking spontaneously in groups.			
I avoid conference calls.			
I avoid initiating.			
I avoid accepting challenges.			

Statement	Frequency	Severity	Work Interference
I'm afraid that if I try something and can't do it, people will think I'm a failure.			
I cut situations short even when I'm enjoying myself because I fear others are bored with me.			
I tend to put things off.			
I often think or say "I don't feel like it."			
I avoid solving problems in a timely fashion.			
I make excuses to avoid things I think I'll do poorly.			
I fear taking on added responsibility at work.			
I avoid interacting with authority figures.			
If I make a mistake, I try to cover it up to avoid a confrontation.			
I avoid conflict.			
I avoid communication in general.			
I avoid talking about my feelings.			
I avoid developing ideas.			
I avoid sharing ideas.			
I avoid being in touch with my feelings.			
I avoid bringing uncomfortable thoughts to a conscious level.			
When people interact with me spontaneously, I try to avoid the situation.			
I avoid asking questions.			
I avoid eye contact.			
I avoid answering the phone.			
I am resistant to change in my work environment.			
Other			
Total Score			

The more avoidance, the more potential there is for inhibited learning of skills. Experience is needed for skills development, whether it's for public speaking, communication, conflict management, relationship development, or performance. The reality is that avoidance kills self-esteem and makes anxiety that much more unbearable. Amy has come up with an interesting way to remind herself to stay on top of her projects as a way of reducing her anxiety.

She devised an "Integrity Cheat Sheet" and has it posted at her desk (see below). You may wish to copy it into your notes or even post it somewhere at your own workplace. If posting it on your cubicle wall seems too public, consider putting it inside a drawer where you can see it and take inspiration and coaching from it every day.

Integrity Cheat Sheet

1. Do what you said you would do and do it on time.
2. Do what others would expect you to do even if you didn't say you would do it.
3. Do it the way it was meant to be done.
4. Acknowledge that you won't be doing it, or won't be doing it on time, as soon as you realize that, and deal with the consequences.

The "I Don't Know" Disease

There are many things I don't know and I'm sure there are many things you don't know. If I were writing a book specifically about the avoidant personality, the title would be "I Don't Know." These simple words often become an unhealthy and unproductive reflex. Consider for a moment: If you have an itch, you don't think before you scratch, you just do it spontaneously and reflexively. The same is true with the words "I don't know." All too often these words serve the purposes of enabling detachment, shutting down communication, censoring the development of ideas, inhibiting risk-taking, stopping the process of sharing differing opinions, killing creativity, and making sure that intimacy does not happen. "I don't know" slams the door on introspection, it slams the door on productivity, it slams the door on success. Let's think of "I don't know" as a door to open—the answers behind it will help you develop a High Performance Mind.

TUNE IN: Think about how often you say "I don't know." Identify times when you really did know. Consider whether those were situations in which you simply did not want to attach to thinking or feeling that would have been required to answer the question. List three examples in which you said "I don't know" although you knew the answer, just to avoid attaching yourself to the thought or feeling surrounding the question:

1. _____
   _____

2. _____
   _____

3. _____
   _____

Dependence Profile

When you don't feel you can depend on yourself—and really, what avoidant person can?—you depend on other things: co-workers, friends, alcohol, your computer. Rather than face reality head on, you get somebody or something else that will serve as a buffer—either by dulling your feelings (as with alcohol or recreational drugs) or by avoiding doing the things you said you would do or know you should do (remember the Integrity Cheat Sheet). Whereas some people avoid learning new technology, other avoidant people rely on it too heavily—blaming their own errors on technology failures rather than taking ownership of them.

Amy told me about a plaque that sat on her father's desk for almost 40 years: "Lemley's Law: If something can go wrong, don't let it." What does that mean? It means you have to give up avoiding the fact that life throws curve balls. It means having a back-up plan—or at least an easy ability and *willingness* to come up with one when necessary. It's great to use a computer or a handheld as a brain that keeps your schedule, contact information, and other important stuff in one place. But what if technology fails you? If your electronic calendar does not pop up with an appointment reminder or your battery goes dead, how are you going to handle it? Plan B thinking is not obsessing over everything that can go wrong. It is being accountable for your commitments and being respectful of other people's time (and your own).

Clearly, dependence is relative. So long as you make conscious, active, empowered decisions about what and on whom you will depend, you will stay on the right track. Humans depend on each other. That's as it should be. It's overdependence you should work to eliminate. Overdependence is the power on which negative avoidance is based. To get a sense of your own dependent behavior and whether it interferes with your work, complete the following profile, as you have done with the preceding ones.

Dependence Profile

Statement	Frequency	Severity	Work Interference
I depend on technology to avoid interaction.			
I use alcohol, medicine, or other substances to deal with stress and anxiety.			
I rely too heavily on other people's advice and opinions.			
I allow others to make decisions for me.			
I rely on others to communicate for me.			
Usually someone else sets up appointments for me.			
Other people answer the phone for me.			
I get another person to make phone calls for me.			

Statement	Frequency	Severity	Work Interference
I screen calls with an answering machine so that I'm not caught off guard.			
I depend on colleagues to do work for me if the task makes me uncomfortable.			
I depend on others to decide what to do rather than initiate.			
When alone, I often have a feeling of indecision when faced with a dilemma.			
I depend on others to solve my problems.			
I depend on others to resolve conflicts.			
I depend on others to interact with authority figures.			
I depend on making up excuses in order to avoid challenges.			
Other			
Total Score			

Obsession

Once I was in New York City presenting to a group of community affairs radio producers regarding the Friendship Connection, a nonprofit organization for which I consult. This group provides social therapy for adults and teenagers with learning disabilities. I was clear on my motivation for being there: The purpose of my presentation was to get air time for the Friendship Connection on the radio. The setting was a hotel conference room, where I sat with 14 producers around an oval table. I had approximately 15 minutes to do my thing, and I was very confident if not a bit cocky. During the presentation, there was good energy and a substantial amount of interest. At the end of the presentation, one of the producers asked me if I had a press release for them. Whoops! Guess what? I had not brought one.

This was a substantial mistake. Without a "leave-behind," I had nothing concrete to remind my audience of their interest in my topic or even a business card to let them know how to contact me. It was embarrassing. While riding the Long Island Railroad back to my office, I lamented my error. What a ridiculous mistake I had made! How stupid! As good as I might have been at presenting, I didn't leave the producers with any concrete contact information. Given that these producers were so busy, the probability was they were not going to contact me. I had thought that telling them the address of my web site would be enough. Such idiocy!

I stayed with this thinking and analyzing for about half an hour. Then I let go of it. The key here is *letting go*. What more could I do? I objectively analyzed. I could not go back and change the situation. Going over and over it in my mind would serve no purpose other than to beat myself up. I had certainly learned my lesson. As I thought it through, I was conscious of how unresolved anger drives obsessive thinking. I was furious with myself and could not give up the anger. Once I realized this, I was able to let go of the anger and move on.

Think now for a moment: Identify a recent situation where you were going over and over something in your mind. Do you see a connection to anger? Do you see how much it wastes your most valuable resource—time?

I define obsessive thinking as "sustained, ingrained worry." Is worrying bad? Not necessarily. There are two types of worry: that which is energy for the sake of problem solving and that which merely torments you because you won't let it go. Maybe you should just learn a lesson, draw a conclusion, or choose an action to take, and then move on. Negative obsessiveness is driven by endless thinking that the situation was bad and must never happen again. This inhibits the development of creativity, exploration, spontaneity, and adventure. Obsessions (thoughts) can become compulsive (behaviors) to different degrees.

Now, measure your obsessive tendencies. Rate each of the following on a scale of 1 to 10—1 is minimal; 10 is the most—and record the rating in the box at right or in your notes.

Obsession

Statement	Frequency	Severity	Work Interference
I have thoughts or ideas that run through my head repeatedly that I would like to stop but can't.			
I become uncomfortable with spontaneous unscripted verbal communication.			
I would describe myself as a perfectionist.			
I would rather go without something than feel obliged to another person.			
I am upset if my regular routine is disrupted by unforeseen events.			
It is very important to me that everything be neat, tidy, and organized to the point that I cannot take action until it is.			
I insist on doing a task myself rather than delegating responsibility.			
I go through a set and rigid routine before going to bed that, if broken, would cause me difficulty in getting to sleep.			
I become uncomfortable taking on challenges where I do not know what's going to happen next.			
I become uncomfortable playing games where I do not know what's going to happen next.			
I consider myself rigid and inflexible in my thinking.			
I think about superstitions or rituals as a way of making sure I am in control.			
Other			
Total Score			

Self-Esteem

Self-esteem is essential for psychological survival. It is an emotional sine qua non—without some measure of self-worth, life can be enormously painful, with many basic needs going unmet. Judging and rejecting yourself causes enormous pain. You take fewer social, academic, or career risks. You make it more difficult for yourself to meet people, or interview for a job, or push hard for something where you might not succeed. You limit your ability to open yourself with others, be the center of attention, hear criticism, ask for help, or solve problems.

—*Self-Esteem* (New Harbinger Publications, 2000)

Consider the difference between a person who says "I failed at my attempt" and the person who says "I am a failure," and between the person who says "I have lost three battles" and the one who says "I am a loser." Failure has more to do with a person's self-concept than with actual unsuccessful experiences. The person who suffers from social or performance anxiety misinterprets unsuccessful experiences. Not winning, making mistakes, rejection, and failing at something are too often interpreted as flaws, or an attack on the core of the person's being. Unresolved emotions from the past are activated.

Self-esteem problems are the root of social and performance anxiety! It is low self-esteem that makes the social anxiety sufferer become overly susceptible to exaggerated feelings of shame, embarrassment, and humiliation. As you learn to develop a High Performance Mind via this self-help program, your self-esteem will grow. Imagine how much better you will feel—and how much more time you will have—once you stop obsessing over how "bad" or "wrong" or "flawed" you are.

Are great home run hitters like Babe Ruth, Hank Aaron, Roger Maris, or Barry Bonds remembered for their strikeouts? As great a bas-ketball player as Michael Jordan was, he missed many more shots than he made. Surely Mick Jagger and Tina Turner sang a few sour notes in their time. Surely Bill Gates has made a few mistakes. Do you think that great scientists never made errors in the process of discovery?

Self-esteem is a sense of liking yourself, liking how you relate to others, feeling personally secure, and not having to prove your manhood or womanhood with external symbols. A professional associate of mine, Dr. Eli Ran Eliaz, an experienced drama thera-pist with whom I worked for many years, has referred to self-esteem as "self as a team." I like that concept!

Self-esteem is not derived solely from feedback you get from oth-ers. As the comedian Katt Williams says, "How could I hurt your self-esteem? It's *self*-esteem!" It comes from within. It is important to guard against variable self-esteem, in which your self-esteem is overly predicated on feedback from others. It can be easy to feel good about yourself when others tell you you've done a terrific job. But the world doesn't work that way most of the time. And what happens to your self-esteem when someone criticizes you? What happens when someone disagrees with you or gets angry with you? Does this mean you are not okay as a person? Honest feedback from others is an im-portant component of personal and professional growth, but you cannot and should not base your self-worth on what others convey. Variable self-esteem is an impossible game to play, although many perfectionists invest in it. When you abandon avoidance, attach to your thoughts, emotions, and actions, and, as Amy says, "manage your integrity as a health practice," you can learn to take satisfaction in a job well done whether anyone tells you you've done well or not. Real self-esteem is not harmed by mistakes or by someone pointing out those mistakes. Variable-self esteem creates much distress and greatly inhibits high performance. Let self-esteem come from within.

Sam, age 48, was married with two children. While Sam played a major role in growing his business through sales as well as developing technology, he began to experience intense obsessive worry regard-ing his performance in conference and sales calls after experiencing the first panic attack of his life. Sam's track record with sales and con-ference calls was very successful, yet he did not allow it to bolster his self-esteem. Sam had a nurturing deficit. He grew up in a trailer park on the "other side of the tracks" and recalled a childhood of poverty. He had had a distant relationship with his father, without any true bonding or emotional interchange and no paternal acknowledgment. Somewhere along the way, he had unconsciously concluded that he had to be perfect before he could feel good about himself.

Seeking perfection has its plus side. Sam's childhood experience was one reason he became successful financially. He learned from childhood what he didn't want in adulthood. He overcompensated, drawing from Michael Jordan's famous saying, "You're as good as your last game." Each "game" or conference call was characterized by an overadaptation—an overly perfectionist attitude. He was too tightly wound and not adaptable to evolving conversations or circumstances. His internal critical script said he had to be perfect for everyone; his feeling good was totally dependent on this process. His nurturing deficit made it hard to acknowledge himself for success and comfort himself after failures. His self-esteem depended on others' feedback.

The following self-esteem chart measures how highly you value yourself. Indicate how much each of the statements represents the way you have thought or felt about yourself during the last few months, using the number ratings in the scale below.

Very Much	Somewhat	Not Very Much	Never
3	2	1	0

I minimize my abilities.   _____

I expect others to fault my work.   _____

I wish I were someone else.   _____

I make demands on myself that I
   would not make on others.   _____

When I succeed I don't think I
   deserve it.   _____

I like who I am.   _____

Under pressure I expect things to
   go wrong.   _____

I blame myself when things do not   _____
   work the way I expect.

Scoring: _____

   0–6 healthy

   7–10 fair

   11–15 guarded

   16+ unhealthy

The True Definition of Success

What does "success" mean to you? A teenage patient once told me that her definition of success was owning a Mercedes. A high percentage of my patients have been perfectionists whose idea of success depended on creating external manifestations of affluence. Yet even those who have attained such things—fancy cars, summer homes, and so forth—feel unsuccessful. It's almost as though nothing is enough (there's that nurturing deficit!). Others have characterized success as being a great public speaker or being the most skilled expert in some field.

With 59 years of personal and professional life experience, I have learned the true definition of success: being in a good mood. *Mood* is defined as an emotional state influenced by varying levels of wellbeing. There are many variables that determine mood. Certainly money is one, but I have seen many very unhappy wealthy individuals. Other variables include work satisfaction (which also plays a major role in longevity, physical health, the quality of relationships, and social life), exercise, nutrition, the ability to manage emotions, the ability to solve problems, manage stress, and so on.

In fact, a review of more than 245 studies from 32 nations around the world found the critical components of happiness include being healthy mentally as well as physically, having good relationships, and feeling in control of your own life. The absence of those things is what can make you nervous at work. "Given the importance of work, both economically and socially, one's achievements and experiences at work and the quality of their working life are a very important component of overall satisfaction," wrote business professor Alfred Michael Dockery in *Happiness, Life Satisfaction, and the Role of Work*.

One thing is for sure. Unresolved anxiety will negatively impact a person's mood because fear will inhibit or handicap his or her proactive journey toward achieving the truth of desire. If you really want that new position, but fear its responsibilities and don't go for it . . . if you really want to be in front of that group but fear being noticeably nervous and don't go for it . . . if you really want to make that discovery, but don't go for it . . . you are not going to be happy!

TUNE IN: What has your average mood been in the last three months? Don't say "up and down" or "it depends." Give it careful thought. Grade your average on a scale of 1 to 10. A 10 is perfect—which is just about impossible for anybody. A 1 is the worst and corresponds to very extreme depression. Seven is the first of the quality numbers. From 8 to 9 you are rocking and rolling. Six means you're not quite making it into the substantial happiness mode. Five means moderate unhappiness and borderline depression, and 4 means you know that depression is present.

My average mood in the last three months has been a _____.

Tip: When you are experiencing that up-and-down feeling in your mood, take some time each day to attach to the feelings you are having. You may want to jot the rating down in your notes or calendar. You could start to notice a trend in which things come up that affect your mood: certain tasks, meetings, interactions, and so on. As we move forward in this book, you'll learn what to do to steady your mood. It is possible to be in a good mood most of the day, every day.

By filling out the profiles in this chapter in a responsible and honest manner, you have created a map for resolving your anxiety and building the confidence to succeed at work. You have more understanding of your F.A.T.E. The brain likes definites! In this chapter you have created a helpful map. You know where you are right now, and you know where you are going. You know the F.AT.E. that you must change and restructure. By redoing these profiles developmentally every few months, you will be accountable for your self-growth and be able to measure your developmental success. Believe it or not, in time you will enjoy looking backward and seeing how far you have come, and that, I promise you, boosts your true self-esteem.

TUNE IN: For the next 60 seconds, focus on deep, rhythmic diaphragmatic breathing. Inhale 1 . . . 2 . . . 3 . . . 4, . . Then exhale 4 . . . 3 . . . 2 . . . 1 . . .

Each inhale–exhale should take between 8 and 12 seconds. Stay in rhythm. Now, tune in to your hands. Are they warm or cold? What are you feeling? Pair the temperature with the feeling. If you like, you can return to the Feelings List in Chapter 1 for ideas.

Understanding Your Five Mind States

Imagine that you are sitting at a conference table with three colleagues and three outside business contacts. You were asked to present a five-minute description of your role in the company. Each of your colleagues will take a turn doing so. You are scheduled to go third. Your turn comes. What are you telling yourself?

1. "People want to hear what you have to say."

   "If you seem nervous, they won't mind. They may not even notice!"

   "Just do the best you can. Your contribution is valuable."

   "There's opportunity here."

2. "You have to be perfect."

   "You don't know what you're talking about."

   "You are a failure."

3. "My hands are cool. My heart rate is increasing."

   "It's my turn to describe my role."

   "I am doing what I was assigned to do."

4. "If people can see I'm nervous, it's the end of the world."

"I'd better stick to my notes. If I say something spontaneously, I could mess up."

"If I fail, I am probably worthless."

5. "It's fun to share knowledge."

"I like talking and listening."

"I am in the zone."

As you imagine yourself sitting there at that conference table, just seconds before you start to speak, which of these internal scripts sounds most familiar to you? Which ones are least familiar? What do you tell yourself when this type of situation comes up?

Glance over the internal scripts again. You probably hear Script 2 and Script 4 more strongly than the rest. In people with workplace anxiety, those two internal scripts dominate. One is telling you that you will mess up, and the other is saying that not only will you mess up, but the consequences of messing up will be devastating. These scripts are saying that messing up means something about you—that you are worthless, stupid, a failure, not good enough. When these two scripts dominate, the other scripts recede.

Consider, on the other hand, Script 1: It is the voice of encouragement and support. Script 3 is "Just the facts, ma'am"—no opinion, no anticipation, no judgment, just logic. And Script 5 is a playful one. It is enthusiastic and has the potential for passion—no fear, no need to please, just being in the moment.

These five internal scripts characterize the five *mind states* that make up a personality. All five are essential to who you are. Balancing all five—not merely trying to ignore or get rid of the ones that spike your anxiety reactions—is the key to success. With all five in balance, you can achieve a High Performance Mind.

Balanced Mind States = High Performance Mind

I have adapted this method of mind state balance specifically to treat social and performance anxiety. The theory has its roots in a type of psychology called transactional analysis, which traces its history from Sigmund Freud to contemporary psychologists and scientists such as Eric Berne. But don't worry: Mind state balance will not be full of psychobabble. We are not interested in abstract concepts here. We are interested in concrete examples that show you, step by step, how to identify and work with your mind states for proper balance. (Remember your most valuable resource? It's time. My own internal atomic clock compels me to be as clear and direct as possible in introducing this process to you.)

Each of the five mind states is a specific form of energy that serves a useful purpose as a component of personality. The mind states are dynamic and cooperative. They work together, and when they are balanced, you are poised for high performance. Chapter 4 will introduce the five-step technique that allows you to integrate and balance the mind states.

All five mind states exist at all times at various levels, so their collective energy is finite or limited. They all work together, which is why balancing them is so important. With all five mind states in balance, a person can "hear" the various internal scripts and take the most productive, effective messages from each. The mind states comprise not just the internal scripts I have mentioned, but also the emotions, actions, and physical sensations that go along with them—each mind state has an associated F.A.T.E. that can be positive or negative.

A healthy mind state balance is the basis on which to build a healthy, productive work life. People suffering from workplace anxiety do not have a healthy mind state balance. Whenever anxiety is present, some of your mind states' internal scripts are too loud, and some are too quiet. Your thoughts, feelings, actions, and physical well-being do not coordinate with each other in support of high performance. The objective, then, is to balance them out—dialing some of them down by bringing others up. Again, their collective energy is finite.

Understanding this objective is critical. Balance your mind states by increasing the energy of some while decreasing the energy of others. Once you achieve mind state balance and learn to sustain it, your F.A.T.E. will have optimum energy. You will be operating with a High Performance Mind.

TUNE IN: How are you feeling? Are you distracted? Are you focused? Mind state balance is an exciting concept, but it also can be intimidating to confront those "internal critical scripts" that tend to repeat over and over in your mind.

Please take a few moments now to center yourself before we move further. Breathe in through your nose 1 ... 2 ... 3 ... 4 ... then slowly exhale through your mouth, pacing yourself 4 ... 3 ... 2 ... 1 ... One more time, slowly inhale through your nose, then slowly exhale 4 ... 3 ... 2 ... 1 ... By now, you should be automatically pacing your rhythmic breathing at 8 to 12 seconds per inhale–exhale. If so, excellent! If you need more practice, spend an extra few minutes throughout the day until you can meet the 8-to-12-second target. The more diligent you are about practicing the breathing exercises in this program, the more they will become a healthy reflex for you. This simple breathing exercise is something to turn to throughout your day whenever you wish to focus, concentrate, or calm down. It's effective, it's free, and it's as portable as they come—and it takes only seconds to work.

How often do you look at your watch during the workday? A lot? A little? Try the following for a while. Every time you look at your watch or check the clock or the time on your computer screen, take in a long, slow deep breath as a means of centering yourself. Try it for 21 days, and you'll establish a healthy relaxation habit. Amy adopted this practice when we started writing this book and raves about it. "When I feel anxious, I experience something called costochondritis—excessive tightness around my ribs," she explains. "Pausing for a deep, expansive breath gave me the stretch I needed to eliminate this symptom, which had been chronic. I was amazed."

Right now, you are in the process of absorbing a lot of critical information. Specifically, you are sifting through your own internal scripts as you learn about the mind states. As you "attach" to this information—recognizing and accepting what is true for you—you are likely to experience variable emotions. The more willing you are to attach to this process, the faster and more completely you will be able to triumph over your anxiety and become a high performer.

TUNE IN: Connect to your dominant hand for a moment. Feel it with your mind. Now place that hand to your cheek. Is your hand warm or cold? Is your hand dry or do you feel perspiration? What are your thoughts? What are your feelings?

Is your hand cold? If your hand is cold, identify the thoughts and feelings that are translating into stress—and remember, cold hands can mean good stress is at work!

Is your hand warm? If your hand is warm, be clear on the thoughts and feelings that are translating into emotional relaxation. Return to the Feelings List at the end of Chapter 1 and clarify the exact emotion you are currently experiencing. Did you take a look at the list? Please follow through on that every time you are asked to do so. Learning to identify and name your feelings is a critical skill that you will use as you work through this program. If you like, you can write down the feelings you identified in your notes.

Know Your Own Mind: Naming the Five Mind States

As humans, we usually think in words. That may seem like a simple thing to say, but it's worth considering for a moment. It's true we can recall images, sounds, smells, tastes, and physical sensations. But we use words to name those things for ourselves even as they occur. When you experience a sensation such as a chill up your spine or you recognize a friend in a crowd, do you use words to narrate the incident? Those words interpret your experience: The chill might cause you to say to yourself, "Wow, that's spooky," or "Autumn's in the air." Seeing your friend may prompt you to say, "This is a great surprise!" or "Jeez, I should have called her back last week." We say things to ourselves all the time.

Think of the mind states as actors, each with a role to play. Below, the mind states are given names and definitions. Read these definitions and memorize them so that the five character names are clear and easy to remember.

Nurturing Parent (NP): NP energy promotes growth, teaches, acknowledges, and provides support. "You're doing your best," "It's okay to make mistakes."

Critical Parent (CP):	CP energy represents authority, evaluates, and passes judgment. "You're doing it wrong," You're doing it well," "That was not your best work."
Adult (A):	A energy is logical and objective. "I have a meeting at 8 A.M.," "I need two hours to prepare."
Adapted Child (AC):	AC energy is conforming, cooperating, compromising, and manipulating. "I have to do this right," "I have to be perfect," "I feel confident."
Natural Child (NC):	NC energy is responsible for spontaneity, exploration, creativity, and joy. It is the truth of desire. "Just do it!" "Do whatever you want."

All five of these inner scripts are present in you all the time. When you are experiencing anxiety, it is the Critical Parent and the Adapted Child that dominate the others. The other three—the Nurturing Parent, the Adult, and the Natural Child—are there, but they are weaker than they should be. Remember, the sum total is finite, so the key is balance. If you strengthen NP, A, and NC, CP and AC recede. (Merely "turning down" CP and AC *will not work*. You *need* those personality components to be effective.) Enhancing your self-nurturing (NP) energy and opening yourself to exploration and discovery (NC), plus opening yourself to logic (AC), creates the synergy that decreases your critical and adapted energy. You do not have to tell those mind states to "shut up"—they will simply fall into proper balance as you increase your NP, A, and NC mind states.

This is something many physicians often fail to take into account when they prescribe medicine—you cannot decrease energy in one area without creating energy elsewhere. Self-medicating with alcohol is a good example of why decreasing CP and AC does not work: Having a few drinks or using a recreational drug to take the edge off may feel good for a short time, but it ultimately has the effect of dulling all the mind states—including those you need to increase. (A very bad long-term solution!)

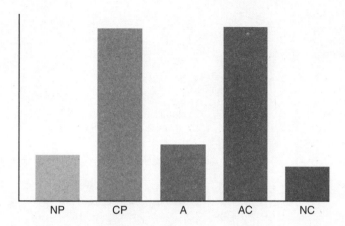

Figure 3.1 Unbalanced Mind States—the Twin Towers Anxiety Graph

Understanding the Mind States Graphs

The Mind States Graphs in this section are valuable visual tools we will refer to throughout the book. They depict the balance—or imbalance—of the mind states. We will consider the Twin Towers Anxiety Graph first (see Figure 3.1). This represents your mind states when you are experiencing performance or social anxiety.

The Critical Parent and the Adapted Child are the twin towers in this graph. They dominate the anxious mind. At the same time, the Nurturing Parent, Adult, and Natural Child are underdeveloped.

Think about each of these mind states and what they say to you when you are experiencing anxiety. It could sound a little something like what's shown in Figure 3.2.

Here, the twin towers stand so tall that they totally dominate your F.A.T.E. (Functions + Actions + Thoughts + Emotions). Those two scripts probably make it hard to even hear the other three messages. That is what you need to change. When you have balanced mind states, you can harness all five aspects of your personality to achieve a High Performance Mind.

See Figure 3.3 to view the balanced mind states—the twin towers are gone, replaced by a more evenly placed skyline of row houses

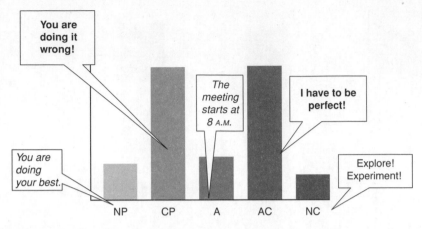

Figure 3.2   The Mind States Speak

that make up a healthy, cooperative neighborhood in which all mind states work together.

When anxiety is resolved, the five mind states are properly balanced. Notice that the Nurturing Parent is now somewhat louder than the Critical Parent, and that the Adult is slightly more dominant than the Critical Parent, Adapted Child, and Natural Child. One thing is clear: You need your Critical Parent and Adapted Child as well as your other three mind states. You cannot achieve balance without them!

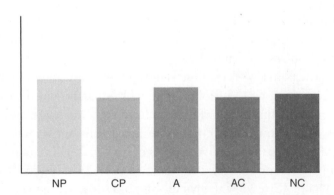

Figure 3.3   Balanced Mind States

Now, let's take some time to explore the internal scripts in your own five mind states. As you learn more about each mind state and its role in your personality, you will begin to identify the ways in which they influence your F.A.T.E.

Nurturing Parent

On our Mind States Graphs, the Nurturing Parent (NP) appears on the far left. The NP mind state is the energy that provides support and promotes growth. It teaches. It is responsible for learning in general and acquiring new skills specifically. The nurturing parent embraces challenges. It includes the dynamics of reassurance and acknowledgment. Picture a father or mother playing catch with his or her son or daughter in the back yard. The child misses the ball. The parent says, "Good try! You will get it next time." This is an example of nurturing. The NP lets you know it's okay to make mistakes. It lets you know that learning is a lifelong process for everyone. It lets you know that you are valued and loved whether or not you perform successfully.

Nurturing is not the same as rescuing. Rescuing, although important sometimes, can inhibit growth. Nurturing is promoting growth while providing support—for example, "I know you can do it! I'll help you learn how" (nurturing) rather than "I'll do it for you" (rescuing). I have worked with countless families with well-intentioned and loving parents who mistook nurturing for rescuing. When this occurs, caregivers are unwittingly teaching overdependence. A typical example is the child who talks when he is at home with family members but is nonverbal with adults and children outside his family. His parents enable this behavior by talking for him. Ask him what he likes best about school, he'll quickly cast his eyes toward his mother, who says something like, "Oh, he likes lots of things, don't you, Scott? He likes math, and reading, and social studies." That type of enabling only inhibits verbal skills development and allows the child's anxiety to flourish. Right now, there is an epidemic of selective mutism among children; one in seven children experience it. Selective mutism is one of the earliest indicators that social phobia and performance problems are developing. It all derives from rescuing—and a person's expectation of being rescued—which is a situation that can perpetuate avoidance and dependence. It happens with adults as well as children.

Rescuing and the expectation of being rescued can be subtle; even so, they can harm both relationships and careers. An adult who refuses to participate in critical meetings may not receive a year-end bonus or a raise. Someone who can't bring himself to participate in networking opportunities may attend an event, but stand mute on the edge of the room—giving up the chance to make connections that could lead to greater effectiveness on the job or even a new and more satisfying job at another company. When colleagues and friends allow this behavior to continue by pitching in on aspects of a project or efforts to network for the person, the rescuing not only reinforces the behavior, but it can also cause resentment.

Balanced mind states work in sync to enhance your decision making and improve your performance. For example, I just invested several thousand dollars in some PR software that I am planning to use to generate publicity for the book we are currently writing. All five mind states are balanced and at work in my decision to do so. My NP and A mind states led me to plan eight months or more in advance as an investment in a realistic and productive learning curve. My CP mind state led me to acknowledge that my assistant and I are not very tech-savvy and may not catch on to it easily; I accept this as constructive, not harsh and demoralizing. My AC mind state is telling me I should make the most of the software in order to maximize my time and financial productivity. And my NC mind state embraces exploration for the purpose of learning: I encouraged one of my staff members to play around with the software now so it will be familiar by the time we really need it. Mind state balance *works*.

Like most people with workplace anxiety, Amy wrestles with a nurturing deficit. Her perfectionism—her "You must be perfect" internal critical script—is too prevalent. Without an inner script telling you that it is okay to need something, okay to try and fail, the twin towers of CP and AC grow too tall.

Roger, the hedge fund banker mentioned in "The Faces of Workplace Anxiety," was 46, married with two children. He was attractive, a good athlete, a nurturing father and good husband. In addition, he made a seven-figure salary. The irony was that he suffered from public speaking anxiety while being the "go to" guy for public speaking in his firm. Only his wife and I knew that he had this issue. His public speaking performances were usually quite successful; however, a month before an important date he would worry relentlessly, often struggling with depressive feelings. He could feel his adrenaline while speaking.

On a deeper emotional level, he did not appreciate and attach or connect emotionally to his accomplishments. His father had abandoned his mother while she was pregnant with him. While he downplayed this issue in therapy with me, stating that his mother was very nurturing, which was true, the absence of his father and the lack of paternal acknowledgment and support nonetheless played a major role in his nurturing deficit. He was adept at learning new skills, which was in some ways a positive way of self-nurturing. His CP and AC mind states also contributed to his being extremely skilled in his profession. His NP mind state manifested as enthusiasm for learning what he didn't know. But the AC and CP mind states were also responsible for his perfectionism—another case of the twin towers being too tall relative to his other mind states. Perfectionism overload is toxic in people who suffer workplace anxiety.

At my suggestion, another patient, an accountant named William, was working Toastmasters religiously—something I often recommend as a laboratory for building public speaking comfort and skill levels. One week, he reported that his Toastmasters group had suddenly grown from 20 to 30 people. He had what I call an "adrenaline blitz," becoming obsessed with pleasing his new audience. "I want to be so good," he said, "that people are going to talk on the street about how great I was!" Talk about perfectionism! Only if the whole world marveled at his performance could he consider himself good enough.

I have heard thousands of similar stories—from people of all generations in all different cultures. Sometimes, a particular culture places an emphasis on one style of communicating or behavior over another. Bella, a native of Colombia, was an interpreter at the United Nations. Ivan, who was from Bulgaria, was a professor at a prestigious university. Both were quite accomplished in their respective fields. Both had public speaking anxiety. And both were very uncomfortable discussing their considerable professional accomplishments. Each one had said to me (I'm paraphrasing here), "In our country we were taught not to boast." Somehow, for these two people who grew up thousands of miles apart, taking credit for achievements was prohibited by the Critical Parent and became a nurturing deficit! Their internal critical script would say, "Don't acknowledge yourself. It's wrong. Don't draw attention to yourself."

Some of my clients have generalized about their own cultures, saying not just their own but also their extended families and their heritage downplayed dealing with emotion and had a critical perspective on therapy. For example, I've had clients of both German and Irish descent tell me that, in their extended families, they were discouraged from talking about their feelings—again causing a nurturing deficit that led to anxiety.

I consider the Nurturing Parent to be the primary state that needs to be developed.

So let's begin. The following exercise will help you to identify your NP mind state.

Identify a situation or event in your childhood where you learned a new skill.

_____

_____

_____

Identify a scenario during childhood where you were acknowledged for doing something well or for trying something new.

_____

_____

_____

Identify a situation in childhood where you were encouraged.

_____

_____

_____

Do some self-nurturing now. Acknowledge that you are currently in motion for learning! You are taking action by working through this book. You have learned the importance of skin temperature. Feel yours for a moment. Identify your feelings right now. Embrace my challenge to do this rather than get annoyed or frustrated. This is "nurturing." Make the Feelings List at the end of Chapter 1 your bible. The more that you attach to your feelings, the more you will be able to control anxiety. Again, whenever I ask you to return to the Feelings List, do it! It is an essential part of this program. (In Chapter 4, you will encounter a similar chart that provides some nurturing statements to be incorporated into your thinking as you learn to balance the five mind states.)

The Clenched Fist Exercise

Now let's go a step further with self-regulation and relaxation techniques. Clench your right hand. Make a fist. Feel the tension. Keep it clenched for 21 seconds, and really tune into the tension. Now slowly release your fist and let the fingers come apart. Feel yourself letting go of the tension. Feel the sensations of looseness replace that tension. Now, do the same with your left hand. Make a fist. Hold it. Keep holding it for 21 seconds, tuning into the tension. Now slowly release your fist and let the fingers come apart. Feel the looseness replace the tension.

Differentiating between muscle tension and relaxation builds your awareness of internal sensations. Of course, you already know what a clenched fist feels like. But doing this exercise labels the sensation as "tension" and labels the release as "relaxation." Developing that awareness will facilitate your learning more self-regulation skills.

Survey your body for a moment. Locate any areas of your body where you currently are experiencing muscle tension. Focus on that part of the body while you take in a deep breath and slowly exhale, pacing yourself 4...3...2...1..., feeling the muscle becoming soft and loose. Say to yourself three times, "My muscles are soft and loose."

Your Critical Parent Mind State

The Critical Parent mind state is energy that represents authority. It makes rules! It teaches "shoulds"! It evaluates and analyzes. It passes judgment and criticizes. And that can be a very good thing. When your parents told you not to touch a hot stove, that was good criticism. You need your Critical Parent for guidance. The Critical Parent serves many important purposes: It keeps our primitive urges in check. It allows us to consider how we performed and how we might do better (For example, I have taped hundreds of my television and radio shows and analyzed and critiqued them for the purpose of improving my performance.) For society as a whole, the police represent the collective Critical Parent, because without them our primitive urges would overtake us and there would be chaos.

But when our Critical Parent gets too loud, it no longer serves us positively. Often the critical script with performance anxiety goes something like "You're going to get nervous," "You will screw up," "You will make a fool of yourself," "People will see who you really are," "People will not get to see who you really are because you will screw up," "You'll embarrass yourself," and so on. Not very helpful, is it? These are obviously negative suggestions. This is a state that must be decreased.

Here's something to remember: It's wonderful to be involved in the pursuit of peak performance. It's absurd to be paralyzed by fear of not being perfect.

Who is perfect? Nobody. The fear of not being perfect is an example of *excessive internal critical script*, which is often a part of perfectionism. While the critical script is important in facilitating achievement and success at work, its excessiveness is a major cause of performance anxiety. Look again at the Unbalanced Mind States graph. See the twin towers? If you suffer performance anxiety, the Critical Parent is a primary cause of your problem because of its unrealistic expectations.

The Critical Parent is a learned script—but it is your own internalized script, not merely the voice of the parents who raised you. It is a product of your values, your parents, your teachers and authority figures, your peers, your culture, and society. It is acquired through experiences that you then interpret as good or bad. For example, Shelly was the CFO of a billion-dollar company. She had experienced a panic episode during a board of directors meeting about a year before she contacted me. Since that time, she had been obsessing that this panic could occur again. As she said to me, "What if I go on television and have a panic attack? The viewers will obviously think there's something wrong and the stock of the company will go down." I did not disagree with her, but I did disagree when she said there was no reason for her anxiety.

When we explored her background, I gained insight into her critical script. Together we began to map out a way to balance her mind states. Shelly's father was a very successful businessman who was also an avid hunter. I'm not an advocate of hunting, but the story has an interesting and important point. When her father went hunting, he took one bullet with him. His thinking? If he could not get the animal with one bullet the animal deserved to live. How's that for a perfectionist challenge? This kind of thinking integrated itself into Shelly's internal critical script and prompted her own endless quest for perfection. That drive to be the best led her to become tremendously successful in her career. But it also caused her anxiety problem.

Again, I ask you: Who is perfect? Nobody. When a person tries to achieve what is impossible, anger and frustration result. Anger, when repressed, recycles. It is a force that drives anxiety and obsession, among other problems. Anger is deep-rooted and may not even resonate on the surface because of detachment. People with anxiety don't want to feel that anger—and so they don't feel it consciously. They are so busy operating in the Adapted Child mode that they don't allow themselves to feel it, and they haven't been conscious of its development. Instead, they stuff it down into the unconscious. It is hidden, but it is by no means gone.

TUNE IN: Take a long slow deep breath in through your nose now, 1...2...3...4...and slowly exhale for 4...3...2... 1...What's the temperature of your hands now? Warm? Cool? Again, I wouldn't be surprised if there is some vasoconstriction going on right now given that you are currently attaching to potentially highly emotional content. What are you thinking? What are you feeling?

It is often our observations, not any words we actually hear while growing up, that help to form our internal critical script. Though Ethan owned a successful construction supply business with 25 employees, he was unable to enjoy his financial success. Looking at his upbringing, he remembered his parents as always "flipping" houses, never staying in one place for too long and always working. He never remembered his parents having fun or enjoying things. Over time, he internalized the message they seemed to be giving him: Work hard, but don't have fun. It's not as though his parents told him directly, "Don't have fun and always work." But this is the script that he learned through osmosis during his growth and development.

As I have mentioned, our Critical Parent script is not only the voice of our actual parents, but also something we ourselves devise based on a number of different experiences and interpretations. The messages can come from anyone, anywhere. Remember Carol, the ovarian cancer survivor who said anxiety was worse than chemo? When Carol was in 10th grade, her Spanish teacher called on her. In front of the class, the teacher said, "Oh, look, you are blushing." For some people, this might not be a big deal. For Carol, however, being singled out in that way caused humiliation and shame that was paired with her blushing. The result was that she hated her blushing and tried to avoid it at all costs. This sequenced into her repressing her curiosity and spontaneity (NC) and her objective understanding that asking questions was sometimes necessary (A); she was that much afraid of being the center of attention. She gave up the career in medicine she really aspired to. (You can hear Carol's interview at www.socialanxiety.com, "Public Speaking Anxiety and Blushing Resolved: Carol: Ovarian Cancer Survivor.")

It's wonderful to set your goals high, strive for perfection, break records, or make a discovery. If your goals are high, it's crucial to deal with frustration and anger. It's vital to learn from mistakes and reposition your definition of perfection as a requirement for success. The closest you can get to perfection is learning to expect the unexpected. When you can "go with the flow," you are in control—not operating from a rigid script. It's those too-rigid scripts that cause emotion that turns into a temper tantrum of anxiety (more on that later). Trust in being yourself. The more you learn this, the more you will be in control. The pursuit of perfection is a never-ending learning process. Fear of not being perfect kills creativity, which is crucial to high performance. Productive performers learn from mistakes. Any other thinking, especially that one should never make mistakes (and believe me, I have worked with many people who have this belief), is dysfunctional thinking. Who's perfect? Nobody.

Perhaps nowhere is failure more visible than in sports competitions, where there is a clear winner and a clear loser. John Madden, the NFL's most popular, now retired commentator, is legendary for his Yogi-isms: "If Dallas has more points at the end of this game, they are going to win." How do athletes cope with failure? Take a lesson in letting go from the Tampa Bay Rays baseball team—well known for being the underdog winners of the 2008 American League Eastern Division Championship and winners of the American League Pennant, beating both the New York Yankees and the Boston Red Sox. After a loss, the team would gather in the locker room for a 30-minute debriefing in which they looked closely at what (and who) went wrong. And then, after 30 minutes—they just let it go. On to the next game! This is an example of engaging the positive Critical Parent mind state.

Amy has a perfectionist streak that is both good and bad. She says:

I see perfectionism in two ways: First, it is the reason I am successful at what I do. But it has also kept me from moving out of my comfort zone or even shooting for something I really wanted, but had no idea whether I could be good at. Writing sitcoms, for example. Or working for a big-time advertising agency. I am feeling anxiety symptoms right now just admitting to those long-ago dreams. I sometimes say that "I am so ambitious I can't even leave the house." What I mean is that I want to do big things and to do them so perfectly that I am afraid to even begin, to even step out into the world and try something. Listening to my internal critical script has, to a great extent, robbed me of the ability to dream big. It always seemed like the cost of failure would be devastating.

Amy is not alone in this. Many people with workplace anxiety don't set their goals high enough because of the critical script that says "You are not capable," "Why bother, you won't succeed anyway,"

"You are not worthy enough," "Be very careful about what people think of you," "Bad things will happen if you make a mistake," "Avoid what makes you uncomfortable," "Taking risks will screw you up," or "You will regret trying." These messages kill the learning process as well as one's self-esteem. They breed frustration, resentment, and anger. Andrea began working as a temp for a luxury real estate agency and quickly demonstrated her ability to manage the marketing tasks at this exclusive firm. The owner offered her a permanent position; one year later, he let her know he was giving her a promotion to team leader. She took the news quietly, then went in to work the next morning and quit. "I couldn't handle being in charge of other people," she explained. "I was awake all night saying that I didn't deserve the new job, that the other people in the department knew I was a fraud, that I had no right to try to tell other people what to do. It was too much. I didn't want the promotion. Looking back, I can see that I really did want it. I just could not handle that internal critical script. It didn't seem like it would ever go away, so I had to!"

Answer the following questions, the purpose of which is to help you identify your Critical Parent mind state.

Identify a message that you learned from your parents (either directly or indirectly) regarding values that you disagree with, or that causes confusion or conflict.

_____

_____

_____

Now give an example of a message that you learned from your parents along the line of values that you agree with.

_____

_____

_____

Identify a situation during childhood when you felt criticized inappropriately or for no good reason.

_____

_____

_____

Identify a situation during childhood when you experienced constructive criticism.

_____

_____

_____

Identify a recent situation where you felt criticized inappropriately.

_____

_____

_____

Identify a recent situation where you felt criticized constructively.

_____

_____

_____

Adult

The middle mind state on the graph is the Adult (A). The A is your
internal computer. This is the energy of logic and objectivity—no
emotion, no influence or contamination from emotion, just the facts
at hand. The Adult is not the same as intelligence—it specifically
refers to facts, not interpretations or opinions. (If you stopped to
consider whether your intelligence was an issue here, take my word
for it that you are intelligent. How do I know? If you are reading
this book and are concerned with performance anxiety and building
confidence at work, it's a good bet that you are an intelligent person.)
What would your Nurturing Parent tell you? It takes a great deal of
intelligence to recognize a problem and tackle it head on as you are
doing—intelligence and courage!

When the internal critical script is too strong, our Adult gets
drowned out. "'Don't take things personally' is good advice," Amy
says. "But when people tell me not to take things personally, I sometimes take that personally!" It's easy to get confused between the

basic facts and the way you interpret what happened. It's the difference between "I failed" and "I'm a failure." One of my patients was
president of the PTA. She seemed hard-wired for stress and anxiety.
Once, when speaking in front of her PTA group, a person at the
back of the room said, "I can't hear you." At that point, she had
a panic attack. When she was in my office for a therapy session I
said to her, "Put yourself in your Adult mind state—all objectivity
and logic, no emotion. What did he mean when he said he couldn't
hear you?" "He couldn't hear me," she replied. It was as simple as
that; however, what he had said was enough to activate her excessive
internal negative critical script, which resulted in her defensive positioning and adrenaline spike. The perceived threat—via criticism
that objectively did not exist—sent her mind to a dark and negative
place. It took only seconds. And it was years before she got a handle
on it.

Once, while driving to a radio station to do a show, I was abruptly
cut off by someone experiencing road rage. This person almost caused
an accident. Emotionally, I wanted revenge—an impulse that came
from my Natural Child mind state. My Adult, however, said to me,
"This guy is so crazy, if I look at him, he may get out of the car
with a crowbar." Operating with logic and objectivity, I avoided eye
contact and looked the other way.

Logic will tell you that you need a learning process to control anxiety and develop confidence at work. Learning does take
time; it can't be accomplished all at once or by magic. Logic will
also tell you that you need to get out of your comfort zone with
F.A.T.E.—Functioning+Actions+Thoughts+Emotions. The next
section will tell you how to do this.

Being Comfortable Being Uncomfortable

This book does not promise that you will never be nervous again.
But it does promise that you will be able to process those feelings of anxiety in such a way that you gain power and improve
your performance at work. Expecting to be comfortable in the first
phases of learning anxiety management and getting out of your

comfort zone is not logical. Far too often, in therapy and in life, it is the desire to avoid discomfort that keeps people from doing the hard work it takes to heal. Real healing means you have to get uncomfortable.

As you experience initial discomfort, employ a nurturing interpretation. Discomfort means "I'm in the process of learning new skills," "I'm in motion," "My health is improving," "I'm learning," or "My self-esteem is in the process of improving."

In choosing to read this book and work through this program, you have obviously realized that learning to control your nervousness at work is an essential part of your self-growth and personal development. As you do so, you will be less susceptible to exaggerated emotion and excessive adrenaline. You'll be more productive with problem solving. The Adult mediates and negotiates between the Critical Parent and the Adapted Child (which is the state of learned emotion, to be considered next).

Now answer the following questions, whose purpose is to help you identify your Adult mind state.

Identify a situation recently where you felt angry toward someone, but you controlled yourself and responded appropriately for the betterment or negotiation of the situation.

_____

_____

_____

Identify a situation where you used logic for objective analysis in problem solving.

_____

_____

_____

Identify an example of where you need to utilize more logic and objectivity and less emotion.

_____

_____

_____

Breathing Exercise

This is a good time to pause for a moment again. Picture a medical diagram depicting how air enters and leaves your body. Take in a long slow deep breath through your nose and slowly exhale 4...3...2...1.... Inhale and exhale, pacing yourself to 8 to 12 seconds. What's the temperature of your hands now? What are your thoughts at this very moment? Pair your thoughts with the awareness of your hand temperature.

Your hands may be cool. That is normal. Often my hands are cold when I am in the process of problem solving and analytical thinking. I've seen that during the process of the actual problem solving my hands are cold due to vasoconstriction, and when I find a resolution to the problem my hands often become warm. This is an example of awareness of subtle internal cues. Think about this possibility for yourself.

Continuing with your Adult, logic and objectivity tell you that there is a difference between performance and identity or personhood. Often the intensity of the Critical Parent (the twin tower on the left) and concurrent nurturing deficit result in confusion about the difference between what you do or have done and who you are. The anxiety sufferer all too often gets stuck with negative feelings and goes too deep into an interpretation of what the discomfort means. In other words, when you do not perform as well as you would like, this does not mean you are not okay as a person. You can fail without being a failure.

You want to develop and sustain the analytical and logical skills of the Adult to enhance your problem solving and skills acquisition. The challenge is to keep moving, whether you think of it as piloting or quarterbacking. Keep going. This is nurturing! You do not want to get stuck recycling or obsessing on negative thoughts and emotions.

I use my Adult as a way of not staying stuck. In 2004, for example, I was booked on the Anderson Cooper show on CNN. I remember the date because the Red Sox were playing the Yankees in the playoffs in New York, and I am a Red Sox fan. The focus of my three-minute presentation was public speaking anxiety. Anderson Cooper was in Colorado and I was in a studio in Manhattan. The assistant producer took me to a small, isolated room where my picture was sent via satellite to Cooper and his to me. I delivered my message well verbally (with the exception that I was cut off before I could get my Web site address on. There went any marketing productivity).

When I returned to the green room where my wife and stepson were waiting, both had disturbed looks on their faces. The camera the producer had directed me to look into was the wrong one; alas, to the television audience, it had appeared as though I were looking at the floor. It was not a good image for a role model for public speaking on international television! I was obviously upset for a number of reasons. I looked ridiculous and the marketing potential of that appearance was very limited.

By the end of the evening, I was beginning to let it go, getting distracted with the Red Sox game and a glass of wine. After lamenting, I analyzed the situation with my Adult mind state. It was out of my control! I did not have the power to replay the evening. I learned then and there that beating myself up was not productive. What sense would it make to beat myself up? That would be excessive critical script. The bottom line was that my performance was horrible. But my self-esteem was intact. I was ready for the next media opportunity. After all, when a member of the Red Sox or Yankees strikes out, he doesn't go back to the dugout and cry.

Now, being a Red Sox and baseball fan, I must say that anything is possible. In 2004, the Red Sox beat the Yankees and finally won a World Series, ridding themselves of the "curse of the Babe" (Ruth). If they could do that, then who knows what else can be achieved! Certainly you can learn to control anxiety and develop the confidence to succeed at work.

Often there are two levels of fear with performance anxiety. Level one goes something like "people can see I'm nervous." Maybe that's true. I have, however, worked with countless people who thought that they were being perceived as nervous when objectively speaking they were not. This is called projection: Like a film projector shining an image from the film inside it onto a screen, you are taking the self-perception inside you and projecting it onto others. You are saying that other people see or hear or believe something that in fact you yourself see or hear or believe. The second and deeper level of fear often goes something like, "They can see who I really am" or "They can see I'm a fraud." That feeling of fraud is common among workplace anxiety sufferers. No matter how accomplished you are, when your critical script is exaggerated, it takes very little to make you believe people don't take you seriously. Logic is needed here instead of exaggerated emotion, which brings us to the Adapted Child mind state.

The Adapted Child

In his role as supervisor of 20 people in a hedge fund, James is supposed to lead group training each month. But he always enlists an associate to conduct the trainings for him, claiming he has schedule conflicts and even deliberately scheduling other meetings so that he can avoid his responsibility. His staff sees what's going on, and his boss has spoken to him more than once about the issue. But he continues to manipulate and avoid—a classic example of a too-strong Adapted Child mind state. This issue developed into a full-on phobia of public speaking. By the time James came to me for help, he had been on antidepressants for six years—yet he still had problems. The attempt to chemically "dial down" his AC was failing because the treatment failed to balance the mind states by bringing up NP, A, and NC.

The Adapted Child is *learned emotion*. It conforms, cooperates, compromises, and manipulates in an effort to please. It is in this state that your negotiating skills are located, as well as many learned successful, healthy, and productive behaviors. It is also in this state that your anxiety and avoidant or phobic behavior are located. As you can see on the Mind States Graph, the twin tower on the right is the Adapted Child, and it complements the excessive nature of the critical script.

The excessive and underlying emotions of embarrassment, humiliation, shame, fear of rejection, and unresolved anger reside in this state. Unpleasant memories, characterized by the previous emotions as well as feelings of loss of control and insecurity also reside in this state. Overdependence on medication or other substances is part of this state.

Historical Link Exercise

Right now, do a *historical link* exercise. Go back in time as far as you can in your own life and identify a situation where you felt embarrassed or rejected. How old were you? Where were you? With whom? This memory is located within your Adapted Child. The Adapted Child makes an important contribution to your success; you can't do without it. It is only when the AC tower gets so tall that it overshadows the other mind states that problems result.

Explore your own Adapted Child mind state by answering the following:

Identify a skill that you learned: _____

_____

Identify a strategy that you use to manipulate: _____

_____

Identify a strategy that you use to negotiate: _____

_____

Identify a recent strategy or rationalization you employed to avoid an anxiety challenge: _____

_____

Identify a recent technique you used to solve a problem: _____

_____

Like all mind states, the Adapted Child is very important, but as one of the twin towers, it must be decreased, along with its counterpart, the Critical Parent.

Natural Child

On the far right of the Mind State Graph is the Natural Child. This is the state of pure emotion. Think of it as containing the truth of desire. It's what you really want—not what you were taught you *should* want. The Natural Child is the energy of pleasure, joy, and fun. It is the energy of exploration, creativity, the development of ideas, discovery, and spontaneity. It is the expression of your most basic instincts, including sexuality. The Natural Child mind state is pure, but it is not solely the source of good emotions or behavior. It is also the source of aggression, of sexuality, and of all our most primal urges. It has no limits. Therefore, it needs the Critical Parent, Nurturing Parent, Adult, and Adapted Child to balance it out. Remember, the CP and AC are only overwhelmingly negative when they appear as the unbalanced twin towers. In proper balance, the Critical Parent and Adapted Child mind states are positive forces in our personality, without which we simply could not succeed.

I saw an example of the Natural Child mind state as I sat on the beach one beautiful summer day. There were two families about 10 yards from each other. Each family had a child who was about three years old. They did not know each other. Yet naturally and spontaneously the children made eye contact and gravitated toward each other to play in the sand. They were not influenced by an internal critical script—there was no "What if she doesn't like me?" No "I'm not good enough." No "I don't know how." These two children engaged with each other spontaneously, creatively, and joyfully.

The Natural Child mind state is not all about play. It is also about openness—the willingness to explore, the willingness to not know something. For example, when I was in graduate school and requested the correctional institution internship, I was operating from my NC mind state. The same was true when I chose to invest in and explore public relations by seeking radio and television appearances. Combined with the other mind states, the Natural Child is a wonderful and fulfilling quality to tap into.

Answer the following to help you further identify your Natural Child mind state. Give an example of something you did for fun as a child and that you still do—or something similar—now:

Identify an idea you developed: _____

_____

Name something that you explored: _____

_____

When was the last time you did something spontaneously? _____

_____

Identify a situation that caused sadness: _____

_____

Identify a situation that caused anger: _____

_____

Identify a situation where you experienced happiness or joy: _____

_____

Identify the last time you laughed or had a sense of humor: _____

_____

Emotions such as sadness, anger, happiness, and joy are the realm of the Natural Child. As adults, we are far more adept than actual children at suppressing those emotions by using our other mind states.

For a moment, picture a child you care about having a temper tantrum—whining, crying, hitting or kicking, maybe lying on the floor. What would you do? Ignore the behavior? Give a spanking? Try reasoning with the child? A nurturing parent would try to comfort the child. Now, think about a time when you have had an anxiety response at work. Take a deep breath in, then exhale 4 . . . 3 . . . 2 . . . 1 . . . Attach to that moment. Access that memory. Now, associate that memory with your AC emotions and the related unpleasant physical sensations. I am positioning your anxiety as an internal temper tantrum because it is an exaggerated emotion coming from your AC mind state. Can you buy this interpretation? Think about it. *Exaggerated* emotion is the basis of your anxiety, perhaps along with autonomic sensitivity. The logic of your Adult will tell you that it's not some unknown organic entity that's causing your exaggerated emotion. (If you think your anxiety response may actually be a physical health issue, go to a physician to get appropriate tests to rule it out.) The exaggerated emotions include anger, frustration, embarrassment, humiliation, shame, and fear of rejection. Therefore self-nurturing is the primary dynamic of healing. What exactly is nurturing? My definition is "to provide support and promote growth."

Look at the twin towers on the Unbalanced Mind States graph (Figure 3.1) carefully now. The left twin tower, your exaggerated Critical Parent, causes your problem. Remember, the energy inherent in all states is important. We are addressing the balance or synergy here. Messages in this state, such as "Don't trust yourself," "Bad things happened before. They could happen again," "You will be nervous," "You'd better be perfect," "You will embarrass yourself," "You are not good enough," and so on, create the excess emotions of fear, worry, and insecurity located in the Adapted Child—which is learned emotion. The twin towers very often become a reflex. Think of the CP-AC as a nervous tic of the mind. Obviously they have to be decreased—not gotten rid of, just decreased, because they are extremely important to your health, happiness, well-being, and ability to perform productively.

Look at the Balanced Mind States graph (Figure 3.2) again carefully, and you will see your objective: a balanced mind state that makes room for the best that each of the mind states has to offer. With balance comes flexibility, and with flexibility come choices. In Chapter 4, we will explore in depth the way to achieve this balance.

Given the definition of Nurturing Parent as providing support and promoting growth and understanding—a multidimensional concept—list three ways that you need to self-nurture:

1. _____
   _____

2. _____
   _____

3. _____
   _____

Given the definition of the Adult as logic and objectivity, list three ways you need to utilize logic instead of emotion:

1. _____
   _____

2. _____
_____
3. _____
_____

Given the definition of Natural Child as exploration, creativity, happiness, and the truth of desire, list three ways you need to invest in this state:

1. _____
_____
2. _____
_____
3. _____
_____

Image Preparation Exercise

Scientific research has demonstrated the power of imagery or "behavior rehearsal" on personal effectiveness. For example, one study showed that a group of basketball players who "practiced" taking foul shots during the week by picturing doing so in their minds, without ever getting on the court, did just about as well as those athletes who actually practiced. Behavior rehearsal is powerful stuff.

Picture your lungs—two expandable vessels that take oxygen in and let carbon dioxide out. Picture the oxygen enriching your blood, which then travels through your body and brain. Really do it! Get a visual. Now, take in a long slow deep breath. Really feel the oxygen as your lungs take it in. Feel the moment. Then, slowly exhale 4 . . . 3 . . . 2 . . . 1 . . .. Be aware of your chest and lungs as you inhale and exhale in a conscious yet natural manner. In a moment, I will ask you to begin the following exercise but read these instructions first: Close your eyes for about 60 seconds while visualizing an anxiety challenge scenario. The goal is to picture yourself accepting the adrenaline. To maximize the power of the image, use your five senses. See the scene. Hear it. Smell it. Taste it if possible. Really feel it!

When discomfort occurs during the exercise, focus on your breathing, then return to the image.

Okay, now for the next 60 seconds do the exercise. Then open your eyes.

Were you able to attach to the adrenaline? Describe the experience to yourself in as much sensory detail as possible. Put it into words—write it in your notes if you like.

I felt _____

I saw _____

I heard _____

I smelled _____

I tasted _____

If you were not able to attach, your excessive critical script is at work, saying "Don't do it." This is a big clue that you need to overpower your critical script with your nurturing self. What sensations did you experience? Could you feel any stirrings of adrenaline? What is the temperature of your hands now? What are your thoughts?

Next, in Chapter 4 we will discuss in detail how to activate and balance your mind states for high performance. But before we begin, stop and pat yourself on the back for having completed the challenging exercises in this chapter. How about giving yourself a few encouraging words courtesy of your Nurturing Parent?

CHAPTER
4

Balancing Your Mind States for a High Performance Mind

"**I**t's all in your head." How many times have we all heard that? Well, guess what? It is! Whether you are talking about good things or bad things, feelings, thoughts, ideas, or even just how your body is working or is not working, it really is all in your head. Am I saying you're imagining everything? Not at all. Let's be very clear what we are addressing here. Just what *is* in your head?

The cranium is the part of the skull that encloses the brain. It's been a long time since most of us have explored the basics of the nervous system, so here's a quick review: Your brain contains 15 billion to 33 billion neurons, each of them linking with as many as 10,000 synapses. These neurons communicate via protoplasmic fibers called axons that pulse messages to distant body parts. The brain controls all the body's physical and mental functioning—its F.A.T.E. Housed deep within the brain are almond-shaped nuclei called "amygdalae." This is the seat of your fight-or-flight mechanism—your basic adaptive reaction to physical or emotional stress. Much research regarding the biology of social anxiety has focused on that area, which is known to play a primary role in processing emotional reactions.

Bear with me a little longer—I realize you didn't pick up this book because you were looking to brush up on neuroscience. But this is important stuff. This is *your* brain we're talking about! And it's *all* in your head.

Here's what I mean: The five mind states we have been discussing exist within your brain. The F.A.T.E. dimensions of each of those mind states have a *biological* base. They exist physically—maybe not as individual "almond-shaped nuclei," but they are sourced from a physical organ that has a capacity for health and a capacity for illness. Doesn't it make the ultimate sense in the world to take care of—or *nurture*—the biological structure of the brain?

Everything Starts with a Thought . . .

. . . whether you are aware of that thought or not. The more you learn to take conscious responsibility for your thinking, the more you can invest in developing a High Performance Mind. As humans, we tend to have a running monologue going all day long. Our mind states—NP, CP, A, AC, and NC—assert themselves in various ways:

Nurturing Parent:	"Have a healthy breakfast—you need the energy!"
Critical Parent:	"Don't eat junk food!"
Adult:	"It's breakfast time."
Adapted Child:	"I'm a pig for eating this doughnut."
Natural Child:	"I want that doughnut!"

Five different thoughts about the same thing—breakfast. Five valuable perspectives. How do you balance the five scripts? *Take conscious responsibility for them.* Remember, all five mind states are essential, so it is not a matter of drowning out or ignoring one mind state or another. Rather, it is a matter of adjusting the dials so that these mind states are in balance.

Here's an example from my own life. I love a great bottle of wine (only white; red gives me headaches), such as a Montrachet or

Corton Charlemagne. But I consciously limit my drinking. At the end of a nice weekend, I would really enjoy sitting down with a few glasses of wine on a Sunday evening. My CP says to be cautious—there is a workweek ahead. My NP says to do what is best to get a good start on the week. My A makes me aware of things such as what time my Monday appointment schedule starts and what effect alcohol—even just a glass or two—might have on my brain health (making it harder to fall asleep, for example). My AC mind state notes that having a drink against my better judgment could make me less effective. And my NC is telling me how much I enjoy wine and how great it would be to have a glass right now!

Over the years, I have factored in the scripts from all these mind states, all of which have valuable contributions to make. The bottom line? I choose not to drink on "school nights." I am not talking about getting drunk; I am just making clear that alcohol can be an inhibitor, depressing overall brain functioning and decreasing all five mind states. Paying attention to my brain health is better for my therapeutic work. It's better for writing this book, since accessing my creativity and organizing my thinking takes brain energy. The same with working out. I want my brain in top working condition! This is not to say you must make this same choice—so long as you think it through from a mind states perspective. A healthy brain requires conscious thinking and decision making. I want my neurons, protoplasmic fibers, and amygdala working as well as possible. I want to nurture brain health as much as I can. How about you?

You know at this point that all the mind states are important. Each contains specific energy, and this energy is finite—not unlimited. Take a look at the unbalanced mind states graph again (Figure 3.1). This is *your* mind states graph. See the twin towers—Critical Parent and Adapted Child? You already have way more of the Critical Parent and Adapted Child energy than you need. Don't worry about that for now. *You do not need to do anything to decrease that energy.* The goal is to grow and develop the Nurturing Parent, Adult, and Natural Child. When you do that, the Critical Parent and Adapted Child mind states will naturally reduce in size to the appropriate level (remember, you need *all five* mind states, so you never want to get rid of those important personality components completely). It's all about balance.

Nurturing Parent

The NP is the energy of promoting growth and providing support. What actions could you take that would grow your Nurturing Parent mind state in a way that will help resolve your workplace anxiety? The following ideas are presented in systematic order. Read each one thoughtfully, pausing to complete the questions along the way before proceeding to the next. Do not detach from a concept or question! Stay with it. Take a deep breath in and out to concentrate as you encounter each new idea.

Invest in good brain health. Invest your time and energy in working through this program, which includes both the carefully designed exercises you have completed so far and the remaining material in this book.

Integrate the belief that your most valuable asset in life is time into your thinking and decision making. *Life is not a dress rehearsal.* Play quarterback. Be the pilot. As you take responsibility for creating motion, you will be in the process of gaining control. Passivity creates more worry, frustration, anger, and poor self-esteem.

Cultivate the interpretation that mistakes and failures are part of the learning process. If you want to be good at anything—controlling anxiety, public speaking, relationships, sports, performing arts, communication—you must understand that mistakes are part of skills development. Let go of excessive perfectionist thinking such as "I should never make mistakes." Believing that mistakes or failures are not part of the learning process would be toxic, if not insane thinking.

Embrace your adrenaline as a source of power. Welcome it!

Sustain your efforts with a persistent attitude. The following quotation from U.S. President Calvin Coolidge hangs in my office: "*Nothing in the world can take the place of persistence. Talent will not; nothing is more common than unsuccessful men of talent. Genius will not . . . the world is full of educated derelicts. Persistence and determination alone are omnipotent. The slogan 'press on' has solved and always will solve the problems of the human race.*"

Realize that anything you do to promote growth is nurturing; therefore, acknowledge yourself for working through this program and realizing what you did not know. Right now, list three new concepts that you have learned thus far. Can you do six?

1.	
2.	
3.	

Invest in attachment. You know that detachment is a defense mechanism anxiety sufferers enact to avoid the pain of feeling. Attach to conscious thinking. Be open to paradoxical thinking—thinking the opposite of what you currently do.

Identify three issues to which you have been attaching *since* starting this book:

1.	
2.	
3.	

Need some examples to get you started? After Amy completed this exercise, she made the following two entries about what she had begun attaching to and—extra credit!—the paradoxical thinking she had opened up to.

1. *Scheduling my time. Paradoxical thinking: Planning carefully gives me freedom.*
2. *Asking for help. Paradoxical thinking: It is smart to ask questions— rather than dumb not to already know the answers!*

Become an expert at identifying (via attachment) your emotions. Make the Feelings List your bible. The more you attach to, identify, and appropriately express emotions, the less you are susceptible to repress and therefore to recycle emotion that drives anxiety, obsessive worry, and mood discomfort.

Develop your awareness of internal physical cues by correlating changes in the skin temperature of your hands to emotions and thinking. (Consider accepting the Biocard offer at www.socialanxiety. com.) Warm hands mean relaxation. Cold hands mean stress—but that can be good stress or bad stress. Use your Adult to recognize that your hand temperature is merely a fact—it is biofeedback information about your physical functioning that lets you tune in and become aware. Adrenaline is not a bad thing.

TUNE IN: Right now identify your skin temperature. Pair it with your thinking and emotion.

Be diligent and precise about learning the self-regulation exercises throughout this program. You must perform each exercise exactly as I describe it—down to the seconds or minutes specified.

Manage your stress. Differentiate between good and bad stress and make stress work for you instead of against you.

Resolve the excessive emotions of embarrassment, humiliation, and fear of rejection.

Understand and resolve your repressed and recycling anger. Express it constructively, and channel it into productive energy.

Validate your achievements! This is crucial for nurturing. We are not talking about boasting; rather, we mean acknowledging yourself for the success you have achieved. It's so easy to focus on negatives and things that do not work out. For example: Jerome taught an IT class at a community college. At semester's end, his 20 students were asked to fill out a course evaluation. Four of the students mentioned that Jerome didn't leave enough time for questions at the end of each class. Sixteen of the students had no complaints, and seven of those said it was the best IT class they had taken. Which feedback did Jerome focus on? The negatives.

Susan, a part-time program coordinator at her church, organized a retreat weekend that 200 people attended; unfortunately, it rained all weekend, which was not what she had envisioned. Even so, the entire group was enjoying the fellowship activities—particularly the improvised indoor scavenger hunt and the fireside sing-along. What did Susan think about? All the outdoor activities she had had to cancel because of the wet weather. Neither Jerome nor Susan was making adequate use of the NP and A mind states, which would have said "Look at all you accomplished!" (NP) and "The entire group participated and the schedule was full" (A). What do you imagine those mind states would have provided by way of encouragement, objective feedback, or playful exploration? Productive performance occurs through focusing on positives.

Right now, think back over the last few months, then list three recent achievements or successes (components of progress).

1.	
2.	
3.	

Now list three more achievements that have occurred within the last year.

1.	
2.	
3.	

What can you say to acknowledge yourself for these achievements?

Cultivate your sense of humor. Developing your Nurturing Parent mind state allows you to look on the bright side and, with the help of the Adult, to put things into perspective. Ultimately, humor helps us not to take ourselves so seriously. Are you willing to lighten up? To let go? To say, "Oh, well!" and get on with things? Amy recalls turning to her Nurturing Parent, Natural Child, and Adult mind states when a particularly stressful day became even crappier—literally:

I was on deadline with my weekly newspaper column. I finished it in the nick of time and raced over with the disk (this was before the days of e-mail!), took my dog to the vet, then made it back home for a phone appointment, after which I had a half-hour to tighten up a book chapter I was working on before dashing six blocks to meet with the coauthor of a book I was writing about dreams and creativity.

But I sure wasn't feeling very creative. It turned out my audiocassette recorder had malfunctioned, so I had had to rely solely on my interview notes for my column. The vet bill was about $100 more than I was expecting. And I had gotten a parking ticket. By the time I was on my way to my coauthor's office, I was pretty stressed.

Then a bird pooped on my head. In that moment, I could have really lost it from the stress and anxiety of the day. But instead I just started laughing. I took it as a reminder that things could always be a little bit worse. That memory still makes me laugh.

In that moment, Amy accessed her NP—it's almost as though her NP put its arm around her and said with a rueful smile, "See? It's always something!" Amy's Adult mind state was also at work. She stayed in the moment, realizing that it was no use wishing things were different. This was the way things were. You could editorialize and say this was a bad day. Or you could use the A mind state and say this was just a day, neither good nor bad. No reason to come to a complete collapse over a little bird doo!

When was the last time you laughed? Not a smile, not a chuckle—a *real* laugh that left you a little out of breath and a lot more relaxed? Laughter truly is one of the best medicines there is. The research of Doctors Lee Berk and Stanley Tan of Loma Linda University has shown that laughter has many health benefits: It decreases stress hormones; it loosens muscle tension for up to an hour after the last guffaw; it gives you a natural high by releasing endorphins that enhance feelings of well-being and ease pain; it boosts your immune system by raising the level of infection-fighting T-cells; and it lowers blood pressure. Plus, it's fun!

TUNE IN: Smile! Make it a big, wide, I-can't-help-it smile. How does it feel? Are your hands cold or warm?

Develop realistic expectations. Unrealistic expectations set your inner child up for anger and frustration. List three examples of unrealistic expectations that you have placed on yourself. To get you started, take a look at one of the examples Amy identified while doing this exercise; then complete each step for yourself, entering your responses in your notes.

Unrealistic expectation:
Be able to take on every new task that comes my way

1.	
2.	
3.	

The result of these unrealistic expectations was what in terms of behavioral outcomes and your emotions?

Results

Felt guilty and ashamed when I didn't complete everything; compromised the completion of my primary responsibilities and caused me anxiety; had to work extra hours to catch up; annoyed boss by taking on too much.

1.	
2.	
3.	

Now change the unrealistic expectation to realistic.
Realistic expectation:
Sometimes I need to say no to a request.

1.	
2.	
3.	

Learn and implement the Five-Step Adrenaline Control Technique described at the end of this chapter.

Work in layers. Often people get overwhelmed when they try to do everything at once. Layering work, doing a little at a time, and working consistently make a nurturing and productive blueprint for success. I learned this concept from a friend back in 1988 in a conversation between basketball games. This person was a best-selling author whose book had been made into a television miniseries; he told me, "Writing is all about layers." He was right. I adapted this dynamic to much of my work and projects in general with much success. Remember that the advice you got about working through this book was to do it *the first time* within 21 days. Take that time—it is a sufficiently long period, yet not so long that the concepts won't stay fresh. Better you spend 30 minutes or an hour here and there than try to absorb the content in just a few days.

Practice using nurturing messages for confidence building, reassurance, and comfort. Incorporate them into your internal script.

Adult

Now that you have a strategy for developing your Nurturing Parent mind state, let's move on to the Adult—the energy of logic and objectivity. Remember, the Adult is not intellectual intelligence. Again, if you are worried about your IQ, don't be: You are intelligent if you have the motivation to improve your performance and control anxiety at work. Unintelligent people simply do not have this desire or motivation.

Here are some exercises for strengthening your Adult mind state:

1. Develop your objective observation skills

   A. Observe a situation for at least a few minutes in an environ-ment that is not too important to you. You could be waiting in line for a movie, waiting for a train, or going through security at the airport. After you observe, describe in your notes what you saw objectively. Omit any value judgment or feelings; just be neutral.

      To get you started, here is an excerpt from Amy's ex-ercise notes; notice where she crossed out the places that included judgment, interpretations, and feelings in favor of sticking with what she knew was objective:

      Two people are ahead of me in line for coffee. One is a young woman, wearing a down parka, jeans, and boots; she is ~~being rude to the cashier,~~ talking on the phone while she is ordering. One person ~~I am glad to see~~ is my friend Robin, ~~who is glad to see me~~.

   B. After A, observe for at least a few minutes a more personal scenario such as your office or a family gathering. Then objectively describe it without value judgment or feelings.

2. Learn from observation

   A. Identify something you learned from a recent observation at work. Write it down, which will help your brain imprint the learning process.

      _____

      _____

      _____

   B. Identify something you learned from a past observation at work. Again, write it down:

      _____

      _____

      _____

Make sure you are actually following through on the exercise. Don't detach!

Use your logic and objective reasoning to hypothesize an answer instead of responding with "I don't know," detaching from, or avoiding the issue altogether. Identify a situation recently at work where you detached from an answer; then hypothesize what the answer would have been.

The situation I detached from:

_____

_____

What the answer would have been:

_____

_____

3. *Validate* the fact that success is not characterized by a straight line up. There are high points and low ones, steps forward and steps back. Success looks like what's shown in Figure 4.1.

Don't be afraid of the success graph. Success is a process—a journey. *Attach* to this image as the shape of steady progress. Celebrate the highs, and learn from the lows, and most important, press on!

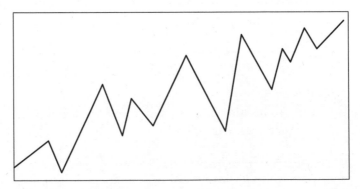

Figure 4.1   The Graph of Success

Identify three past situations where your emotions got in the way of your learning from mistakes or where embarrassment or humiliation impacted objective reasoning and forward movement.

1. _____
2. _____
3. _____

Identify options for utilization of logic and objectivity instead of emotion in these scenarios.

1.	
2.	
3.	

Heaviness Exercise

This is a basic version of a very effective exercise we will return to in an upcoming chapter. For now, practice giving yourself over to the present as you master this 60-second version. Sit in a comfortable chair. Allow yourself to feel passive. Take in a long, slow, deep breath 1 ... 2 ... 3 ... 4 ... then slowly exhale 4 ... 3 ... 2 ... 1.... For the next 60 seconds, focus on your rhythmic breathing, pacing your inhales and exhales to between 8 and 12 seconds. Then say three times, "My right arm is heavy and limp." Then say three times "My left arm is heavy and limp." Close your eyes and repeat the phrases again—three times for each arm. Next, feel yourself sinking into the chair. Feel like a rag doll. Feel loose. Feel limp. Feel very limp. Become comfortable with, and focus on, the sensations of heaviness and limpness for two to three minutes. Then, open your eyes and take a deep breath in and out.

Learn and implement the following problem-solving technique. A good thing to tell yourself is, "Don't stress out about that which is doable." When a problem comes up, the objectivity of your Adult will tell you that with most problems, resolution is possible. Resolving is a process, and it requires proactive thinking. What usually gets in the way is anxiety. It is anxiety that inhibits forward motion. To give yourself courage, apply a nurturing interpretation: Tell yourself that feeling uncomfortable can mean "I am improving my skills," "My self-esteem is improving as I am moving forward," "I will be less angry when I take responsibility for motion instead of being passive," and so on.

Problem-Solving Technique

A. Identify the problem or stressor.

B. Identify the cause.

C. Identify the choices.

D. Set priorities.

E. Make a decision.

F. Follow through.

G. Keep following through.

Here is an example of the Problem-Solving Technique in action. Caroline was the executive secretary to a bank's senior vice president. When Mike, a midlevel executive, was transferred from another branch, things got a bit complicated. Caroline's anxiety increased because Mike started asking her to do research for him although she was not assigned to him. Caroline found herself falling behind in her own work. She left work daily feeling resentful, angry, and powerless. Here is how she applied the Problem-Solving Technique:

A. Identify stressor: Mike gets me to do his work for him.

B. Identify cause: I can't seem to say no.

C. Identify choices:

1. Keep doing the work.

2. Tell the vice president it's an issue.

3. Go directly to Human Resources.

4. Get feedback from other colleagues.

5. Flatly refuse to do the work.

6. Do it, but make clear that it's extra.

7. Tell Mike "I'd be glad to, but I have to check with my boss."

8. Tell Mike "I'll do it as soon as I'm finished with my other work."

D. Set priorities:

1. Keep my job!

2. Get my own work done first; do it as well as I can.

3. Maintain good working relationship with vice president.

E. Make a decision:

   I will keep it between Mike and me. I will tell him I'm glad to help once my own work is done. Going to HR could backfire. Refusing to help could cause more conflict. If I'm lucky, Mike will learn to do it himself rather than having to wait for my help. I know I'll experience some adrenaline anticipating and following through with Mike. The "nurturing" interpretation of adrenaline as positive energy gives me courage.

F. Follow through:

   The last time Mike asked for help, I did just as planned, and he found another assistant with more time to help him. No hard feelings. Actually he was pretty nice about it, so if I ever do have time, I really wouldn't mind pitching in.

G. Keep following through:

   I have begun to feel less nervous about saying no—and at the same time, Mike seems to have gotten the point, because he asks me less and less.

Caroline succeeded in allowing her Adult to step in to provide a solution that kept the emotion in her Adapted Child from getting out of hand. A key dynamic was her "nurturing" interpretation of adrenaline. She experienced an increased adrenaline flow at two points: first, when she anticipated talking to Mike, and second, when she was about to talk to him. She was able to use the Problem-Solving Technique to ride the adrenaline wave without giving in to any past negative association she had with that feeling.

Give the Problem-Solving Technique a try right now.

1. Identify problem or stressor: _____

2. Identify the cause: _____

3. Identify choices: _____
   A. _____
   B. _____
   C. _____
   D. _____

4. Set priorities:
   A. _____
   B. _____
   C. _____

   Important: Identify the points at which you will face an adrenaline challenge and consider how you'll have to utilize the nurturing interpretation.

5. Make a decision: _____

6. Follow through: _____

7. Keep following through: _____

Follow through means follow through! This is not merely a practice run. Return to your notes as you follow through and keep following through so you have a record of what worked and what didn't. As with any technique, this one has a learning curve, and practice is critical.

Listen when your Adult tells you there is a difference between performance and identity. This is one of the most profound if not the most profound beliefs necessary for controlling social and performance anxiety.

We've all had times when our performance has not been good. Coping with that has certainly required logic in separating performance from personhood. Kirk Rueter was a pitcher in the major leagues for 13 years, playing for the Montreal Expos and San Francisco Giants. During his career, he won 130 games. Sometime later I had the opportunity to talk with Kirk about performance issues, and I asked him facetiously, "Did you ever have a terribly bad game?"

"I was once pitching against the Colorado Rockies," he recalled. "I was losing 7–0 in the first inning with no outs." Just imagine—a full stadium, on television, everyone focusing attention on a losing effort. I asked him how he dealt with that.

"I have to pitch every fifth day," he said, "so I concentrate on what I have to do to be better then next time out." He makes it sound so easy! But think for a moment. Isn't that the perfect winning psychology? A true example of high performance thinking? So simple, so perfect. What would keep an individual from investing in this thinking? The answer is a too-critical internal script—things you say to yourself in your mind so constantly that you may not be able to consciously hear yourself. But I will teach you to hear that script. And more important, to change it!

Kirk's attitude of focusing on the keys to "doing better the next time out" is characteristic of a winning attitude and proactive thinking. To resolve anxiety and develop confidence and success, you must *embrace proactive thinking*. Realize that there are some things you do not yet know—and understand that this is good news. Learning something new means you can change what is not working for you and build confidence.

To view a free Webinar in which Kirk Rueter and his wife discuss selective mutism, visit www.socialanxiety.com.

We've all had bad conversations, bad meetings, bad days, bad weeks, bad months, and sometimes even bad years. That's not much of a consolation, but it does tell you something: We got through it. How you performed is not who you are; it's simply how you performed. What gets in the way of this logic are the emotions of embarrassment, humiliation, shame, fear of rejection, and the unhealthy and unproductive expectations of perfection. The capability for embarrassment is substantially exaggerated for the person with social and performance anxiety. The reason for this exaggeration, and often toxicity, is trauma or feeling loss of control, both of which are usually based on an over-concern regarding others' perceptions of you.

Attach to your own feelings of embarrassment. Describe the following situations.

A typical situation that I now dread due to my fear of being embarrassed is

_____

_____

_____

What my fear tells me *others* would be thinking is

_____

_____

_____

If I addressed the situation using my Adult mind state, being totally objective and rational, others would be thinking something more like:

_____

_____

_____

Projection

Recall that "projection" refers to putting your thoughts or projecting them onto other people. To give a very simple example, Kathleen dislikes her speaking voice, but instead of consciously realizing that, she instead ascribes that dislike to her colleagues (who may or may not actually feel that way). Another example is Alex, a college student working in a sub shop; he had a very strict manager who appeared to anger easily. Alex's thinking was that this manager, given her constant state of agitation, did not like it when she was asked questions. But Alex didn't ask questions because he thought having questions meant he was ignorant; he was projecting that thought onto the manager.

Using the logic of your Adult, list three scenarios where you hid your feelings from yourself by imagining that that was how another person felt about you:

1. _____

2. _____

3. _____

The Natural Child

The next state for development is the Natural Child. To review for a moment: This state is the truth of desire, creativity, exploration, discovery, the development of ideas, creativity, spontaneity, as well as basic urges such as sexuality.

Here are some ways to "raise" your Natural Child. To begin, become aware of the times you may have stifled your Natural Child—for either productive reasons (holding back road rage during your morning commute) or less productive ones (refusing to dance at the company holiday party even though you wanted to). Note: There are many questions here, and you will be making many lists, so you should definitely use your notes to answer the following series of questions.

1. Acting on a desire
   A. List as many examples as possible where you did not act on a desire.
   B. List as many examples as possible where you want to act on a desire.

2. Expressing yourself
   A. List as many examples as possible where you wanted to express yourself verbally but did not because of anxiety (worrying what others would think, fear of saying something stupid, etc.).
   B. List as many examples as you can where you want to express yourself verbally.

3. Exploring something

   A. List as many examples as you can where you wanted to explore something (a relationship, a problem to solve, a challenge scenario) but you did not because of anxiety.

   B. List as many examples as you can where you want to explore.

4. List as many examples as you can where you wanted to be spontaneous but censored or stopped yourself because of anxiety (in the last day, week, month, year).

5. List the activities that you want to do for fun, recreation, and enjoyment.

6. Give as many examples as you can of situations where you used your instinct well.

7. Make a list of ideas you need to develop.

8. Make a list of where, or to whom, you need to express your feelings instead of detaching.

These lists will become an important part of your behavioral game plan as you learn to implement the Five-Step Adrenaline Control Technique.

An important tip: On a daily basis, take a minute or two to identify in your notes examples of how you engaged (and therefore increased) your Nurturing Parent, Adult, and Natural Child. If you like, you can write in more detail.

The Five-Step Adrenaline Control Technique and Mind States

Realistic expectations are a necessity for anxiety management and confidence at work. Realistic expectations are nurturing. Your adrenaline is going to be there when you encounter anxiety challenges. That's a fact; knowing it is using your Adult. You'd better learn to accept and embrace this reality. Acceptance is nurturing. Investing in the interpretation that adrenaline is your friend and source of power is also nurturing. Believing that the adrenaline should not be there is characteristic of the unrealistic standards of the excessive Critical Parent. This unrealistic thinking will set your Adapted Child up for a temper tantrum of panic and anxiety. Non-acceptance of the adrenaline—getting angry and frustrated with it when you experience it—is the excessive Critical Parent telling you it should not be there. Your Adult will confirm that adrenaline is a source of power; therefore, accepting it makes a lot more sense than rejecting it.

Experimenting with Mind State Balancing is itself a process of nurturing your Natural Child. Creating a hierarchy of anxiety challenges will require use of your Adult's objective analysis. Learning breathing, acceptance, and surfing/acceptance skills are nurturing activities. Being proactive at implementing and sustaining the Five-Step Adrenaline Control Technique is nurturing. (See Figure 4.2.) Adult (logic) will tell you that implementation must be sustained in order to truly learn confidence with the skill. Your A will tell you that you have to feel or attach to whatever you wish to control (in this case, adrenaline). You can't do it via osmosis (as your Adult knows!).

Hyper Vigilance

"After my first panic attack," says Anne, office manager at a medical practice, "I could not stop thinking about when it would happen again—not whether it would happen, but *when*." Anne felt tension as soon as she pulled into the parking lot and she stayed on edge all the time—prepared for fight or flight.

The clinical term for that sense of defensive arousal is "hyper vigilance." It is typical of panic attack sufferers to become hyper vigilant *even after just one panic attack*. Essentially, the nervous system is on overdrive, consciously or unconsciously expecting a threat to occur. Hyper vigilance integrates thoughts, feelings, and physiology. Anne's thoughts raced, her emotions were close to the surface, and she felt physically uncomfortable.

Anne worked six days per week and had not taken time off in many months. With so little down time she was seldom able to come out of this state. It was a typical vicious circle: The more time she

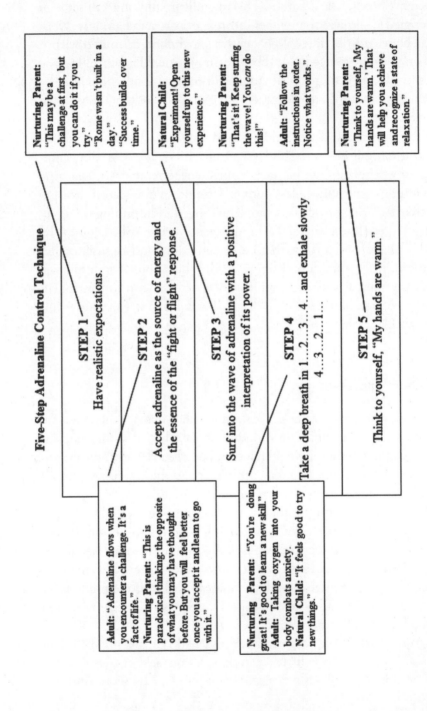

Five-Step Adrenaline Control Technique

STEP 1
Have realistic expectations.

STEP 2
Accept adrenaline as the source of energy and the essence of the "fight or flight" response.

STEP 3
Surf into the wave of adrenaline with a positive interpretation of its power.

STEP 4
Take a deep breath in 1...2...3...4... and exhale slowly 4...3...2...1...

STEP 5
Think to yourself, "My hands are warm."

Nurturing Parent:
"This may be a challenge at first, but you can do it if you try."
"Rome wasn't built in a day."
"Success builds over time."

Natural Child:
"Experiment! Open yourself up to this new experience."

Nurturing Parent:
"That's it! Keep surfing the wave! You *can* do this!"

Adult: "Follow the instructions in order. Notice what works."

Nurturing Parent:
"Think to yourself, 'My hands are warm.' That will help you achieve and recognize a state of relaxation."

Adult: "Adrenaline flows when you encounter a challenge. It's a fact of life."
Nurturing Parent: "This is paradoxical thinking: the opposite of what you may have thought before. But you will feel better once you accept it and learn to go with it."

Nurturing Parent: "You're doing great! It's good to learn a new skill."
Adult: Taking oxygen into your body combats anxiety.
Natural Child: "It feels good to try new things."

Figure 4.2   The Five-Step Adrenaline Control Technique: Integrating All Mind States

116

spent in hyper vigilance, the more her energy depleted, and the more susceptible she became to both panic attacks and burnout.

Some people's hyper vigilance begins with childhood expectations of perfection. When a child grows up believing he or she must be perfect to be valued, the slightest slip-up can cause anxiety. Demanding parents only reinforce this response. For some children, the pressure leads to high achievement coupled with high anxiety; for others, it leads to a kind of paralysis—doing nothing at all (avoiding) so as to do nothing wrong.

Sean was the oldest son of two college professors who had high academic expectations for him from the time he was a kindergartner. At the age of 30 and a self-described "IT geek," Sean said his ongoing nervousness at interacting with colleagues and customers felt natural to him: "My parents often had professors over when I was little," he told me. "I was shy around them. I sort of hid behind my mom. I guess she was trying to make light of it when she would tell them, 'Don't ask Sean where he goes to school or what grade he's in. Apparently he doesn't know!' That always got a big laugh. She may not have meant anything by it. But the feeling I get at work is the same feeling I had back then."

Sometimes, serious childhood trauma causes hyper vigilance—whether the trauma is abuse, neglect, or loss of a loved one. Extreme embarrassment or rejection early in life are traumas too. Trauma imprints the brain with a familiar and terrifying feeling. A person who was bullied as a child, for example, may feel bullied by his or her boss. In people who were sexually abused as children, hyper vigilance is quite common. Norma, a 45-year-old middle manager in a market research company, suffered from public speaking anxiety; she never realized the problem was her unresolved emotional conflict, anger, and hyper vigilance resulting from her stepfather's sexually abusing her during her adolescence. Children who grow up in a home environment characterized by discord, conflict, and fighting also become conditioned toward hyper vigilance. They will develop vigilance as a defense mechanism—in answer to some unconscious thinking that goes something like "When will I have to defend myself next?" "When will the peace be broken?"

TUNE IN: Use your Adult to identify a scenario from the past (childhood or more recently) in which you may have learned hyper vigilance. Can you remember two or three?

1. When _____, I felt _____, and I reacted by _____.

2. When _____, I felt _____, and I reacted by_____.

3. When _____, I felt _____, and I reacted by_____.

The Critical Parent–Adapted Child Adrenaline Reflex

Let's do a memory exercise. Go back as far as you can in your memory—back to your childhood if possible—and identify a scenario where you felt a loss of control, panic, embarrassment, or uncomfortable rejection. Notice how you made a negative association to adrenaline. Recognize the hyper vigilance that could have resulted from this scenario.

You probably remember Carol, the ovarian cancer survivor who said she preferred chemotherapy to public speaking. She traced her workplace anxiety to a grade school experience in which her teacher pointed out that she was blushing during class. Jerry, the military surgeon mentioned in Chapter 1, also had public speaking anxiety; his had manifested itself on hospital "rounds" with his peers as well as in formal clinical presentations. His father was an alcoholic who often displayed unhealthy and inappropriate behavior such as attending Jerry's medical school graduation drunk. Jerry learned to be on guard and hyper vigilant from a young age. This hyper vigilance was accompanied by adrenaline flow, which registered as anxiety. In a public speaking challenge, Jerry's *critical script* said, "There's going to be danger," "Be on guard," "You will be nervous and embarrassed." His learned anxiety and deep negative imprint of adrenaline existed in his AC mind state.

The more this CP–AC syndrome of hyper vigilance and excessive nervous system activity occurs over time, the deeper and more ingrained a reflex it becomes. It can become automatic, which is why the NP, A, and NC need to be consciously developed. This reflex can be the result of ongoing hyper vigilance or, in some cases, one-time trauma.

When I asked Amy what early memories she had that could have led to hyper vigilance, she told me this.

When I was three, I was the littlest kid in the neighborhood. All my friends were five or six years old. When the group of girls would get together to play, the older sister of one of them (she was maybe eight) would always seek me out and punch me in the stomach when no one was looking. I'm talking hard! I never cried, never said a word—I was that determined to be one of the "big girls." My defensiveness when Ana was around definitely reminds me of the hyper vigilant feeling I have had in certain work or social situations: "Brace yourself for whatever's coming next," "Don't trust anybody," "Keep your fears and feelings to yourself," "Big girls don't cry"—all that stuff. It amazes me that my hyper vigilance of today has its roots in such a long-ago experience. I had forgotten all about Ana until I started working on this part of the program.

Opie and Anthony: A Performance Ambush

The following story of my appearance on the *Opie & Anthony* radio show represents productive mind state balance.

Warning! This is an X-rated story told as exactly and graphically as I can remember.

A few years ago, a PR firm booked me on this show. The PR firm did not tell me the nature of the show, and I had not done any research—which demonstrated *not enough Adult* and *too much Adapted Child* on my part. It would have been more effective for me to use the logic of my Adult to do some research about that particular show. But I was rocking and rolling in general—going with my Natural Child—doing a lot of shows, one after the other. Frankly, I was a little too cocky; I felt like I could handle anything, and it didn't occur to me to stop and use my Adult to decide which shows were truly worth my time and energy. All I knew was that *Opie and Anthony* was on a good station in New York with a substantial audience. I was completely unaware that Opie and Anthony were two shock jocks who made Howard Stern look tame.

I was waiting to do the show by telephone from my home in East Hampton. My wife was in New York, where she heard the promos for "Bad Guest Day." The purpose of the show was to embarrass and humiliate the guests—the hosts' Natural Child instincts gone wild. It was an ambush! My wife tried calling to warn me, but was unable to reach me. The phone rang. I started the interview with my usual two-to-three-minute introduction geared to generate audience attention on the subject of social anxiety.

The first listener call came in: a man who sounded like he was in his twenties. "Doc, can you tell me how I can get the guy in the urinal next to me to hold my penis?" My response after a moment of thought? "I guess you need assertiveness skills."

The next caller: "Doc, how can I get my girlfriend to bend over?" "What do you mean?" I responded. "To have anal sex," he said. After another moment of thought, my response was, "You need to teach her how to relax."

At this point, realizing something was a bit screwy (Adult), I went on the offensive (Natural Child), saying, with a hint of humor, "You know, I work with a lot of socially handicapped people; it sounds like you have many in your audience." To top it off, after subjecting me to this absurdity, they bleeped out my 800 number as the show ended. Opie and Anthony were eventually taken off the air for orchestrating a couple having sex in a church (more primitive Natural Child) and putting it on air. They are since back in action.

There are two clinical points to this story. They are profoundly important for the resolution of performance anxiety.

1. Opie and Anthony were trying to humiliate me. They orchestrated their attempt very well. But they were not successful. Embarrassment is an internal dynamic. I was angry, but I was not embarrassed. A person can't embarrass you. Yet they can provide a stimulus. You decide. Humiliation is a result of the Critical Parent–Adapted Child interaction, the twin towers on the graph. You and I determine internally if we will or will not be embarrassed by an external stimulus. To paraphrase Eleanor Roosevelt: "No one can insult me without my permission."

2. After I'd cooled off a little, I took some time to analyze my performance objectively (Adult). I realized I was pleased with my performance (Nurturing Parent), especially my creative answers under stress (Natural Child). I had by then done hundreds of shows, so I was adept at controlling adrenaline and performance stress. I was able to be centered under pressure enough to access my creativity, my Natural Child, and keep from getting rattled on air by this ambush.

In other words I had become relatively desensitized to the stress of performance. This was the result of developing my Natural Child over time. I had given myself a lot of permission to experiment, explore, and discover during my many years of public speaking experience. I had taken a Nurturing Parent approach to performance by seeking out ways to develop performance skills and I was able to access my creativity (Natural Child) under stress.

Create Your Behavioral Hierarchy

Anxiety is a relative phenomenon. Creating a hierarchy of behavioral and situational challenges gives you a list of much-needed laboratories within which you can experiment with your adrenaline. You are going to need as much practice with attaching and utilizing the Five-Step Adrenaline Control Technique as possible. Your investment in this belief will very much determine your degree of success with performance anxiety control. Experiment with the Five-Step one step at a time. *Doesn't it make sense that if you are going to learn to control something you first have to feel or attach to it? (Adult)*

The ideal strategy is to make the pursuit of your challenges gradual, consistent, and sustained. Create a hierarchy of the situations that make you nervous on a scale of 1 (lowest) to 10 (highest). These lists are different for each person. One client, for example, rated speaking one-on-one with his boss or other authority figures as a level 5; speaking to his sales team was a 7; the board of directors meeting was a 12 (on a scale of 1 to 10!) (See? That's a joke! [Natural Child]). For another client, participating in Toastmasters, a worldwide self-help program for public speaking, rated a 10.

For still others, Toastmasters was only a 3 because she perceived the forum as a safe place to take risks. It's all subjective and relative. For some people talking spontaneously in a staff meeting is a 2; for others, a 9. You get the point. Create your behavioral hierarchy list of performance challenges now. It may take some thought. Do not continue with reading until you do this.

1. _____
   _____

2. _____
   _____

3. _____
   _____

4. _____
   _____

5. _____

6. _____
   _____

7. _____
   _____

8. _____
   _____

9. _____
   _____

10.

_____

_____

Before continuing with the next chapter, can you experiment with a level 2? Try it.

Imagery Exercise

Close your eyes for a moment and identify how many windows there are in your kitchen. How did you get the answer? You pictured it with your mind's eye. You can use this technique to picture anything. This exercise can become an important tool for behavior rehearsal.

Now, do rhythmic breathing for 60 seconds. Pace your inhale–exhale at between 8 to 12 seconds—so that this 60-second exercise comprises about six inhale–exhales. Sixty seconds. I mean it. Do it. Next close your eyes and picture yourself implementing the Five-Step for a level 2. Stay with the image for about 20 seconds, and then open your eyes.

TUNE IN: What's the temperature of your hands? What thoughts and feelings are present?

CHAPTER 5

The Positive Power of Stress: Make It Work for You

"Stressed out." "Under a lot of stress." "Stress-related illness." "Stress relief." "Stress management." We hear the word stress a lot. But what exactly is stress? Is it something good? Something bad? How do you define it?

How about "physiological adaptation to change"? That is how it was characterized by Hans Selye, the scientist who in 1936 identified and defined "stress" as we know it today. "Adaptation" occurs on emotional, behavioral, and lifestyle levels—switching gears in response to an alteration in circumstance. That's all it is, isn't it? You notice a stimulus and respond to it. For example, if you are crossing the street and a car closely whizzes by you, your pulse will increase, your muscles may tighten, you might perspire. And you would no doubt get angry instantly. I know I would.

Or how about if your boss tells you "something just came up" and you have to address a group of your colleagues in one hour about your latest assignment. Would you have any physiological adaptation? How would your mind react? What would your body feel?

When I was a freshman in college, a psychology professor staged a scenario where someone unexpectedly burst into the classroom, pointed a pistol at him, and fired! The gun was a starter pistol and the bullets were blanks, but of course we had no way of knowing that. Talk about adaptation! All of our bodies instantly went into fight-or-flight mode—and rightly so. Our senses heightened, our pulses quickened, blood rushed from our extremities to the areas of our bodies where we'd need it most. Such an adrenaline rush is the appropriate response to a stressor of that magnitude. (In light of the last few decades' school shootings, it's a good bet that this educational exercise will not happen again.) Extreme adaptation is not, however, especially useful to you when you need to focus your energy and clear thinking on a last-minute assignment or other challenge. Adrenaline is not bad; it is an important source of power. You can manage it. You can *use* it. What you can't do is avoid it (unless you are dead or heavily tranquilized—neither of which we recommend!).

There Is No Stress-Free Life

We all experience stress. We can't avoid it. We don't have to. In fact, in this book you are learning to welcome stress. The flow of adrenaline itself is not bad. It is *useful*. Stress can be an asset. Of course, some stressors are negative, and these situations are called "distress." But most of the anxiety-causing stress we are discussing here is good stress, or "eustress." "Eustress" is power! The more you can convert your perception of stress into "eustress," the more positive energy you will have to pour into your performance. Think of "eustress" as a command: *Use* stress. Use it as fuel for success. Draw on your Natural Child as you explore this new way of thinking about stress.

In the early 1980s I did a number of stress management workshops in corporations and organizations. At one preliminary meeting with a human resources rep at a major television network, he said, "There's no stress here." Maybe everyone was dead? Otherwise, what he was saying was simply not possible.

Distress exists when physiological adaptation manifests as panic, headaches, insomnia, gastrointestinal problems, and a myriad of other physical symptoms as well as substance abuse and phobic avoidance.

Eustress occurs as anxiety before those events you fear—confronting a challenging problem, dealing with conflict, interacting with a difficult colleague, taking risks. In the past, you have associated adrenaline flow sensations as distress. What you are learning now—and will put into practice—is that stress simply exists, and that you yourself can create an interpretation that transforms it into eustress.

One of my clients was a champion skydiver who jumped hundreds of times a year. He specialized in group jumps. Yet he was petrified of speaking to groups from a podium. Another client experienced less anxiety as a soldier in the Israeli army involved in door-to door confrontations than he did when he had to make a presentation to a group of six colleagues about a topic he knew well. Personally, I'd rather handle the stress of public speaking than skydiving or being in the infantry in a war zone.

Skydiving. Presentations. Combat. Conference calls. It's all a matter of individual taste. It's not the adrenaline itself that scares people into avoidance. It's the association of adrenaline with something bad. Once you decide that the adrenaline means, "You are terrible at this!" or "You're not good enough," or you associate it with losing control and feeling embarrassed, you interpret adrenaline in that situation as bad. Were those skydiving clients courageous? Many would say yes. *You* can be courageous too: Courage is action in the face of fear. You're afraid? Do it anyway! As Amy says, "It takes so many hours and so much energy to dread something. Go ahead and do whatever it is, then, if you still need to dread it, go ahead and do so after you're done."

Of course, once you are riding the high of accomplishing whatever you had feared, you probably won't feel the need to second-guess yourself. Instead, you'll be creating a powerful personal history of success. Nurture yourself by celebrating that success. Let your Critical Parent mind state acknowledge you for a job well done. Use your Adult to note that you completed your assignment and can remember the positive response. Listen to your Adapted Child remark that you prepared as you should have, you rode the adrenaline wave, and it worked. And let the Natural Child's sheer joy at the pleasure of experimentation and being in the zone take over.

Adaptation to stress is a healthy part of life. But overadapting to stress can have profound implications. At work, avoidance may take the specific form of getting out of any public speaking assignments, dealing with authority figures, or taking on new responsibilities. It may be as general as avoiding any scenario where there is fear of being noticeably nervous because of, for instance, blushing or sweating. Adapting to stress is normal and healthy. Overadapting, or adapting in a way that has an extremely negative influence, won't get you anywhere, and it could cost you quite a lot.

Give Up Believing You Have Control Over Everything

Life happens. There are life events over which you have no control that will create stress and require you to adapt. Some of these events may be considered positive and some negative. For example, getting a promotion or getting fired both create adaptation. Believe it or not, if you won the lottery, it would create stress. According to Holmes and Rahe, two pioneering researchers in the area of stress, there are many life events—happy, sad, disappointing, exciting—that can cause stress and put you at risk of illness. They devised a deceptively simple test that instantly depicts how various events in our lives affect our mental and physical health. Interestingly, its official name is the Social Readjustment Rating Scale (note that the term "Readjustment" is there to indicate that these stressors require you to adjust or *adapt*). This famous inventory, commonly called the Holmes and Rahe Stress Scale, is available for free on the Internet and takes about five minutes to complete.

According to Holmes and Rahe, even a vacation has some degree of stress—just two more points than "minor violations of the law"! Getting fired is a 47. Getting married is a 50. The point is, both our triumphs and challenges, both our joyous celebrations and our darkest moments, stimulate us to adapt. Life is not static. It is dynamic. Consider this list in light of the situations that cause your adaptation.

TUNE IN: Focus on your rhythmic breathing for 30 seconds—three inhale–exhale sequences. Consider how you may have foregone good career opportunities because you wanted to avoid the feelings associated with them. Realize that stressors outside work can affect your effectiveness on the job.

Avoidance Harms Self-Esteem

Avoidance may be your default adaptation to stress. But along with that default comes another one: anxiety. Avoidance can successfully mitigate feelings of anxiety in the short term. But the longer the avoidance is in place, the more underlying worry, frustration, anger, and self-loathing develop! After a while, you might simply condition yourself to a feeling of worthlessness—to you, it seems that "worthless" is just a part of who you are.

Mindy, age 32, parlayed her master's in accounting into a job with a firm she really liked. A week after she started, she made a few errors—small ones that any entry-level professional might make. Her colleagues told her everyone made mistakes at first. As a joke, they gave "Newbie" (their nickname for her) a stack of grade-school addition and subtraction flashcards. These were signs of affection and acceptance, but Mindy was mortified. She kept her feelings to herself, but everyone could see she had withdrawn into her work and did not want to be part of the friendly, informal office culture. Mindy was hyper vigilant—always sure someone would make fun of her. She was sure she was underqualified and terrified every single day that she would make another gaffe. In the end, her fear slowed down her productivity, and she was passed over for several promotions because she simply wasn't cutting it.

Believing you are worthless and have nothing to contribute sets you up for a myriad of problems including obsessive worry, panic, depression, substance abuse, headaches, insomnia, overeating, and hypertension, which is, by the way, the classic disease of adaptation. (Indeed, one in three Americans has hypertension, yet, according to the Associated Press's Laura Neegaard, "doctors too often don't treat it aggressively and the government hasn't made it enough of a priority, either.") It would be worthwhile for you to review the Physical Anxiety Profile in Chapter 2. If you think about these stress-related illnesses for a moment, you will see one common thread: They are for the most part invisible. They are a way of internalizing, and in some ways keeping secret, the degree to which you are unable to deal with stress out in the open. Overeating and substance abuse are less easy to conceal—yet even they often occur under a cloak of secrecy, especially when they become serious disorders.

On the Edge of Your Seat

Being on the edge of your seat is not a good feeling unless you're at the movies enjoying a thriller. For anxiety sufferers, that "Oh, no, what's going to happen next?" feeling is constant. And it builds on itself: Anxiety causes you to overadapt by avoiding the thing that makes you anxious. Avoiding it makes you even more anxious. So you avoid it more. Hyper vigilance increases until it cannot sustain itself. This excessive state of arousal can create "burnout"—sustained emotional and physical exhaustion. When you overuse your nervous system, your energy gets depleted.

One of my clients was a commercial airline pilot. Given how much of an obsessive perfectionist this man was, I'm sure he was skilled at his profession. Believe me; I would feel very comfortable being a passenger in his plane. He sought treatment with me for a very specific problem, which occurred only when a senior pilot was sitting next to him. He was afraid his voice would crack when he had to make an announcement on the plane's loudspeaker (even something simple such as, "Sorry, ladies and gentlemen, there will be a delay") with another senior pilot in the cockpit. He was afraid of not appearing perfect in front of the other senior pilot.

This client shared an interesting bit of aviation history that is worth mentioning here. Historically, passenger planes had one pilot and one navigator in the cockpit. The navigator would provide the information, and the pilot would make the decisions. Here's an interesting question for you: Who has more stress, the pilot or the navigator? The answer may surprise you: It's the navigator. The pilot makes the decisions, whereas the navigator must wait for those decisions, without the authority to act on them. Decision making itself can cause stress and anxiety, but the lack of control—being required to wait for the decisions of others—is very stressful. Research has proven that people with very little autonomy in their jobs are generally more stressed and unhappy in their positions than those with decision-making power. Is this a factor for you?

In your own life, you are not the navigator. You are choosing to work this program. In doing so, you are training yourself to be the pilot—or the quarterback if you prefer. The pilot makes decisions. The quarterback makes decisions. Mistakes are inherent in decision making—you won't always be right—but you, as the pilot, as the quarterback, must take control. This concept is crucial to your management of stress and anxiety at work. You cannot control your environment or the people in it, but you can control your reaction!

Let's apply the adaptation to stress to the actual process of working through this book.

Attach and Connect

How are you adapting thus far to the concept of piloting or quarter-backing? Are you creating productive motion? Have you been doing the exercises in the book diligently? Do you have your hierarchy of behavioral challenges identified and in place ready to take action? Are you making notes as you complete the exercises? Have you been experimenting with the Five-Step Adrenaline Control Technique?

At this point you should have developed an increasingly productive sense of hand temperature and its correlation to specific emotions and thoughts. Have you attached to the breathing exercises? Have you utilized the problem-solving strategy of the Adult mind state? If you have been in motion, really on the court with this program, make sure to acknowledge this fact. Pat yourself on the back. This is nurturing.

And if you find yourself answering no to some of these check-in questions—ask yourself why. Do not "should" on yourself! Don't tell yourself you *should* be doing a better job, *should* be less afraid, *should* be more committed or disciplined. Instead, use your mind states to form a fully rounded picture of where you are. Do not let this become a component of the negative critical script. Just notice whether you are or are not following the program as instructed.

So where do things stand? Being honest with yourself—without judging—is the only way to stay in this game. Do not tell yourself, "Well, I haven't been doing it right, so I should just quit." Do not tell yourself, "This program isn't really helping me" if you have not been following it to the letter. Don't do that to yourself. You deserve to be treated better than that, Just take inventory, notice what you may have needed and not put in place to support your effort—dedicated time to read, a simple system for note-taking?—and consider how to put it in place so you can continue. Not only that, but by all means return to earlier chapters and get up to speed before you continue. And if for any reason you feel like you have lost ground or missed some concepts, go back and review. After all, this is your book. You can read it as many times as you want to.

Don't step over anything, though. Ask yourself why you have avoided certain aspects of this program. If you realize you have not attached to the exercises and strategy up to this point, be even clearer about the specific thinking that allows you to detach and avoid. What did you tell yourself that made it okay to avoid and detach? What mind state was dominating when you said or thought those things? Probably it was your Adapted Child. Identify whether this AC thinking is characterized by illusion or possibly delusion.

Pay Attention Here: This Is the Gold

Before going any further, take in a long slow deep breath through your nose and slowly exhale 4 . . . 3 . . 2 . . . 1 . . . . Focus on the following statement:

Developing your mind states to achieve mind state balance is the ultimate stress management strategy because the process creates structural change in the personality.

Make yourself clear on the steps you must take in order to develop NP, A, and NC. Use your A now—logic and objectivity. Should you do a review? What enhances your learning curve? Implement it. This is nurturing.

A new skill that you have been learning is self-regulation/ relaxation. The more you are investing in the technique, the more you are nurturing yourself. The fact is that *anxiety and distress are incompatible with relaxation.* The self-regulation technique that you are learning is the most direct natural tool to help you control the energy of stress. In addition, using this technique effectively will allow you to access the Adult mind state; its logic and objectivity are necessary to resolve the problems that cause distress and anxiety. When I am under stress, I often rely on exercise as a therapeutic technique, not only because of its profoundly positive impact on mood and self-esteem, but also because the mind-body impact of working up a good sweat allows me to productively access my Adult.

Your exercise choices aren't limited to sports. Three years ago, Amy discovered salsa dancing, which is as intense as an aerobic workout. She reports, "Even if I'm feeling lazy, I manage to drag myself out to the salsa club. Within 20 minutes, I am feeling only pleasure and well-being, just in the zone, giving in to my Natural Child and feeling those endorphins rush."

The Five-Minute Integrated Biofeedback Exercise

Let's return to the Heaviness Exercise we introduced in Chapter 4. This time, you will spend a full five minutes completing it. Give yourself over to it. Do not think of it as a quick or a slow exercise. Just be in the moment as you explore and then complete it. It integrates all the techniques you have learned thus far. Rely on your ability to concentrate and to attach to the psychophysiological (mind-body) process of letting go, which—paradoxically!—is true control.

Take time to read the instructions slowly and attentively first. Then do the exercise.

1. During the exercise, look at a clock so that you can get a sense of time only at the beginning and at the end. Then let go.
2. Focus on your hands to assess the temperature.

3. Focus on your diaphragmatic breathing for about 30 seconds. Using the 4...3...2...1...pace of exhale, you should take three breaths of about 10 seconds each. (If you wish, practice that timing for a few minutes before you begin the full exercise.)

4. Close your eyes.

5. Make mental contact ("feel" with your mind) with your right arm. Say three times slowly to yourself, "My right arm is heavy." Pace yourself with each statement. Feel each word as you verbalize it. Say it three or four times, and notice the sensations in each arm after each statement.

6. Make mental contact with your left arm, saying three times slowly to yourself, "My left arm is heavy." Pace yourself at 30 seconds again as you repeat these words.

7. Make mental contact again with your right arm, saying three times slowly, "I feel the blood flowing through my right arm." Use the same pacing.

8. Make mental contact with your left arm, saying three times slowly, "I feel the blood flowing through my left arm." Use the same pacing.

9. Focus on your breathing again for 30 seconds. Slowly and fully in, then out.

10. Open your eyes.

11. Assess your hand temperature.

12. Look at the clock to check your timing.

You've read the instructions. Now go back to Step One and complete the exercise.

Letting Go

How did you do with this exercise in *letting go*?

Letting go is true control. Use your Natural Child to welcome this idea as true. Say to yourself: "Letting go is true control." Were you able to pace yourself, or did you rush through the exercise? Did you detach from doing it? (Was a little voice in your head interrupting with thoughts like, "This isn't working," "How long is 30 seconds?" "Five minutes is too long" or "too short"? Often the anxiety sufferer has learned that control is defensive positioning—*holding on* or being hyper vigilant. This may feel like being in control, but it is the opposite. When you are hyper vigilant, you are feeling and behaving as though you are under siege from an outside threat. You are obsessed with defending yourself—and overarousal is the result. Anxiety does not diminish if that is the way you adapt to it.

It's a paradox: Let go to *gain* control! Learning self-regulation and relaxation is a difficult challenge for the anxiety sufferer because hyper vigilance is so ingrained. But stick with it. The benefits are tremendous.

Letting go is an attitudinal, emotional, and physiological process. To attach to this concept, read the following passage slowly, line by line, breathing deeply and regularly as you take in the concepts and then let go of stress.

Letting Go

To let go doesn't mean to stop caring, it means I can't do it for someone else.

To let go is not to cut myself off, it's the realization I can't control another.

To let go is not to enable, but to allow learning from natural consequences.

To let go is to admit powerlessness, which means the outcome is not in my hands.

To let go is not to care for, but to care about.

To let go is not to fix, but to be supportive.

To let go is not to judge, but to allow another to be a human being.

To let go is not to be in the middle arranging all outcomes, but to allow others to effect their own outcomes.

To let go is not to deny, but to accept.

(continued)

> *To let go is not to nag, scold, or argue, but to search out my own shortcomings and correct them.*
> *To let go is not to adjust everything to my desires, but to take each day as it comes and to cherish the moment.*
> *To let go is not to criticize and regulate anyone, but to try to become whatever I dream to be.*
> *To let go is not to regret the past, but to grow and live for the future.*
> *To let go is to fear less and to love more.*

Isn't that inspiring? Please refer back to this passage whenever you wish to nurture yourself. You may want to copy it and keep it where you can access it daily as a kind of meditative pep talk: *Letting go to gain control.* What a concept. And what a gift. Give that gift to yourself and you will see a change in how you choose to adapt to stress.

A Magic Trick

All hyper vigilance has its roots in trauma. Sometimes that trauma seems small to others (a teacher humiliating a young student), sometimes inarguably significant (sexual abuse). For example, Jan was a 22-year-old college student who had been involved in a carjacking. During this episode, he was shot and remained in critical condition for a number of weeks. He almost died. For many years before this happened, Jan had been experiencing severe social anxiety with facial blushing. It was just horrible. After he recovered from the carjacking, with the help of his state's victim assistance program, he obtained therapy with me. Even though he had almost died after the carjacking, he gave that fact very little attention compared with his shame and embarrassment about blushing. He hardly cared about the shooting and the prospect of testifying in court and facing his attackers. All that was on mind was his blushing. He was completely obsessed.

After a number of sessions with me, he told an interesting story. He had done a presentation in front of one of his college classes. As he began, he told his fellow students, "In a minute you are going to see a magic trick. My face is going to change color." Guess what? He did not blush. Do you have any idea why?

By being proactive, which took quite a bit of courage (action in the face of fear), Jan was not on defense; hence, his nervous system was not working as hard as it usually did. He preempted his negative critical script by utilizing this paradoxical technique. This was a major investment in nurturing the risk taking and creativity of his Natural Child.

If you happen to have a blushing or sweating issue, try to blush or sweat right now. I dare you. Can you do it? Probably not, because this symptom most often is the result of defensive positioning and thinking. It is an adaptation. Like Jan, however, you can disarm it!

The pressure for productivity and high performance at work is stressful by nature. Many people feel their jobs are on the line with any given mistake—whether that's true or not. To give you a personal example: Several editors did not want to take the risk of publishing this book, even after our first book, *Beyond Shyness: How to Conquer Social Anxieties* (Simon & Schuster), had solid sales. Such reactions are just a fact of life in the world of business decisions. For the person waiting for a favorable decision, it's important to stay in the Adult mind state, since much potential emotion will result from either a favorable or unfavorable outcome. Our editor, Dan Ambrosio, took an educated and productive risk, which is often the key to high performance and productivity. But it always requires negotiating stress and anxiety.

When I was talking to the producer of *The Sally Jessy Raphael Show* in 1989 after my appearance on *Oprah* in 1988, his first response was, "You were on Oprah; we don't want you." I stayed the course, fielding his challenging questions. He asked an interesting one: "Why do you have a public relations firm?" I took a risk (Natural Child) with my answer. "I want to educate the world about social anxiety." I grossed over $1 million during the next few years as a result of this one "performance" on the phone with this producer.

"It's Scary at the Office"

This was the title of a 2009 article in *Newsday* by Judith Sills, who does an excellent job of describing the pressure that workplace anxiety can exact. She wrote:

> *Fear is stalking us at work. It's a nameless dread slithering through the vents. The whiff of flop sweat has spread well beyond those sectors openly marked as bruised and bleeding; car dealerships, newspapers, real estate fiefdoms. Whether reasonably or irrationally, we find ourselves looking around and asking each other, what's going to happen here? And then, for want of any information, we make up a scary answer.*

At the time this article was published, late in 2009, profits were down, expenses up, layoffs and budget cuts abounded, and desperate, anxiety-ridden managers were faced with deciding whom to fire. Entire projects were being cut out, and the tension of business leaders was contagious. You can double that tension for a two-income household with expenses that won't quit, and the climate at home can be as tension-filled as the climate at the office.

Worry continues to be rampant on both fronts. But worry is also normal and can be productive. There are two types of worry: first, the kind that goes round and round without searching for an action to take—worrying for the sake of worrying; and second, worry that manifests itself as energy you can channel into productive action. At different times in life, you may have gone one route or the other. Both are adaptations to stress. The recycling worry is the kind that leads to avoidance—and bores your friends because you won't get off the dime and just confront your boss, complete the assignment, or submit that résumé for the new job you keep saying you wish you had. You choose paralysis through cyclic worrying as a way to avoid doing what there is to do.

Productive worry—worry as fuel—is what we are after here. You've worried productively before—worried that an accident on the freeway might delay your arrival, you choose an alternate route that gets you there more quickly. Worried that you might make a bad impression by arriving late (again!), you take action by leaving not 15 minutes but a full 30 minutes ahead of time.

In other words, worry can be either energizing or paralyzing. It's all in how you use it.

Give two examples of times when you worried without taking any action:

1. _____

_____

2. _____

_____

Note the results you got for each:

1. _____

_____

2. _____

_____

Now give two examples of channeling worry into productive action:

1. _____

_____

2. _____

_____

The results:

1. _____

_____

2. _____

_____

What was the difference? How did you feel? Were you nervous? Did you take action anyway? Why or why not? No one is expecting you to have acted on your worry without any fear. Fear is probably your default response to worry or anxiety.

Here's something to understand: Courage is not doing some brave, confrontational, or outrageous thing. *Courage is action in the face of fear*. *Action*—not avoidance—even though you feel fear (anxiety, paralysis).

Sometimes Amy plays a game with herself that gets her to snap out of avoidance: "I pretend to be someone else. I may tell myself, 'Oh, you are not articulate or outgoing enough to make that phone call.' Then I choose to pretend that I am that articulate, outgoing person. I ask myself, 'What would that person do? Make the call.' So I take on that persona, take the action, and get the good result that I so deeply wanted all along."

The Boss Factor

It's not just employees who feel anxiety in the present economic climate (or even when things are going very well, as our many case studies have shown). Managing staff in this economy can be extremely daunting. Often managers take out their stress on those managed. Don was an $80,000 per year hard-working and productive employee in a major corporate event planning organization. He came to consult me about his public speaking anxiety. At one point his boss sent him an IM saying she was taking away his $90 per month stipend for a cell phone because he was not sending her e-mails on weekends. That was it—no discussion. The boss had never said, "Please send me e-mails on weekends to check in so we can get the best use out of your cell phone." She never said, "This is important to me, so please follow through." She just cut him off. Was his boss having a temper tantrum or was she using a productive negotiation strategy? In this instance, it was clear that it had nothing to do with necessary financial cutbacks.

My client's interpretation was that the boss was doing things in a childish fashion, and I agreed. I have learned very clearly, after supervising staff in many professional environments, that you do not engender good feelings by taking anything away. That's something to avoid unless absolutely necessary! A conversation between Don and his boss would have been a suitable step toward clarifying expectations for both parties. In my opinion, this example was a very poor management technique (Adapted Child) and showed primitive emotion uncensored (Natural Child). It certainly was effective in increasing Don's anger and decreasing his morale.

Employers dealing with avoidant workers often face tough challenges. They may feel sympathy for their employee, yet they can't enable that person at the expense of productivity. For example, a manager I know, Arthur, supervised about 125 individuals in an advertising agency. In his mid-sixties, he was much respected in his field. He not only knew the advertising business inside and out, but he also truly cared for his employees. I asked him to share some stories about employees being "nervous at work" from a manager's perspective.

One story he told me was about the vice president in charge of television buying, Marie, who had suffered a stroke but had recovered almost fully. Yet since her return to her work three years earlier, she had never volunteered for new assignments and never stayed late, which was often a necessity in her position. Rather than confront her changed abilities head on, she hid from the problem: Whenever possible, she orchestrated scheduling conflicts so she could avoid being assigned difficult projects. On days when Arthur would be in the office, she would call the receptionist to say she was working from home that day or had a medical appointment and wouldn't be in. Because she avoided the topic, Arthur was left to interpret things for himself: Was she incapable of continuing in the same position? Had she come to a point that she simply didn't care enough to do a good job? What support did she need—she hadn't asked for any, which he later ascribed to her avoidance and perfectionism. With no feedback from Marie, Arthur faced the issue of possibly "stepping her down" after further personnel reviews.

Elena, a staff member from Eastern Europe, was sensitive about her lack of fluency in English. She avoided phone conversations and instead relied on e-mail for all communication. Yet she toiled for hours over those memos and asked an associate to correct her work before she sent it out—even one-paragraph e-mails! The associate complained to a supervisor rather than confront Elena directly—creating a circle of avoidance and resentment that was destructive to morale.

I found these stories especially interesting because they presented unique challenges for the manager. Managers get nervous, too. They don't always know how best to handle things. And they do not know what work is like for you unless you tell them. All the more reason to get a handle on your anxiety so you can discuss what would enable you to do a better job. As a manager, Arthur had to draw on a combination of compassion (NP), complex negotiation skills (AC, NC), and his knowledge of human resource allocation (CP, A). Arthur had the bottom line to think about.

Incorporating the concept of mind states balance into management style offers great advantages. Dupont, for example, views its paternal management style and commitment to nurturing creativity (combining NP and NC) as essential to remaining competitive. "We have experienced the power of setting an environment for employees to think and act creatively with remarkable results," said one of DuPont's vice presidents. In 1997, David Tanner, PhD, who served as director of the DuPont Center for Creativity and Innovation, published a book about the success of his program, plus many other business initiatives, called *Total Creativity in Business and Industry*. Dr. Tanner wrote: "Many companies are discovering that total quality is essential—but not enough. Sustained success requires the ability not only to cope with change but to command it. Creative thinking provides the fuel for leadership in innovation."

Entrepreneurs and Mind States Balance

Owning their own business is a professional dream many people share. Entrepreneurship, too, requires mind states balance. Got a great idea? Wonderful. That's the Natural Child at work. How do you decide if the market is there? Uncovering that information requires your Adult to play a role. Sticking with it despite the many headaches of owning your own business requires encouragement from the Nurturing Parent. And doing things well so your customers will come back again is the role of the Critical Parent and Adapted Child.

Richard is one of my favorite examples of balanced mind states leading to a successful venture. When we met in 1978, Richard was directing an after-school center for elementary-age children. The same mind that was so good at providing fun for children created another enterprise, this one for adults: A traveling disco. This evolved into a major event-planning business serving hotels and corporations. Here is an example of his creativity. Once, when pitching a major corporation for an event, Richard brought with him a mime, a firebreather, and an elegant and exotic six-foot-six model to pose in the background and create atmosphere during the meeting. He got the job. Richard's Natural Child mind state kept his ideas fresh and his Adult paid attention to his market. His Nurturing Parent encouraged him, and his Critical Parent-Adapted Child combo kept his company on track. The last time I saw him was on a television show about self-made millionaires.

As so many anxious-avoidant people know, sheer talent is never enough. You also must access the drive to make something of that talent—and to rise above the fear of failure that threatens to keep you where you are. Stephan was a martial arts instructor whom I hired to work in a children's program. He was an interesting guy. He had once wrestled a criminal to the ground and held him until subway security officers arrived, an incident that made the news. He had choreographed fights for a few movies. Yet he was willing to commute a great distance to teach in our program for very little money. Eventually I discovered why: He collected unemployment benefits and therefore worked as little as possible. Stephan, it seemed, did not like to work. I never discussed it with him, but I began to suspect that something else was afoot: Was Stephan merely afraid to pursue a fight choreography career? Was he simply giving in to both his Natural Child mind state and also his internal critical script? Some people would think it ironic for a "subway superhero" to feel fear. But I have seen far more powerful men and women than Stephan simply freeze up in what others would consider benign situations.

You Can Change Yourself, But You Can't Change Your Boss or Co-Workers

Working for You Isn't Working for Me. This is the title of an excellent book by Katherine Crowley and Kathi Elster about dealing with different kinds of bosses who just plain drive you nuts—which can mean making you angry, making you feel unacknowledged, making you feel worthless, and so on. Any of these emotions can escalate into a full-blown anxiety response. Co-workers can cause these same feelings, so much of what we say here applies to anybody you encounter during your workday. It's way too easy to blame others for making you feel a particular way. But your anxiety is not their fault—even though your co-workers may be what triggers it. Part of it comes down to chemistry: If your personalities or communication styles don't mesh well, working together can be a struggle, to put it mildly. As Crowley and Elster write: "Far too often, the people placed in positions of authority are unable to manage, guide, or direct us adequately. In fact, the person in charge often becomes the biggest obstacle to his or her employees' success. Instead of feeling supported, guided, or encouraged, employees working for less-than-adequate managers begin to feel thwarted, persecuted, undermined, or trapped."

Your F.A.T.E. is your own, however. Your reactions are your choice. And as you learn to manage your adrenaline flow, you will gain control over how you view your supervisor and his or her actions. No one is saying your boss *isn't* a jerk. Your boss is your boss. But we are saying to take your jerk-o-meter off the table because no matter how much evidence you have, it won't change anything, and it will just cause you to obsess. You can't control your boss. Whom *can* you control? You. Your role in the matter is to gain control over your own F.A.T.E. by managing your anxiety. When you are less nervous, you have more options.

Provided you know what your organization expects of you, you can align your integrity with those expectations. If you don't have a copy of your job description, ask for one in writing. Job descriptions, production schedules, task lists, protocols. Those are your objective measurements—the biofeedback of your work life. Did you complete Task 1? Yes. Did you complete task 2? No. Those are facts—the realm of the Adult. There may of course be consequences for the "No's," but operating from a position of integrity will actually take away some of your anxiety, rather than adding to it. You don't have to hide or deflect blame—you just have to tell the truth. And then you will know how you are doing. You can use your Adult to determine areas where you could improve, then form a committee of your NP, CP, and NC to figure out what resources would help you succeed. In all that you do, "manage your integrity as a health practice." In fact, if you measure your To Do list against your Integrity Cheat Sheet, you will have a true measure of how you are doing at work—whether your boss ever gives you a thumbs-up or not.

Remember that gem of a quotation from Eleanor Roosevelt. Your Adapted Child will do all it can to *allow* those insults to happen. Here's a paradox: "If you think you work for someone else, you're wrong." *You* are the pilot. Strive for excellence to please yourself. Do the very best you can, maintain your integrity, perform "a day's work for a day's pay." What do you have to do to feel like you have done a full day's work? If you can go home at the end of the day feeling satisfied that you have done a day's work—realizing that no one can do it all each day—you can let go of obsessing about whether you are good enough or have done enough. You need some down time, and obsessing about work or staying late each night like a typical Type A will only lead to burnout.

We would be remiss in failing to address another problem avoidant people come up against: *Not* doing enough. We all have times when, for one reason or another, we have been unable to give our all. But—and answer honestly—are you aware of times when you could give more to a project but you don't? If you fear doing a bad job, or fear doing a good job that goes unacknowledged, you may not feel like doing your best. Often, a micromanaging boss can play a role in actually getting less from his or her employees. When someone is a bottomless pit of criticism, it is difficult—particularly for people who are nervous about their work performance or some aspects of their job responsibilities—to stay engaged. If you believe that you can't possibly succeed in the eyes of your supervisor, your CP and AC twin towers grow. Your avoidance escalates. Your obsessive second-guessing of yourself takes over, and you become paralyzed. One wrong move, you believe, could be the end of you. *Give up this kind of thinking now!* Do your best because that's who you are—whether anybody is supervising you or not. When adrenaline shows up, ride that wave by balancing your NP, CP, A, AC, and NC.

Invoking the ADA: A Lawyer's Perspective

Anxiety disorder is a medical diagnosis that the U.S. Department of Labor classifies as a disability. Under Title I of the federal Americans with Disabilities Act (commonly known as "the ADA"), private employers with 15 or more employees are required by law to make certain changes so that disabled employees can perform their jobs—so long as the changes are reasonable and effective. The federal Rehabilitation Act covers public employers and tracks the ADA. Many states have similar laws, some of which apply to employers with less than fifteen employees.

Whether or not to "invoke the ADA" is a personal choice of the employee. Often, a simple (and courageous!) private conversation with a supervisor or human resources director is enough. You can't use it to get out of your responsibilities—nor should you. But requesting certain arrangements that will help you manage your anxiety in such a way as to be more productive is good for you *and* good for the company.

Jane Rasmussen is an employment attorney practicing in the Washington, D.C., metropolitan area. Her clients include both employees and employers, which makes her an excellent source for a balanced discussion of the ADA as it applies to anxiety disorder sufferers. Here is her perspective on social anxiety disorder and the ADA. (Note: This information is included for education purposes only and is not legal advice. Individuals should contact the appropriate legal resource for specific legal advice regarding their particular situations.)

Question: What is the purpose of the Americans with Disabilities Act?

Answer: Title I of The Americans with Disabilities Act requires employers to, among other things, provide reasonable accommodations to disabled employees and prohibits employers from discriminating against employees because they are disabled.

A disability is a physical or mental impairment that substantially limits a major life activity, such as eating, sleeping, concentrating, thinking, communicating, and working. A major life activity also includes the operation of major bodily functions, such as the neurological system. Recent changes to the ADA reinforce court rulings that mental illnesses such as generalized anxiety disorder and panic disorders are covered by the ADA.

Question: What are "reasonable accommodations"?

Reasonable accommodations include job restructuring, providing assistive devices, permitting intermittent leave to attend medical appointments, and providing prolonged leave for periods of hospitalization. One common accommodation for individuals with depression and anxiety is allowing leave to attend psychiatric and therapy appointments and, in some cases, leave to undergo hospitalization.

To benefit from the ADA's protections, an employee *must* be able to perform the essential functions of his job with or without a reasonable accommodation; that is, an employee who *cannot* perform the essential functions of his or her job because of his anxiety disorder *even with* a reasonable accommodation is not protected by the ADA.

Question: Can an employer refuse to provide an accommodation?

Answer: Yes. An employer is not required to provide an accommodation that would constitute an undue hardship (i.e. is prohibitively expensive) or employ an individual whose disability poses a direct threat to himself or others.

Question: Does the ADA apply to schools?

Answer: Yes, Title II of the ADA applies to all educational institutions, and the ADA and the Federal Rehabilitation Act apply to both public and private educational institutions that receive federal financial assistance. Like employers, these educational institutions may not discriminate against students with disabilities and must also provide reasonable accommodations. Typical accommodations for a student with anxiety disorder include seating modifications, testing modifications, the use of taped materials, and providing class syllabus and lecture summaries.

Question: What is the best way for an employee suffering from anxiety to make use of the ADA?

Answer: Here's a story that illustrates the positive application of ADA. It has a productive outcome that pleased both the employer and allowed the employee to "heal" by finding a way to perform the essential duties of her job.

Julie, a midlevel project manager at a consulting company, suffered from depression and generalized anxiety disorder. Although she was on medication and undergoing therapy, her symptoms persisted. In particular, her anxiety affected her ability to sleep, eat, and concentrate—three of the "activities of daily living" the Americans with Disabilities Act identifies. At work, her anxiety negatively affected her ability to concentrate in team meetings, interfering with her ability to retain the critical information discussed. Julie's performance also suffered because her cubicle provided little privacy, causing her to feel anxious because her colleagues could overhear her telephone conversations with important customers. And every fourth Friday, Julie was in charge of ordering takeout for her team's Friday lunch meeting. Each time it was her turn to collect her colleagues' orders, she experienced a disabling anxiety attack because she feared she would mess them up. Her office mates noticed her odd behavior and lost confidence in her ability to perform other, more important responsibilities. Julie began to fear she would lose her job, and, consequently, her anxiety increased exponentially.

Julie approached her boss and explained to him that she suffered from an anxiety disorder and asked whether the company could provide her with some reasonable accommodations that would allow her to perform her job more successfully. The company's human resources director became involved and, through a positive interactive process, approved several of her proposed reasonable accommodations. The company permitted Julie to tape-record all meetings and provided her with the tape-recording equipment. In addition, the company erected an inexpensive partition to provide her with more privacy. It also excused her from the minor responsibility of ordering lunch for her team. Her boss also agreed to meet with her weekly to review her performance and provide her with feedback—one of the accommodations the Department of Labor's guidelines suggests specifically for employees with issues such as anxiety.

If Julie's anxiety disorder prevented her from, say, conducting training classes and training was an essential function of her job, then she would not have been protected by the ADA, and the company could have terminated her employment for this reason. Because ordering lunch every fourth Friday was not an essential function of her position, the company was required to excuse her from this task and assign it to someone else.

Julie's performance improved significantly. Although her concentration remained a problem at meetings, the tape recordings enabled her to revisit the meetings and follow through on assignments. The partition greatly reduced her anxiety and allowed her to work more productively. She no longer dreaded the Friday lunches and her colleagues' confidence in her grew. The weekly feedback kept Julie's anxiety in check, grounding her thoughts in actual accomplishments and specific areas that needed improvement. Julie's anxiety actually decreased as her success at work increased.

How the ADA Can Help You Work This Program

The ADA can be a wonderful tool for employees suffering from anxiety in the workplace—if and only if it assists those employees in actively addressing the anxiety issues and finding positive ways to perform, not to avoid performing, their jobs. What is your opinion of Julie's utilization of the Americans with Disabilities Act? Was it productive? Or by invoking it, did she avoid confronting and overcoming her anxiety? Maybe it's a mixture of both. The critical question is, When does the ADA support recovery—giving you room to succeed—and when does it allow you to hide from what makes you anxious and thus perpetuate the problem? (What you resist persists!)

The ADA is never a license to avoid doing your job. Its sole purpose is to enable everyone to be able to perform the "essential functions of their jobs." My client Ted is someone who, I think, tried to abuse the benefits of the ADA.

Ted worked in customer service for a luxury and sports car automobile parts catalog. He spent most of his workday surfing the Internet and playing computer games—letting the phone orders roll over to other customer service reps. They complained about Ted privately, but nothing was done at first. Eventually, however, Ted was told he had to shape up or ship out. At that point, Ted smiled and told his boss that he had social anxiety and referenced the Americans with Disabilities Act—which he had been reading about online.

Neither Ted nor his employer could, however, identify any reasonable accommodations that would enable him to perform the essential functions of his job. Despite the company's best efforts, Ted continued to shirk his responsibilities, and he was eventually fired. Simply put, the ADA does not entitle a disabled employee to get paid for doing nothing. Rather, the ADA entitles a disabled employee to reasonable accommodations that make it possible to do the work he was hired to do. It is designed to level the playing field. If a company makes those accommodations and the employee still doesn't do the work, then the employee can be terminated.

Another client of mine, Chris, left a good career in computer-aided design to go to business school. Then, for the first time in his life, he began having panic attacks. The Socratic method was to assign blame: Professors cold-called students, which meant they always had to be extremely well prepared just in case they were asked a question (talk about hyper vigilant!). While Chris logically understood the value of this method of teaching, he felt that one professor in particular was picking on him. He approached the professor after class and stated that he had social anxiety, which was triggered when he was singled out in class.

"I don't know what to tell you," the professor said. "Class participation is a third of your grade. Our whole program is based on this type of classroom experience."

"Anxiety disorders are covered under the ADA," Chris said. Then, working up considerable courage, he added, "I was hoping we could come up with a way that I could still participate in class discussion, but perhaps have a little warning beforehand." The professor considered Chris's request, and made a suggestion that he thought would both meet the program's class participation requirement as well as ease Chris's anxiety without letting him off the hook. They agreed that the professor would not cold-call Chris, but that Chris must make two comments during every class discussion. This worked. The spirit of the ADA is to devise ways to make the required tasks possible—not to reduce someone's responsibilities or obligations. You must use it to solve your problem—not to avoid solving it. Chris's speaking to his professor had a permanent and favorable impact, his confidence was healed, and he was able to finish his MBA without further issues.

Would changes in your work environment help you perform your job better while you work to control your anxiety? Which changes can you put into place on your own? Connect with your Natural Child for a moment—be creative. Are you frustrated by new software? Could you request training or obtain it on your own? Is the noise in your office distracting? Could your office provide you with noise-canceling headphones? Making such requests need not be a big deal—you don't even need to mention the ADA or go into detail about your anxiety disorder.

Of course, if you do experience anxiety prior to asking, you now have the Five-Step Technique to empower you. What might you say? Follow this formula when making a request:

1. State the benefit to the person you are asking (e.g., more productivity).
2. State the options you suggest (e.g., training, headphones).
3. Make the request.
4. Always thank the person for considering your request even if he or she disagrees.
5. If the person does agree, follow through as soon as possible with a concrete action, such as identifying and ordering an item or locating a class and obtaining registration information to pass along to your supervisor.

Here are some examples of what to say:

"I think I could increase my productivity if I got more training with our new CAD software. Here are some training options I've discovered. May I pursue one of them? Which one do you recommend?"

"I would be able to focus on my work a lot better if the noise in our office weren't distracting me. Could we order some noise-canceling headphones for me next time we order supplies?"

If you are interested in other ideas for accommodating anxiety disorders at work, visit the Department of Labor's Office of Disability

Employment Policy. Again, you can request or implement many such changes even without an official ADA reasonable accommodation request; even oral requests for a modification that do not contain the magic words "reasonable accommodation" count. See "Maximizing Productivity: Accommodations for Employees with Psychiatric Disabilities": www.dol.gov/odep/pubs/fact/psychiatric.htm (accessed February 29, 2010).

Panic Control

Panic is anxiety in extremis. When panic occurs, it is because of excess adrenaline activated by a perceived threat. In other words, it is the stress of excessive physiological adaptation. The sensations associated with panic—an overall loss of control, mind going blank, voice shaking, sweating or blushing, heart palpitations, increased pulse, thoughts such as "I'm going crazy," and overall fear of being "noticeably nervous"—occur to different degrees. Often, the first experience is traumatic because, in addition to those symptoms just described, acute feelings of embarrassment, shame, and humiliation are experienced. The extremely uncomfortable anxiety symptoms get linked in your mind and body with the extremely uncomfortable emotions. For the social anxiety sufferer the memory of panic is stored in the brain, often with a deep imprint resulting in the fact that once the panic is experienced the person does not want to experience it again. This often leads to avoidant behaviors and defensive thinking and behaviors. Therefore, the quicker the sufferer becomes proactive, the better. To be proactive, you must control the adrenaline. To do that, you must feel or attach to the adrenaline (a paradox).

It won't work to simply hope the adrenaline will not be there or will magically disappear. You have to accept it. Pushing it away or numbing yourself with substances will not work.

Kevin, age 42, a single man with an active social life, maintained a private law practice in his suburban town and served on some local government committees. He was considering running for a seat on the town council. Kevin often had to leave court, hurrying off to the men's room to compose himself, because of major sweating episodes associated with panic. His perspiration was so intense that within minutes his entire shirt would be wet and his forehead would be dripping. This was hyperhidrosis caused by social anxiety. Aware that the problem was interfering with his career, Kevin sought therapy and achieved extraordinary success. For example, in the later stages of his therapy, he described a business meeting where he started to sweat, but he knew what to do to stop it: He controlled his critical script, which stopped the sweating after about a minute. Very impressive! This was a fantastic example of psychophysiological (mind-body) control. In fact, Kevin's therapeutic success was so phenomenal that it is featured on my Web site at www.socialanxiety.com. The title of the interview is "Kevin: Successful Lawyer—Performance Anxiety and Hyperhidrodosis Resolved." If you listen carefully to the interview, you will gain much insight into the problem and the process of healing. Kevin resolved all of his avoidant tendencies and continued to develop a rewarding and lucrative career.

Kevin's Nurturing Parent learned to say at different times:

"The adrenaline is my friend."

"Go with it."

"Surf the wave."

"I'm in control."

"Use the power."

"I'm okay."

Instead of the Critical Parent mind state, which used to say:

"I am panicking."

"I'm going to sweat."

"Oh, shit!"

"People are going to see I'm nervous."

"I'm going to have to get out of here."

"I'm not okay."

Very specifically, Kevin learned not to be *angry* at the first sensations of panic. He learned not to resist. He learned the *nurturing* power of acceptance and he gained control.

In Touch with Your Panic

Have you experienced panic? Then do the following: Take in a long slow deep breath and slowly exhale. . 4 . . . 3 . . . 2 . . . 1 . . . .

Think back to a recent scenario where you experienced panic. Use your Nurturing Parent and Natural Child skills to allow yourself to remember the situation as vividly as you can. Note: It is okay if this experience upsets you. Go with it. Take my coaching. Just do this exercise and know that it will empower you greatly.

Place yourself in the panic-causing situation in your mind. What were you looking at? Who was there? What were you doing? What was the very first sensation or feeling that you experienced as the panic started? Remember exactly what you did at that moment. Make a note of the feelings you remember.

What was the situation?

1. _____
   _____
2. _____
   _____

What did you start to say to yourself?

1. _____
   _____
2. _____
   _____

It's a good bet that you got angry and activated your critical script. It is at that moment that you needed to employ the *nurturing acceptance* that Kevin demonstrated. "What you oppose controls you" is a saying prominent in many self-growth programs. Oppose the adrenaline and it will control you. Accept it and you are the master. When you accept the adrenaline it looks like the bell curve shown in Figure 5.1, gently flowing up, up, up and curving down.

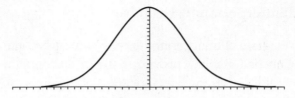

Figure 5.1   The Adrenaline Flow Curve

When you do not accept the adrenaline it looks like what's shown in Figure 5.2: up, up, up.

When you experience a surge or spike in adrenaline, ride the wave—accept the rise and fall of the bell curve.

ACCEPT...ROLL...BREATHE...

ACCEPT...SURF...BREATHE...

ACCEPT...FLOW...BREATHE...

Take in another long slow deep breath and then slowly exhale 4...3...2...1.... Remember to pace the inhale–exhale to between 8 and 12 seconds.

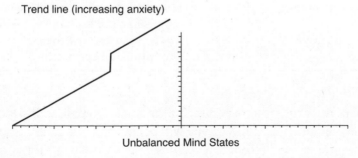

Figure 5.2   The Anxiety Curve

Stress Reinterpretation Exercise

To achieve a state of high performance, you must become comfortable being uncomfortable. This may sound like a contradiction, but as we have said, a nurturing interpretation of the discomfort caused by the stress of adrenaline must be developed over time.

Developing confidence and success at work requires controlling stress and anxiety, which will require you to get out of your comfort zone. Your life is your laboratory, so consider this your homework:

1. On a regular basis, write down three tasks or interactive situations that cause you anxiety.
2. Imagine yourself doing those things or having those interactions. Really picture it. Feel the adrenaline.
3. Choose one of those things and go do it.

To complete this homework assignment, you have to develop a new interpretation of stress and learn the self-nurturing that will allow you to reach higher levels of performance. When you experience a surge of adrenaline in the form of physical symptoms, follow the advice in this chart:

Instead of believing . . .	Believe . . .
This is no good.	This energy is necessary.
This makes me not okay as a person.	Every person has the same adrenaline.
Things are not right.	I am getting better because I am facing my fear and/or learning new skills.
I am out of control.	I can apply my new awareness/ knowledge and gain control.

The next time you experience a surge of adrenaline, instead of believing_____, you will believe_____.

Feel the fear and do it anyway!

Type A or Type B?

Are you a go-go-go type, or a get-around-to-it-whenever type? By now, you are well aware of my philosophy that time is your most valuable asset. Using time optimally is a critical part of stress management and career productivity. We're talking quality here—not just going full speed and doing an okay job at everything but never really excelling. And as for managing stress and learning to relax—that does not mean wasting time or ignoring deadlines or obligations.

In the 1950s, two doctors, Meyer Friedman and fellow cardiologist R. H. Rosenman, developed the Type A personality theory, hypothesizing that Type A people were more likely to experience heart problems. Although that initial conclusion proved controversial, the fact remains that their theory is extremely valuable in identifying two different types of people. This is especially true in the world of work.

At its core, Type A attributes can be described as "hurry sickness": A severe sense of time urgency. In addition, as Friedman wrote in 1996, Type As suffer low self-esteem and free-floating hostility. Type Bs, on the other hand, may appear calm. They may even seem detached from the job at hand—or willing to tinker endlessly without concern for completing a project. But not all Type A and Type B characteristics are negative. Both personality types offer many advantages as well as disadvantages.

You can learn a lot about yourself by taking a simple Type A personality test; many are available online at no charge. For example, the Discovery Health television network offers one on its Web site: http://discoveryhealth.queendom.com/type_a_personality_access.html (accessed January 19, 2010). A Google search will provide other links to such tests.

Time Urgency: The Type A Personality

The Type A personality is bad for a person's health. Research has demonstrated a direct correlation between heart disease and Type A personality. What may surprise you is that research has also demonstrated that Type As are very much locked into middle management.

The hurried, frenetic, pit-yourself-against-the-clock mentality does not necessarily correlate to management success. One research project where the heads of successful corporations were interviewed showed that the Type As would interrupt the research interviews with phone calls. The Type Bs would have their secretaries *hold* the calls. This particular research showed that Type As were locked into middle management while Type Bs were at the top and at the bottom. Generally, Type Bs are more easy going and able to delegate responsibility.

Cardiologist Meyer Friedman, who co-developed the Type A personality theory, learned something interesting when he had the chairs in the waiting room of his office reupholstered. "I have never seen anything like this before," his upholsterer told him, because only the edges of the chairs needed reupholstering. Friedman's cardiac patients were literally on edge waiting to be called in to the doctor!

When I talked about Type A in my corporate workshops, with a sense of humor and seriousness I would say: "To a Type A, a green light means go, a yellow light means go faster," and "the Type A appreciates a restaurant named Eat and Run." You get the picture.

Enhancement of self-esteem, anger resolution, especially a modification of free-floating hostility, and learning to make adrenaline your friend are essential concepts for Type A modification. Growing your NP, A, and NC mind states will help immensely with Type A restructuring.

Skin Resistance

Let's think about where you are at this point in the program. You now have a solid understanding of the importance of skin temperature. You are well on your way to differentiating "eustress" from "distress" as it applies to skin temperature and have been practicing a self-regulation technique geared to consciously increase the temperature of your hands by increasing peripheral blood flow through vasodilation.

Remember the physical cues and sensations related to stress and think about how they apply to stress management. You understand that dry and warm hands indicate relaxation, while clammy or sweaty hands indicate stress.

In biofeedback terms this perspiration is measured in terms of galvanic skin response. Very interestingly, I have observed with extensive use of a Galvanic Skin Response biofeedback machine that the arousal is measured on the machine one to five seconds after a thought. So far, you have been correlating skin temperature to emotions and thoughts. You can do the same with perspiration. When your hands are moist or clammy, take note, and then use the same technique to solidify your awareness as to whether "eustress" or "distress" is present.

Quieting Response Exercise

Now I am going to give you a biofeedback-based relaxation exercise designed to help you learn, step-by-step, how to relax. Nurture yourself by setting a time aside for this exercise when you are alert, not tired. Wear loose, comfortable clothing. Turn off your phone. Close the door if others are nearby. Give yourself permission to be free of distractions. Focus only on the moment. The goal is relaxation, not sleep, so do not begin this exercise after a heavy meal or shortly before bedtime. Remember, you are trying to learn a new skill, and the learning process deserves your full attention and energy. If you fall asleep, it may be a signal that you are burnt out (emotionally or physically exhausted), or depressed. If that happens, give into sleep if you have time. Return to the exercise at a different time or day when you can be fully present and focused.

Before you begin, make a list of the physical sensations you are aware of at this moment. Use whatever words come to mind. For example, are your hands warm or cold? Are they dry or is perspiration present? Do you feel calm or stressed? Is your body generally tense or loose? Use this list as a basis of comparison for what you are experiencing now compared with when the exercise is over. Do not judge or try to change anything as you make your "Before List." Just use your Adult to objectively write down your observations.

Make the "Before" list now:

_____

_____

_____

_____

If you follow these directions, there should be no tension. Assume a comfortable position in the chair. Hold your head, neck, and back in a straight line. Try not to slouch or arch your back. Your feet should be resting flat on the floor, and your hands should rest on your thighs. Do not let your hands hang at your sides. If you wish to use armrests, you may do so, so long as your shoulders are not hunched. You should not feel any pull or strain on your shoulder muscles. The goal is comfort and ease. The more comfortable your body is, the less it will distract you.

Give yourself permission to be passive. Concentrate only on this exercise and how your body is feeling. If you find yourself losing concentration, or experiencing any intruding thoughts, let them flow through you until they pass. Allow yourself to breathe them away. Acknowledge them while breathing in 1...2...3...4.... Then exhale them out 4...3...2...1.... As always, pace your inhale-exhale for about 8 to 12 seconds.

Now focus on your breathing. Inhale through your nose, slowly drawing the oxygen down into your abdomen. Hold it for a moment and then slowly exhale 4...3...2...1.... Again, breathe in, hold it for a moment, and slowly exhale. Don't push or force the air in and out of your body. Continue to breathe slowly and deliberately until the pace feels natural. Concentrate on the process. Inhale the oxygen, exhale the carbon dioxide. Inhale the energy, exhale the tension. Feel yourself settle further into your chair and becoming more passive with every breath.

Next, focus on your muscles. Start with your right hand: Make a fist. Hold it. Feel the tension. Then slowly let the fingers open up, releasing tension. Feel the tension disappear as relaxation overtakes it. Repeat the exercise until you have memorized the difference between a tense muscle and a relaxed one.

Make mental contact with your right arm. Feel it with your mind. Feel the muscles in your shoulder, then focus on your biceps, elbow, forceps, wrist, moving into your hand and the very tips of your fingers. Imagine the muscles releasing their tension, becoming soft and loose. Think the words "soft" and "loose" to yourself. Then begin to experience your right arm as heavy and limp. Say three times to yourself, "My right arm is heavy and limp."

Once again, if you experience any distracting thoughts, let them go by breathing them away.

Switch sides now, making a fist with your left hand. Hold it, feel the tension, and then release. Replace the tension with relaxation as your fingers open up.

Next, make mental contact with your left arm. Feel it with your mind: shoulder, biceps, elbow, forceps, wrist, hand, fingertips. Feel the muscles relaxing. Feel them becoming soft and loose.

As you feel yourself settle further into your chair, resume concentrating on your breathing. Slowly inhale through your nose, drawing the oxygen into your abdomen. Hold it for a moment, then slowly exhale counting backward 4...3...2...1... pacing your inhale-exhale at 8 to 12 seconds.

Reestablish your mental contact with your right arm. This time, say to yourself, "My right arm is heavy and limp." Repeat this three or four times, which should translate into saying the phrase three to four times slowly then pausing for a moment after each statement. Then expand your focus to include the sensations of warmth, saying for about 30 seconds, "The warmth is flowing through my right arm." You must feel very passive with all your thoughts focused on your right arm.

After a minute or so move your awareness to your left arm. What does it feel like? Say to yourself, "My left arm is heavy and limp." Repeat these phrases for about 30 seconds three or four times, slowly pausing between. Then for another 30 seconds say, "I feel the blood flowing through my left arm." Note any sensations you feel in your left arm. Tingling is a good sign during the relaxation process.

Let go of all intruding thoughts. Focus on your breathing, slowly, naturally, passively.

Now, move your awareness to your face. Allow the muscles of your forehead to soften. Picture your forehead smoothing. Feel the tension melt away. Let your jaw slacken and drop slightly. Let go of the tension in your jaw. Move up to your temples, then to your eyes, releasing the tension as you go. Find a comfortable position for your eyes and let them rest. Feel them become still and calm.

Focus on the tension in your stomach. Hold the muscles of your stomach in, and then let them go. Let everything sink, and feel your weight being pulled into your chair. Allow all the muscles of your torso to let go completely.

Let your whole body become more passive as you sink deeper and deeper into your chair. As you continue to breathe deliberately and deeply, bring your focus back to the abdominal area. Fill the area with air, and then count backward from four as you exhale slowly. Feel the tension flow from your body every time you exhale: energy in, tension out, energy in and tension out.

Continue this process, focusing on your abdomen moving in and out with each deep breath. Let go a little more with each exhale.

Allow your body to take on the breathing naturally. Again three times say, "I feel the warmth flowing through my right arm." Now say three times, "I feel the warmth flowing through my left arm." Breathe consciously for a few moments. Stay with the feeling of passivity. Next, take in one more long slow deep breath 1 ... 2 ... 3 ... 4 ... and exhale 4 ... 3 ... 2 ... 1 ....

Now, write down the sensations that you are aware of. How do you feel? Relaxed or stressed? Are you experiencing heaviness, limpness, warmth, tingling, dry hands, regular, even breathing?

This exercise is intended to build relaxation into your life as an ongoing ritual. Each time you achieve a state of relaxation, make note of it and commit the sensations to memory so that you can go back to them when you want to come down from excess stress.

Continue to practice. Just as an athlete relies on a muscle memory to execute the same basic moves again and again, so must you develop a relaxation memory, a blueprint to refer to every time you want to relax or regulate your body.

I Gave You the Gold, Now Here Is the Platinum

Your ability to invest in the preceding exercise is key. No one expects you to be an expert at this point or even actually experience the various sensations that were suggested. What matters is the process of learning and the effort of trying. If you invested, acknowledge this as a positive step (NP). If you detached or skipped over the exercise (AC), not only is this unproductive behavior, it may also be a sign that high levels of obsessive or Type A energy are present!

CHAPTER 6

Going Deeper

C hrista was heading for the kitchen to grab a snack when a television commercial grabbed her attention. Could the medicine they were advertising to treat anxiety really be the answer to her obsessive nervousness? Instead of getting some chips and a soda, she reached for the Yellow Pages.

Brian was at the end of his rope. After a year of therapy, he felt as anxious as ever. He had spent so many sessions talking about his fear of interacting one-on-one with his co-workers. But nothing had changed. If therapy didn't work, then what would?

Steve led a double life. By day, he seemed confident and capable. After hours, though, he spent most evenings at home drinking to stave off his anxiety about work. Each morning, he attended his team's Q&A meeting with trepidation. He hated being put on the spot; even when he knew the answers, he would just go blank out of fear. "There is something seriously, permanently wrong with me," he thought.

Maybe you've considered going to a therapist for your performance anxiety, but you haven't. Maybe you've actually gone to a therapist or two but have not achieved productive results. Or maybe you are simply convinced that you suffer from some serious and permanent character flaw. From my professional perspective, I've concluded that most people with performance and social anxiety do not seek therapy because they feel embarrassed and ashamed. They do not want to expose themselves—not even to a therapist. Most social anxiety sufferers who do seek therapy end up disappointed with the results. Often, therapy fails to pinpoint the specific dynamics at work. The resulting lack of progress leads to frustration and, understandably, can cause the anxiety sufferer to conclude that there is simply no hope for a solution. And in cases where the therapy is potentially productive, the anxiety sufferer's avoidance habit may kick in the minute the therapist raises issues that create discomfort.

Now, more than ever, we all expect instant results. Lose 10 pounds in two weeks! Make $10,000 a month in your spare time! The average social anxiety sufferer also wants a magic fix and does not want to do the real work. That's the nature of the avoidance: Don't feel it. Detach! Run, baby, run! Many clients come to me only after things get bad enough that their careers are on the line. Those clients realize that their very survival is at stake. Like an alcoholic who hits bottom, a workplace anxiety sufferer often finds the strength to reach out for help only at the last, most desperate moment.

The job market today is more competitive than ever, with hundreds of thousands of layoffs occurring each month. In this economy, even superior job skills may not protect you. But learning to access your adrenaline flow as positive energy and abandoning your avoidant behavior in favor of balancing your mind states will give you an edge over your colleagues. When your mind states are in balance and you operate with a High Performance Mind, you are able to give your best and demonstrate not only your capability, but also your potential as an ever more valuable employee when belts are tightened. Do not detach from the fact that times are tough; instead, confront that challenge with proactive steps. Working through this program may be the best career move you have ever made. (Nurturing Parent—but, let's face it, Adult, too!)

So How Long Will It Take?

That depends on your learning curve, which has many variables:

- Length of the problem.
- Severity of the problem.

- Your motivation.
- Your expressive ability.
- Your ability to integrate new concepts.
- Last but certainly not least, your readiness to face fear.

What I am saying, although it is a cliché, is "No pain, no gain!" That's why it is so important to nurture yourself by investing in the new stress reinterpretation formula. Feeling comfortable with the necessary progression of feeling uncomfortable as you evolve out of your comfort zone is crucial for your success!

In this chapter you are going to concisely and directly pinpoint the deeper issues you need to address in order to resolve the anxiety that makes you nervous at work. You will engage your five mind states throughout this process.

Nurturing Parent: Pat yourself on the back for coming this far. Tell yourself it's okay to feel scared, confused, angry—in fact, it's important to let those emotions out. Remind yourself that this may be hard, but you are up to the task.

Critical Parent: Acknowledge that working this program is critical to your well-being. Admit things are not as you want them to be and that learning new skills is necessary—the sooner the better.

Adult: Follow the instructions. Take the coaching.

Adapted Child: Accept that you need to do this important work—otherwise you won't get the result you want. Imagine yourself as you wish to be and use that image to spur you on.

Natural Child: Explore! Experiment! Be open to new ideas and perspectives.

Too many people get stopped by their fear of exposure. Not only are they incapable of sharing their problem with close friends, family members, and therapists—but they are afraid of exploring it themselves, using detachment and avoidance to stay stuck. Obviously, you have made a major breakthrough in acquiring this book and getting this far in the program! If you think about it, you are lucky because you can work through your difficult emotions in privacy with this book.

An Embarrassment Challenge Exercise

Here's a simple but effective lab experiment in dealing with the adrenaline flow that you perceive as embarrassment; you probably have several opportunities a week to practice it, so give it a try. When you are at a store or restaurant and paying cash, give the wrong amount to the cashier and allow yourself to accept the possible adrenaline associated with being the focus of attention for a moment. Notice or reflect on how that feels. What sensations were you experiencing? What emotions? What were you thinking? Did you use any of your new stress management skills? If not, why not? If you like, make a few notes and track your progress as you continue doing the exercise from time to time.

Where Anxiety Begins

At age 50, Sarah was a successful and talented artist whose paintings brought as much as $2,500. Her father, a successful businessman, had established a trust fund for her so she could attend art school five days a week; she had no bills to worry about and could devote herself full time to doing what she loved. But she felt conflicted about investing time in school versus time for creating artwork, which would allow her to sell her paintings and build her reputation. Feeling divided about it was causing constant worry that was getting in the way of both pursuits. She was stuck—and had developed the painter's equivalent of writer's block. I helped Sarah understand that much of her work paralysis was due to her perfectionist CP mind state. Much of this excessive CP was the result of unresolved emotion coming from her relationship with her father. When he had provided her with the means to do her own thing, he had made an offhand remark that continued to haunt her: "I expect a return on this investment. Don't waste your time or my money."

Eventually, we discovered that she had a lifetime history, beginning in childhood, of feeling that she fell short of her father's high expectations. He was generous with his money—but also his criticism. She recalled an example of how hard he was on her: "I remember struggling through algebra. I was an A student in other classes, but math was really tough for me. My father paid for a tutor, which helped me go from being a C student in math to getting a B on my final exam. I was so proud of that B; my teacher even commended me for my improvement." But when she came home from school that day, her father reacted sternly. "I paid for that tutor for three whole months and that's all you have to show for it? What a waste of money!" Sarah was devastated.

Sarah had internalized that criticism into her own excessive Critical Parent mind state. Beneath her feeling of failure was unresolved, repressed, and recycling anger in response to her father's excessive criticism when she was growing up. In time, she learned to channel her anger into productive action.

When I relate such stories, I am *not* parent-bashing, and that's not what I do in my therapy. I am just teaching the facts as to how cognitive, emotional, and behavioral responses are learned. Those responses derive not only from parental influence, but also from relationships with teachers, coaches, and peers. The messages in the internal critical script are crucial to identify. That can be a challenge, since much of this content has been repressed and, more often than not, channeled into extreme perfectionism. That perfectionism can lead to avoidance—the feeling that "If I can't do it perfectly, then I can't or shouldn't do it at all." Often when I start therapy with perfectionist clients, their initial response is to be protective and defensive of their parents, with a conditioned reflex to detach from important dynamics and issues: anxiety → detachment → avoidance.

Here's another example. Jacqueline was an intellectually gifted lawyer in her mid-forties; she specialized in contract negotiations. Her anxiety at work arose out of her belief that in many situations she had nothing to say. Each year, her performance evaluation included phrases such as "lack of assertiveness," "too passive," and "needs to contribute more to discussions and client meetings." Jacqueline desperately wanted to make partner, but she was passed over and for several years had seen younger, less experienced attorneys pass her by. With thousands of lawyers losing their jobs during the 2008 economic crisis, she began to fear for her job. That fear caused her to participate even less in meetings; she felt, and wanted to feel, invisible in order to avoid conflict. In treatment, Jacqueline told me that her parents had moved to the United States from the Caribbean, where "children should be seen and not heard." Her father had reinforced that cultural belief throughout her childhood. This critical content inhibited the development of the spontaneity and creativity of her Natural Child. She did not trust her instinct enough, and had overdeveloped her Critical Parent mind state. She had been repressing substantial frustration and anger—both at her father and at herself, the result of the CP inhibiting the expression of her NC.

Resolving anger is critical to your success. Any client of mine who has achieved a high degree of resolution to social and performance anxiety has done productive work with anger. Yet at the beginning of treatment, many of these clients said, "I'm not angry" or "I do not consider myself to be an angry person." They had detached from their anger, often years before seeking treatment; confronting that emotion was simply too intimidating.

As I mentioned, it's not just parents who contribute to our internal critical scripts. I was brought up in the state of Maine. When I was in the eighth grade, I played on the basketball team. As a junior member of the team, I spent a good deal of time on the bench, and only got to play about five minutes a game. At one point a new player joined the team. He had moved to Maine from Brooklyn, New York. He was a tough guy. He picked on me somewhat with an anti-Semitic attitude, which was hard to take. If I met him today, I would kill him! *Just kidding!* That was my Natural Child and an attempt at drama therapy—designed to get your attention. In reality, if I met him today, I would ask him if he wanted to play hoops—having channeled my anger into confidence a long time ago. Without sounding too narcissistic, I cannot imagine that at age 59 he would be in as good a shape as I am. And I always thought I was a better ball player than he was back in the eighth grade. The point here is that I was very aware of my anger and I have learned how to channel it productively though the years. Anger is energy!

Don't Try *Too* Hard

For example, Margie owned a community newspaper. She had a lot of stress regarding day-to-day operations and was coming to me for general stress management and biofeedback training. I had been teaching her temperature training (hand warming). One day I had her on a temperature machine, which required her to hold a temperature sensor. Her beginning temperature was 78 degrees Fahrenheit, which you now know indicates stress. After 25 minutes of practicing relaxation assisted by the machine's feedback, her temperature remained at the starting point. She was pressing too hard, which created sustained stress. That told us something right there: She was too anxious to let go—literally! After her relaxation exercise, I was talking with her while she remained connected to the machine. As she was talking about her stress at work, without focusing on the machine, an interesting thing happened. During the next 10 minutes, her skin temperature increased about 10 degrees. Without trying to relax, instead just talking, she was releasing frustration and anger, thereby creating vasodilation.

When your hand temperature is warm and dry, do you have a sense of ease or release? When it is cold, cool, or sweaty, are you aware of a sense of urgency or tension? You know the drill. TUNE IN. What's the temperature of your hands now? Your thoughts? Your emotions?

Lifestyle changes—even simple ones—can help manage negative stress and the exhaustion it causes. Cindy was a would-be singer and disco queen, a singer and dancer, age 45. Her role model was Madonna, and her act was intended to express creative freedom and self-expression, the realm of the Natural Child. She suffered stage fright before every performance; training was a challenge because of an alcohol and marijuana habit as well as substantial back pain. I knew of a doctor, John Sarnow, M.D., who treated back pain as both an emotional and physical condition, and I suggested she read his book, *Healing Back Pain*. She skipped the book and (drawing on both NP and NC) went directly to the doctor. She reported her experience to me in therapy, and I was impressed when I learned more about his specific beliefs and therapeutic blueprint. His take on back pain treatment was similar to mine for anxiety. His work helped me refine my therapeutic knowledge.

Sarnow treats back pain with emotional workshops. Like Sigmund Freud, who is considered the father of psychiatry, Sarnow discovered his patients' physical symptoms were the direct result of strong feelings repressed in the unconscious "We are all under one kind of pressure or another," he explains. "We all have internal reactions to those pressures, and all of us will have physical symptoms in response to those inner feelings. No matter how we react to life's pressures consciously, another world of reactions exists in the unconscious."

The Unconscious Mind

The concept of the unconscious mind originated in antiquity and has been explored across cultures. It has been a foundation of many psychologies including that of Freud, who developed a vertical hierarchy of consciousness: the conscious mind, the preconscious, and the unconscious. While neuroscience supports the existence of the unconscious, this concept is still in its infancy.

As it relates to work, the unconscious mind is a repository for both current assignments and past knowledge and perspectives. It is capable of processing and ruminating without your being aware that it is doing so. The unconscious mind played an important role in the writing of this book. "Not working" was part of working. My typical schedule would involve a few hours of deep concentration at the computer, then exercising, just thinking, watching television, contemplating my navel, or whatever, and creative thoughts and additional content would come into my mind. The conscious writing stimulated content from my unconscious. Another way to understand this is that ideas were formulated by *passive concentration*. For whatever it's worth, I *consciously* scheduled my writing and creative time for days when I was not doing clinical work. My brain has finite energy (like yours) and I know my limits. In other words, I invest in nurturing myself with realistic expectations.

Back to Dr. Sarnow

In a nutshell, Dr. Sarnow believes repressed anger and rage inhibit the flow of oxygen into the bloodstream, causing back pain—not all back pain, but a specific syndrome called tension myositis syndrome (TMS). I believe the same occurs with anxiety as well as depression, which is often a byproduct of anxiety: When oxygen levels are inhibited, anxiety can result.

Sarnow identifies three potential sources of pressure and rage in the unconscious:

1. Infancy and childhood
2. Perfectionism
3. Reaction to everyday life pressures

"The brain tries desperately to divert out attention from rage in the unconscious," he says. "We can influence unconscious thought processes by the application of conscious thought processes." This is what the attachment process in this book is all about! The more you bring issues to a conscious level, the less susceptible to anxiety you will be. Stress accrues over time. Just as you put money in the bank to collect interest, your unresolved anger and rage is collecting interest internally. That's not the kind of interest you want to earn.

Let's consider anger from a mind state perspective. The Natural Child is the seat of desire. When your true desires are not *nurtured* by the Nurturing Parent mind state, the result is anger and rage, whether conscious or not conscious. For example:

- If you wanted to express yourself at the work meeting but did not.
- If you wanted to address the group, but did not.
- If you wanted to go after that promotion, but did not take it because of fear of new responsibilities.
- If you wanted to learn a new skill, but avoided the learning process due to discomfort.

- If you wanted to market yourself and your skills and abilities at work, but did not because you feared being the focus of attention.

- If you wanted to clarify an issue or resolve confusion with your boss, but did not because of fear of what he or she would think about you.

These are common examples of investing in anger and rage. Your decisions are "rage in the bank"—and the cumulative anger makes anxiety worse and worse.

TUNE IN: What's the temperature of your hands now? This process of temperature awareness, and the concurrent challenge of identifying your thoughts and feelings, has been an important exercise in bringing unconscious content to a conscious level. Have you been doing it?

List three scenarios which may be an investment in anger for you:

1. _____
   _____

2. _____
   _____

3. _____
   _____

Anger Is for Real

When Howard Stern blew me off his show (we were going to talk about "involuntary virginity") in favor of a hermaphrodite and the largest rubber band ball in the world, I was goddamn pissed off. Come on Howard, call me now; I'll give you a good show! Amy feels enraged and marginalized in situations where her contributions are not acknowledged. But she is better able now to use her Nurturing Parent mind state to give herself credit for a job well done. Her Adult reminds her that this is just what's so—and just because her clients or supervisors fail to give her credit doesn't mean the work was not valuable. She is even able to laugh about her tendency to overreact: "A friend of mine told me a long time ago never to confuse malevolence and stupidity, and I see the point," she says. "If someone fails to give even a thumbs-up, he's not necessarily out to get you. He could just lack the managerial skills to keep you motivated!"

Being angry at yourself for failing to do a good enough job derives from an excessive Adapted Child. When the CP-AC dynamic interferes with the Natural Child's pure desire, the Natural Child becomes enraged. Unconsciously, you become furious at the powerlessness. This gets established at an early age. A person may mask that anger by expressing resentment over the assignment or procrastinating rather than taking care of it. Accountability is easy when you're on track, but much harder when you face a challenging project or an unanticipated roadblock. Susan had one month to complete a budget for a series of promotional events at the auto dealership where she worked. She was excited about these events, and she used her Natural Child to brainstorm ideas such as an Oktoberfest to highlight Volkswagens and a tempura station to draw attention to Toyotas. Some printed pieces were necessary to promote these events, but they were not Susan's focus as she planned the marketing effort. She saved the pricing portion until the week before her deadline only to discover that the graphic designer she always used was on a two-week European vacation and therefore completely unavailable to provide an estimate. Susan didn't enjoy the nuts and bolts part of planning, so she avoided it. She was furious at herself and dreaded explaining her delay to the dealership owner.

Can't Get It Out of Your Mind?

Obsessions are intrusive, unwelcome, distressing thoughts and mental images. The word "obsession" comes from the Latin word *obsidere*, meaning "to besiege." Previously, I defined obsessing as sustained ingrained worry. Often obsessing is characterized by unpleasant thoughts that do not go away and keep intruding in to your mind against your will, thoughts like these:

"Oh, God, I said something stupid."
"What will they think of me given that mistake I made?"

"I should have done that differently."

"I blushed. They will think I'm a fraud."

"They saw that I was nervous."

"I feel guilty about doing that the wrong way."

"They will find out who I really am."

To get a handle on this type of obsessive thoughts, you must attach to the memories of incidents that caused these feelings. Do not push those memories and emotions away. Obey your coach! Use your NP to support yourself as you delve into the realm of anger. Use your A to objectively analyze these obsessive thinking patterns. You will see that *unresolved anger is the emotion that drives the repetition*.

There are always options, but anxiety may prevent you from seeing them. These options may take some work. You may have to use courage—action in the face of fear. You may have to confront your own failure to be accountable for your poor performance or lack of skill. You may have to acknowledge that the job you are in is not the right position for you for whatever reason (corporate culture, essential responsibilities, etc.). At some point, following through on an option will require anxiety management. In that way, you can think of anxiety management as a job skill. Recall the Problem-Solving Technique on page 108 in Chapter 4. Now might be a good time to go back and review it.

Compulsions are behaviors that people perform in a vain attempt to control the fears and anxieties caused by their obsessions. While the sufferer often is aware that these behaviors are ridiculous, the feeling is so strong that he or she gives in to the compulsion and magical thinking—superstitions such as "If I ever wear the outfit I wore that day my boss yelled at me in front of everyone, I will make another major mistake" or "I have to push the elevator button with my thumb or I'll have a bad day."

Jim wrestled with compulsions related to his anxiety. He grew up in a small southern town and was being groomed to take over the family business. Jim was intelligent, attractive, a good athlete, and a good soul. As a teenager, he developed a blushing problem. "I began to blush in nerve-wracking situations such as being with groups and dating," he recalls. "During this time, I became very confused and angry, because I could not figure out why this was happening to someone like me. I was very popular and an outgoing person and assumed I lived the perfect life."

It was all Jim could think about. "This blushing thing was terrifying," he says. Jim was constantly looking in the mirror, touching his face several times a day, all to try to control his blushing. Nothing worked. "My blushing obsession led to many forms of checking compulsions," he says. "I would obsess about things that had happened. There were times I would become brain-locked for days over a silly blushing episode. In the midst of all this obsessive-compulsive behavior, I developed a mild case of panic disorder because I would misinterpret bodily sensations that would cause me to have anxiety." He learned to avoid spicy food, bright sun, and other sensations that would make his face feel like it was blushing. Diagnosed with "facial hyperhidrosis," Jim found himself in a surgeon's office, having a consultation about an endoscopic thoracic sympathectomy (ETS) to cut his facial nerves. "I decided to have surgery to magically fix the problem," Jim recalls. "Little did I know that the majority of my issues were mental, not physical! Thank goodness I did not follow through with that procedure."

In therapy, he found the roots of his problem in his early childhood experiences. "My anxiety issues began when I was a young child," he says. "I would do things such as have to tie my shoes 'perfectly' or have to say what time it was 'perfectly.' But the anxiety did not become tormenting until I was around the age of sixteen." He was able to go deeper and discover that he believed his blushing was "a punishment from God." Having grown up in a Southern Baptist environment, he believed that "God would punish people for not abiding by the religious doctrine" and that he was being punished for his partying (dating many women, going to bars, etc.). The CP he internalized from that religious doctrine inhibited his NC's ability to express himself freely. "Eventually I learned to let the uncomfortable thought/anxiety be there without reacting to it," he explains. "If the compulsion was physical"—say, checking the mirror many times a day to see if his face was red—"then I would resist performing the compulsion until the anxiety subsided."

Time to Take the Plunge

Now, let's go deeper. You are going to learn a strategy geared to get the brain to stop creating your anxiety. I respectfully credit Dr. Sarnow for his input into the following concepts.

1. Accept your anxiety symptoms as the result of a mind-body interaction.

2. Accept that unconscious emotional things play an important role in creating the symptoms. Therefore, the process of learning, which includes thinking and writing about many things that are related to your unconscious mind, is very important. This process may be uncomfortable or create anxiety in the moment. You have to just go with it. Understand that one purpose of the anxiety is to protect you by keeping certain content out of your conscious mind. You can work through it. Learning about hidden feelings sends a message to your mind that says, "I appreciate the love you show by protecting me, but now I have to supervise you more closely."

Sarnow refers to a "reservoir" within us where rage, unresolved anger, emotional pain, sadness, and feelings of unworthiness are stored. The F.A.T.E. patterns developed in early childhood carry over into our adult lives. Shame, embarrassment, guilt, and loss of control—four categories that fill Sarnow's reservoir to the point that the brain must produce symptoms to protect us from these feelings. The reservoir is located in the AC: learned emotion, albeit, not conscious. Sarnow's point of intervention has been back pain. Mine has been anxiety. Sarnow adds that "all of the above result in feelings of unworthiness as we enter adult life, and these in turn lead to the next contributor of the reservoir."

Daily Attachment Exercise

On a daily basis, or as often as you can, write about the things you would rather not think about. (Remember, paradoxical thinking!)

Take a few minutes and just do it—using the notebook, handheld device, or computer files you have been relying on throughout the program. Seriously, just a few minutes each day. This process will help you connect your conscious mind with your unconscious. After you write, if you don't want to keep the material, you can tear it up or erase it. Doesn't matter. It's the act of giving words to those fears you usually detach from that has value. This will develop your NC and A mind states. Trust the process!

Ed, a successful businessman and entrepreneur in his mid-forties, found this exercise extremely useful. He had everything in place to have a great life—plenty of money, a wonderful family, plenty of vacations, a motorcycle he loved to ride. The reason for his unhappiness was his difficulty with letting go of his internal critical script, which told him that he should always be working. This script was inherited from his parents, who were always working; they never encouraged Ed to play as a kid but always to be working. Yes, this excessive script did result in anger, a lot of which was unconscious. Although Ed was quite intelligent, he had a difficult time identifying specific thoughts and emotions. Ed's anger was the result of his early experiences: Don't enjoy, don't play, don't let go. Taking the time to put those feelings into words helped him get in touch with the specific, deeper issues.

Nurturing Attachment Exercise

At the end of the day, before you go to bed, go to a private comfortable place. Take a few minutes and do your diaphragmatic breathing. Focus only on your breathing for a few minutes. Breathe intruding thoughts away. Imagine a six- or seven-year-old you sitting in front of you. Tell this child that you love him or her and that you are going to give him or her the love and support he or she needs. Accept any emotions that you experience. Do this often.

Anger Under the Microscope

You have been learning the importance of anger as it relates to social and performance anxiety. Identifying it, expressing it, and channeling it into productive energy is the goal. Anger is often unconscious, so the key is to bring it out in the open. I mentioned previously that when I initially bring up the issue of anger, many of my clients say they have never related their anxiety to anger. In my office, I have a little hole in the wall that has been there for 15 years—it was caused by a teenager who stormed out of the office, slamming the door in a state of rage because of what her parents were discussing. I decided to leave it there as a point for therapeutic discussion with clients. Anger is not always this obvious.

As a means of helping clients identify and express anger, I use an exercise I call "Anger Under the Microscope." Here are my instructions: Write about your anger. Do not censor yourself (turn down your CP). Use whatever language you want. In fact, be as descriptive as possible (NC). I encourage you to use colorful language (NC). Really let it out. Talk about people, situations, events, past, present, anything you want. Do not be concerned about grammar, spelling, typos, or messy handwriting. You are not being graded (turn down your CP!). Let go!

The following is an excerpt from a client named Ray's writing exercise. Again, this exercise is all about expression, not perception. Do not obsess about writing quality or even how well you say what you choose to say. Just get it out there. You don't even have to dot your i's and cross your t's if you don't want to. Remember, we are going deeper. Everyone with an anxiety disorder has his or her own issues, but many of Ray's are common. The goal with Ray was to get him to express the repressed and recycling energy that drove his distress and anxiety.

Anger is many things to me. First off, I get angry with myself when I feel I lose control. Losing control can be drinking, eating, smoking, spending money, not making wise decisions. Anger can also include my past such as being angry that I didn't do certain things, and being angry that I did do certain things. I also feel that I let myself get frustrated and this builds up inside, frustrations such as not having enough time to do everything I need to do, always being under the gun at work and home, never having time just to relax and not worry. Worry is the key word, I believe. Even though I am not outwardly angry I find myself losing patience, something I had always had a tremendous amount of. I am worried I am becoming more and more like my father in terms of being short on patience, something I never thought would happen. I am at a point where I don't know if I am frustrated, overly worrisome, or angry, or all three. Somehow they are all intertwined, though.

This client went on to resolve his anxiety problem: He would avoid communicating with his senior partner, and he became more proactive because he learned to control his adrenaline in challenging situations. Recognizing his tendencies, he chose to combat his self-loathing with self-esteem-building affirmations and activities. He also put some systems in place to control the avoidant behavior.

Now, while this issue is fresh in your mind and your brain has just been stimulated by the previous essay, write your own "Anger Under the Microscope." Take a deep breath and do it! Stop reading, put the book down, and do it. Then return.

So, what are your thoughts? Be clear on what they are. TUNE IN: Connect your skin temperature right now to your feelings and thoughts. As you progress with your healing, when you are consciously aware of your anger, also be aware of the temperature of your hands.

The Critical Script and Anger

When your CP is excessive, putting unrealistic demands on your AC and NC, the result is anger. "Be perfect, don't make any mistakes, don't be nervous, don't have adrenaline; you have to be the best, you should know everything already, and most of all, you should not have feelings!" This CP content is not only excessive, but toxic. It will set the AC up for rage, anger, and implosion. Note: I am not saying "don't strive for perfection." I am saying if you are striving for perfection, you'd better have realistic expectations. Plus, you have a better chance of achieving it if you are loose instead of tense.

Want to make sure that you have a lot of rage? Let your CP tell you that "if your performance is not good, you are not okay as a person." That message will guarantee you a myriad of problems. Logic and objectivity, your A, will tell you that there is indeed a vast difference between a performance and identity and personhood. Believe me, I still thought I was an okay guy after the camera showed me looking at the floor during my CNN appearance, even though I was upset and pissed!

Now, list three ways your CP is currently putting unrealistic demands on you, causing frustration or anger:

1. _____
2. _____
3. _____

The Natural Child and Anger

Another way to guarantee anger and rage is to be aware of your true desires and not act on them. For example, you may want to talk to that difficult authority figure at work, give a presentation, resolve a conflict, or take a risk at expressing yourself to co-workers. But the thought of acting on that desire causes you anxiety. Trust me. I am aware of this. But the truth of reality is that unless you nurture yourself by learning how to control your anxiety in such a way that you are free to take actions, the anger and rage will build (consciously or unconsciously), working against you at a very deep level.

Think about three work situations in which you want to take action and have been holding back. Get in touch with your anger over those situations. Now, list them.

1. _____
2. _____
3. _____

Often a symptom of unresolved anger is brooding—obsessive negative preoccupation. Irene was a special education teacher, age 30, with a lot of social anxiety. It was a difficult challenge for her to interact socially with her peers at work. She put pressure on herself because she thought she should know it all. She would avoid asking for help because she didn't want to look or feel stupid. She would greet each morning with dread and come home at night exhausted. At home she would spend endless hours on the Internet, compulsively researching a multiplicity of subjects, primarily issues related to pregnancy. She was having difficulty conceiving, and went so far as to say she was glad when one of her work associates had a miscarriage. Sometimes anger can run amok. Anger at her own situation. Angry at herself. This is typical of many avoidant and anxious people. "Life is not fair." "Why do they have it and not me?" These people convey an attitude that the world owes them something—even though, deep down, they may realize they are not pulling their own weight because anxiety is holding them back.

Embarrassment . . . or Death?

Remember Carol, the ovarian cancer survivor who told me that she would "rather be back in chemotherapy than speak in front of a group"? That's a very compelling remark—and makes clear just how debilitating anxiety can be. I have often started radio shows and lectures with that story to get the audience's attention. Really, think for a moment: Death versus embarrassment. For someone with social anxiety, embarrassment is excruciating. Where others may laugh off a misstep or fumble, a workplace anxiety sufferer will experience extremely uncomfortable physical symptoms and a seemingly endless internal monologue of Critical Parent–Adapted Child judgment and disgust. Embarrassment has an impact on social anxiety sufferers at a very deep, if not molecular level.

But remember what you have learned: Embarrassment is an internal dynamic. Consider both my setup on *The Opie & Anthony Show* and my appearance on *The Anderson Cooper Show*. I had a choice in those situations: Let my confidence sink or swim with the tide. You *choose* if you are going to be embarrassed by external stimuli. *You* are in control. *You* make the decisions. It all depends on how you manage your mind states. Resolving embarrassment requires that you develop self-esteem and actualize the NP and A mind states. The mind states are dynamic: Raise your NP and A, along with your NC, and your twin towers—CP and AC—will naturally recede to a productive and comfortable level.

Embarrassment-Logic Exercise

This is a typical situation that I currently dread due to my fear of embarrassment:

_____

While being totally logical and rational (Adult), I know others would really be thinking:

_____

I know my exaggerated emotion of embarrassment stems from situations in the past which may have been traumatic, such as:

_____

_____

Use your Adult logic to answer the following:

What is the worst feeling that can result when you experience embarrassment?

A. Everything in life is over.

B. I will panic.

C. People will think I am not okay as a human being.

D. All of the above.

E. None of the above.

F. Other.

I understand that there are situations where anxiety sufferers believe they will lose their jobs if they are noticeably nervous at work. Sometimes this could be true, depending on whether your visible anxiety symptoms somehow compromise your effectiveness. For example, a hotel front desk manager who gets flustered and cannot concentrate when a customer has a complaint may simply not be suited to or effective in that job. A cruise director who develops stage fright will not be very good at energizing a crowd. But even in those situations, a solution exists that a person can try before dismissal comes to pass. Learning to manage anxiety through mind states balance and the Quieting Response could mean the difference between employment and a new job search. Recall that research shows the fear of losing one's job is even more anxiety-provoking than actually being laid off or fired.

And if you have already lost your job or resigned from it because you hadn't yet beat your anxiety problem, you now have the opportunity to build stress management skills so that, next time, you'll be able to handle what comes up. In any event, call on your Adult mind state to remind yourself that you are not alone. According to Estelle H. Rauch, L.C.S.W.: "Today's treacherous economy, with its deteriorating job market in most sectors, has created a level of shared stress approaching dread in even the highest functioning members of our society," she writes in an article entitled "The Psychology of Uncertainty: Surviving the Job Search." "Many who had followed their superior educations with gratifying careers now join the always-vulnerable underclass in experiencing profound uncertainty in their work lives."

Your Adult logic is also the place to turn to combat embarrassment—a prerequisite for healing and anxiety resolution at work. Take a moment to define embarrassment for yourself:

Focus on your AC, where embarrassment is located, to answer this question:

To me, embarrassment means:

_____

Now, switch your focus to the NP. What message does your NP need to communicate to the AC?

_____

This is an excellent exercise in nurturing. You are the best person to come up with the NP words of encouragement that you'd like to hear. The words you choose may not be the same as the words others would pick. Use the Nurturing Statements Guide for inspiration if you like. Here are some situations and their outcomes to get you started.

Andrea was a Web designer for a small publishing house. As the publisher expanded, he decided to add an online distribution arm to his enterprise. In a previous job with a large company, Andrea had received the same directive. But that company had had the budget to outsource the assignment, leaving Andrea to focus on the design and production work she did so well. This time, there was no money available. It was up to Andrea to do the whole job. She made her best effort, and even worked with the PR person at the company to launch a promotional campaign advertising the site's new functionality. The launch date came. And went. Andrea's attempt had failed to work, and phones started ringing off the hook with customers complaining about the problem. The problem would take Andrea a day to fix. "In the past," she says, "I would have left the office immediately and gone home to bed—just to avoid the physical and emotional torture that I would go through if I stayed." But this time was different. "Because I'd learned to use my Nurturing Parent mind state, I was able to comfort myself and lower the anxiety to an acceptable level. By the time I had begun working on the fix, my anxiety had dissipated." What were the phrases she used? "This is just a temporary setback and a normal part of being a Web developer." "You're handling this well, and you can press on and do what needs doing." "Your colleagues have confidence in you, and that includes knowing you can fix what's broken."

Carolyn was a REALTOR with a major agency. Since getting her real estate license six months earlier, she had had three listings of her own, and had also had some co-listings with another, more experienced agent who was mentoring her. When she was unable to sell one of the properties after three months, the clients let their seller's agreement lapse and ended up with another agency. Carolyn took this as a sign that she had failed. Nothing her mentor said could persuade her otherwise. Finally, Carolyn got herself together enough to remember the power of Adult logic: "The fact of the matter was that my clients had not renewed with me." That was a fact. "I also acknowledged the plain truth that it was a very difficult market at the moment," she said. "I also observed that I had done everything I knew how to do—including holding open houses and printing color flyers for the other real estate agents. I was straight with myself about the fact that I could have advertised more heavily or targeted my promotions more effectively (that one was hard to swallow, but it was a fact)." And finally, she says, she offered herself true comfort with the words "You are doing the best that you know how." "And that was absolutely true," she says. "It took my Nurturing Parent to point that out!"

Going Even Deeper

The deepest manifestation of embarrassment and shame as well as unresolved anger is the feeling of being flawed as a person. The concept of flaw is at the root of self-esteem problems. Obviously, everyone has flaws because there is really no such thing as being perfect. Who determines what is perfect anyway?

Stan, for example, considered himself deeply flawed. From the outside looking in, Stan had it all: a good job, a lovely wife, two healthy kids. He was an award-winning architect and avid triathlete. But he had a secret, something he could tell no one but that was on his mind every second of every day: He was sexually attracted to men. For a man with a wife and family, this was a major emotional conflict, to say the least. Stan loved his wife and his married lifestyle. But he was finding it increasingly difficult to deny these other feelings—and he was sure that his face told the entire story. "When you are nervous, people can see who you really are," he said. He really was a high-achieving, if overly perfectionist, man who was well liked at work and socially. But he couldn't see that; his CP/AC was too much at the forefront of his thoughts. It was not until Stan did some very intensive therapeutic work that he was able to develop self-acceptance.

Cathy, age 52, a systems design engineer, believed she was flawed by her blushing, which was a major issue with her performance anxiety and avoidant behavior. She avoided expressing herself and being generally proactive at work. She avoided interacting with her supervisor. She was terrified about speaking in and in front of groups. Her self-esteem was handicapped. Her mood was negative. Using her Natural Child mind state, she tried something unusual while in therapy: She wrote a letter to her blush. These are her words:

For years I feared your arrival, like an unwelcome last minute guest who spoils the party every time, humiliating me in front of all my other, important guests. At first I had a hard time seeing you coming and was always caught off guard; then I came to expect you, so I stopped planning so many parties.

After a lot of work and introspection, I thought I had learned how to keep you at bay. But what I didn't realize was that my life became about keeping you at bay. You became my focus. When you failed to show up so often, I took it as a sign that I was doing well. And in many ways I was doing better. But I was measuring how well I was doing by the frequency and intensity of your appearance.

Now, I'm coming to realize that although dealing with you has been so very hard in many ways, just getting to that point is a very low threshold to reach in terms of having a good life.

At long last I'm learning that you are not some scary interloper bent on doing me harm. Actually you are really just a part of me, a mirror of my insecurities. You've actually been trying to do me a favor, showing me in a way that was literally "in my face" that I was not respecting myself, wasn't valuing myself above the assessments of others. Instead you were trying to tell me that I've been so preoccupied with what other people think that I have all but shelved my own natural impulses and desires about what I want out of life.

Unfortunately, for the longest time I misinterpreted your message. When I feel you coming, my tendency is to think, "Oh no, not you again. What if people see you? I'll be mortally embarrassed and humiliated." And when I do that my focus stays on what people think. But now I know better than to stop there. My response, which is starting to come more naturally to me, is I am interested in getting the most out of this situation, both for myself and for others. Of course I am showing some signs of nervous excitement—that is normal. But I don't have to worry if these people think I'm a good and worthwhile person, because I know I am—that's a given!

It has taken a really long time to get to this point. Part of me is angry about how much of my life I have wasted worrying about you. But there is nothing that I can do to change that and I have good years still ahead of me. I'm excited!

I'm putting more stock in what matters to ME. I'm putting my focus on envisioning things that I want to happen, rather than on things I fear happening. I've started asking for what I want, instead of assuming I can't get it and never trying. Great new people are coming into my life. I find it easier to prioritize demands rather than being in a constant state of being overwhelmed.

The shift is energizing, but it's still new and a bit scary. But I know this is the way I want to be.

Kathy resolved her problem, as you can see from her letter. She even went on to win a public speaking award at her regional Toast-masters competition.

I have had many clients with similar issues. Everyone wants to fit in—that is true from the time we are little children. Being singled out in any way is the anxiety sufferer's worst nightmare. Different = bad. Stan who was afraid his colleagues could detect his same-sex attraction, about which he was highly conflicted. Stan did not want to appear different. Being different can be difficult. Imagine, for example, being

- The only Asian-American working for a Latino cable television station.
- The only non–college-educated employee at a medical research corporation.
- The only man at a woman-owned company.
- The only waiter with a PhD.

These distinctions are not always discernable to the naked eye. But that medical research employee may feel sure that everyone is judging him for his lack of a college degree. That waiter just knows all the other servers are talking about what a bad fit he is and how he must not be very smart if his PhD only got him as far as this. People have feelings of shame about coming from an impoverished background, and even embarrassment about physical features such as buck teeth or a deformed finger. "When you are nervous," as Stan put it, "people can see who you really are." Unworthy. Damaged. Flawed. Raising your NP and A will turn down the volume on that CP/AC voice, allowing you to begin healing and build self-esteem.

Many individuals with the struggle of being noticeably nervous, especially with blushing and sweating, believe they are genetically flawed. Countless numbers of social anxiety sufferers believe they are flawed by a lack of intelligence even if they are obviously quite bright. Believing you have a flaw is the result of excessive CP. The biggest challenge is when an anxiety sufferer believes the anxiety is totally the result of a genetic flaw. This belief inhibits the person's ability to develop compensatory strategies. Self-acceptance is the key; it is the ultimate example of the positive Critical Parent mind state.

Believing you are flawed also gives you the perfect out—if there's "nothing to do about it," you can avoid taking action. Do not fall for this Critical Parent trap! Use your Nurturing Parent to remind yourself that even baby steps result in steady progress. Use your Adult to reinforce the fact that there is nothing permanently wrong with you. Your current problem with anxiety is a fact of life—it is not permanent and you *can* resolve it. Use your Natural Child to continue exploring new ideas by working this program. As you raise these mind states, the twin towers will fall in line, and you can use the Critical Parent and Adapted Child for the roles they serve best: Your CP will tell you that you are capable of anxiety management. And your AC will say that achieving anxiety management is necessary for improving your work and your life.

Narcissism, Avoidance, and Anxiety

There is a high degree of self-centeredness associated with workplace anxiety.

Narcissism is at its core self-love. It manifests itself in different degrees, from a healthy self-esteem to the root of much mental illness. A sense of self-centeredness is integral to all anxiety sufferers. You may feel like the center of attention—closely scrutinized, heavily judged—when in fact no one is paying attention or even really cares. We are all busy paying attention to ourselves, not zeroing in on someone else's trembling hands or blushing cheeks. (Sigmund Freud, the father of modern psychiatry, believed every one of us is a born narcissist.)

There is a great degree of selfishness in missing a deadline, in failing to return a phone call, in dropping the ball. If this resonates with you, stop to consider the ways in which you are detaching from the impact you have on others. Use your Adult to note instances where you have set integrity aside or made excuses for your behavior. Then, access your Critical Parent mind state (without that internal critical script); attach to the effect your behavior has on other people. Then, using the Problem-Solving Technique, outline a plan of action that would have taken care of those situations. Are there current areas of life in which you are being narcissistic? What can you do to nip that in the bud and restore your integrity?

What I did   *The effect it had on other people (name them)*

_____

_____

_____

Plan of action

_____

_____

_____

Some Words of Encouragement

Attaching to your fears rather than avoiding them, "going blank," or ducking out of uncomfortable situations will make an extraordinary difference in your life. This is hard work, and you deserve kudos for taking action in the face of fear. In the words of Jerilyn Ross, one of the pioneers of anxiety therapy, who died in early 2010:

The moment you understand that you have a living, breathing relationship with your anxiety—a relationship whose qualities and character are of your making—is the moment you free yourself from the tyranny of fear and assert your right to challenge, subdue, and even embrace it.

The Healthy Brain: "The Hardware of the Soul"

I can drink a double espresso and go to sleep one hour later. My wife cannot drink coffee after 12 noon or she will not be able to sleep that night. Person A can smoke marijuana and sustain productive and creative energy for hours. Person B can smoke the same pot and have an anxiety attack or get depressed. Person C can have a glass or two of wine and leave it at that. Person D cannot stop drinking once he starts. Person E can take prescription medicine to ease nervousness and stop obsessing and gradually regain calmness and control. Person F can take the same medicine for the same reason and become agitated and more anxious. You get the picture. This is called "chemistry," and it varies from person to person.

Have you ever thought of your body as one big chemical reaction? The fact is, the human body undergoes hundreds of billions of chemical reactions every second. "The brain is fundamentally a chemical system," Susan Greenfield writes in *The Human Brain: A Guided Tour*. "Even the electricity it generates comes from chemicals. Beyond the fluxes of ions into and out of the neurons, a wealth of chemical reactions are occurring incessantly in a bustling but closed world inside the cell."

Indeed, the brain is a dynamic organ with properties and reactions to physical substances and neural stimuli. It's all in your head, remember? Inside your cranium are neurons, protoplasm, nerve cells, axons, dendrites, blood vessels, cerebrospinal fluid, and much more. These are the things that make up your mind—you didn't think the "mind" was an abstract entity, did you? It is a living organ that requires care and feeding—nurturing—to operate at its best. *Nurturing brain health is the most important singular investment you can make to control your nervousness at work and beyond!* Promoting healthy brain chemistry is an absolute must. Do everything you can to maintain the "hardware of your soul."

TUNE IN: Take in a long, slow, deep breath 1 . . . 2 . . . 3 . . . 4 . . . . And exhaling 4 . . . 3 . . . 2 . . . 1 . . . . One more time. Now look closely at the picture of the brain in Figure 7.1. Take your time. Consider this extraordinary organ. Notice how it is housed inside the head, behind the eyes, nose, and mouth that make up the human face. It is the seat of your senses, the source of your soul. Take in another long,

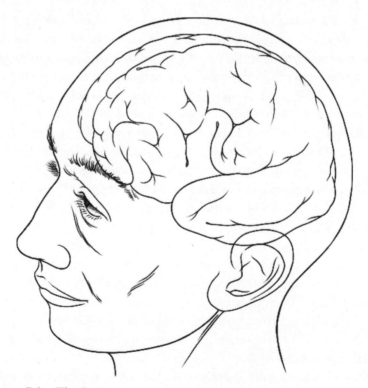

Figure 7.1　The Brain

Patrick J. Lynch, medical illustrator; C. Carl Jaffe, MD, cardiologist. Used with permission.

slow, deep breath. Imagine the oxygen feeding your brain. Picture the neurons firing. After a minute or two, return to your reading.

Inside your head, behind your face, between your ears, is an extraordinarily powerful yet delicate machine. Do you see the complex, intricate, and potentially fragile makeup of the brain? Your brain is home to your knowledge, your memories, your hopes, and your dreams. It holds the secret to ending your anxiety and moving forward in life and your ability to perform successfully at work. Don't you want to do everything possible to ensure its health? Do you want to take chances by disrupting its chemistry?

Brain health is not merely mental health. A healthy brain requires the same healthy habits we all know about—good nutrition, regular aerobic exercise, and good, restorative sleep each night. When your neurons are firing properly, you are better equipped to balance your mind states when stressors arise.

Many of the substances people typically turn to in an effort to ease anxiety are actually at odds with optimal brain health: Alcohol, sugar and other foods, caffeine, tobacco, prescription and non-prescription drugs, marijuana, herbal remedies, and vitamins can all compromise brain chemistry. I am not saying you should not consume them—we'll talk more about that later. But it's time to understand their effects on brain health. Lack of exercise, air pollution, poor lighting, physical pain, repressed emotion—all of these affect the brain's *chemistry*. Chemistry is physical. It is not an abstract concept. Attach to the knowledge that your brain is affected by your decisions. Don't "should" on yourself if you have failed to protect it. This information is likely very new to you. The brain is a living organ that can heal itself quickly if you take the right actions. Stay present. Use your Adult's logic and objectivity. Now is the time to gather information so you can make a rational decision about the way you wish to care for your brain.

Looking at the Brain

Evolving technology has led to a new understanding of brain functioning. For example, the MRI machine shows blood volume to different parts of the brain. The different degrees of volume are depicted by changes in color. With the individual who is a drug addict, blood volume is lower in specific areas. It is the same dynamic with anxiety. Therefore, one of the therapeutic objectives for anxiety management is to increase blood volume to the brain. Now, many activities will accomplish this—self-regulation/relaxation exercises, the healthy expression of emotion rather than repression, specific substances, both prescription and otherwise, brain-challenge exercises, and more. *But the most direct way to increase blood volume to the brain is with quality aerobic exercise.*

Get Moving: Aerobic Exercise for Your Brain

Do not avoid reading this section! If you are not a regular exerciser, you will be tempted to skip over this. But stick with me here. This is a critically important topic. Don't dismiss it by saying you've heard this all before or you know you won't follow these guidelines or you're thin or too busy or anything else. First of all, the guidelines are simple: Do something—walk outdoors, march in place, dance, or participate in a sport—for 20 minutes (or more) five or six times a week. (That's more than the three times a week recommended for basic heart and lung health—but this is your brain we're talking about!) The more you can oxygenate your brain, the better—not just for your anxiety but for your mood and brain power as well. If possible, get in the habit of doing your exercise outdoors—fresh air, Vitamin D from sunshine, a sense of solitude, and a chance to connect with nature will boost your spirits and leave you feeling grounded yet energized.

It's only 20 minutes a day—the length of a couple of coffee breaks or a phone chat. You can find the time. You must. Just 20 minutes of exercise at a moderate pace can mean the difference between mental (and physical) fitness and major imbalances that put you at risk of both more severe anxiety symptoms and heart disease and other illnesses. Not convinced those 20 minutes will be worth it? Read on.

Imagine a brain that scientific researchers would characterize as "biochemically, molecularly calm." A brain that functions at a higher level, able to fire its neurons for maximum performance. A brain that allows you to do your best, to be your best. Imagine a brain that is as fit as an Olympic athlete, able to adapt quickly and appropriately to challenging situations. A brain that uses the energy of adrenaline to fuel its excellence.

Aerobic exercise can give you that brain. Scientific studies indicate that exercise actually improves the brain's ability to handle stress. "It looks more and more like the positive stress of exercise prepares cells and structures and pathways within the brain so that they are more equipped to handle stress," Princeton University researchers report. "Exercise changes your brain for the better at a molecular level."

In the Princeton study, rats that were physically fit coped better with stress than those that were not. "Scientists have known for some time that exercise stimulates the creation of new brain cells (neurons)," the *New York Times* reported, "but not how, precisely, these neurons might be functionally different from other brain cells." The scientists found that the rats that exercised responded more calmly to stressful conditions than the rats that were kept on an exercise-free regimen. The brain cells they developed during exercise, the researchers said, were "specifically buffered from exposure to a stressful experience."

Hands down, aerobic exercise is the most effective technique for increasing blood flow to the brain. In fact, long-term research has shown that *quality aerobic exercise is more effective in treating depression than antidepressant medication.*

I must confess that I am addicted—to exercise. This addiction started during my senior year of college. In high school I was on the cross country and track teams. Although I was able to run a five-minute-four-second mile, I hated the pressure of the clock correlated to my running. In fact, I often succumbed to performance pressure. My senior year, in the first cross country meet of the season, I placed fourth out of about 35 runners. The next meet I placed last. I choked. It was in my final year of college that I really discovered aerobic exercise as a mood enhancer. At that time I was making it a point to run about five miles a day.

In my early 30s, I gave up running because of the stress it placed on my joints, but I kept up basketball. Now, at age 59, the additive stress on my back is taking its toll, but I am more addicted to the sweat than ever. I use aerobic exercise machines to get a workout that does not put stress on my ankles and knees; I have used a stationary bike and a Nordic track (I went through five of them), and now use an elliptical and stepper. I crave a good sweat. It gets my endorphins flowing. It greatly enhances my mood, self-esteem, and confidence, and helps me access my Adult mind state for problem solving. It has been and remains my therapy.

The power of sweating (via exercise) is enormous as it applies to anxiety management. Exercise-induced sweat rids the body of excess adrenaline and other biochemical activity associated with anxiety and panic. The key to creating a productive exercise program is to nurture yourself. This includes realistic expectations. If you proceed too quickly or intensely your inner child will have a temper tantrum (loosely interpreted) and will sabotage your efforts. Proceed with caution and a gradual methodology. Find the pace that works for you. It's better to reach quality objectives within a month's time than to try to get there within a week, find it too difficult, and stop. The more you can find an activity or sport that you genuinely like (Natural Child), the more potential you have to stay with it.

Your minimum therapeutic exercise objective for anxiety control is to work up to exercising three times a week for 20 minutes at your target heart rate. Measuring your heart rate is a simple form of biofeedback: observing information then taking targeted action in response to that information. To figure out your target heart rate subtract your age from 220, and multiply by 0.75 (e.g., if you are 40 years old: $220 - 40$ years old $= 180 \times 0.75 = 135$ beats per minute). Inexpensive pulse monitors are available. If you don't own a pulse monitor, here is a simple way to check your heart rate as you exercise: Place your index and middle fingers on a pulse point such as your wrist or neck. Using a stopwatch or clock, count the number of beats in 10 seconds and multiply by 10 to get your total. Alternatively, you can count for the full 60 seconds to determine your total. For more information on achieving your target heart rate during exercise, consult a reliable health Web site such as Discovery Health or Mayo Clinic. If you have any concerns about beginning an exercise program, consult your health care practitioner before you start—especially if you have not exercised in quite some time.

The Blood Flow Image Exercise

Take in a long slow deep breath and slowly exhale 4...3...2... 1..., pacing your inhale–exhale. Inhale the oxygen and its energy. Exhale the carbon dioxide and tension. Inhale the energy. Exhale the tension. Do this three times, and settle into rhythmic breathing for a few moments.

Now I want you to access your mind's eye. How many windows do you have in the living room of your home? You will probably get the answer quickly because of the image imprint stored in your mind. You just used your mind's eye. Take in one more long slow deep breath and exhale 4...3...2...1....

Read the following description carefully. Then close your eyes, using your mind's eye to create the image:

The oxygen-rich stream of blood is flowing through your right arm smoothly as the muscles around the blood vessels are relaxing, which opens the blood vessels up wide, allowing the blood to flow through with no resistance.

Focus on this image for two minutes as you breathe rhythmically. You may experience a tingling sensation. If so, embrace it. Next, the oxygen-rich stream of blood is flowing through your left arm smoothly as the muscles around the blood vessels are relaxing, which opens the blood vessels up wide, allowing the blood to flow through with no resistance as you continue to breathe rhythmically. Focus on the tingling sensation if present and the image for another two minutes. Then open your eyes and take a deep breath.

TUNE IN: Get a sense of your skin temperature and match it with your thoughts, feelings, and energy. Now do the exercise. The more you practice this, the better you will get with hand warming.

A Good Night's Sleep

Getting enough sleep sounds easier than it is. Everyone has concerns that keep them up at night from time to time. But people who have anxiety about work have a lot of trouble making sure they get the right amount of prolonged, restorative sleep—the kind that lets you wake up refreshed and reenergized. How much sleep should you get?

For most adults, seven to eight hours is about right. But the reality is that few of us establish the habit of getting that much sleep. I strongly recommend devoting eight hours to sleep. You need energy for all five mind states.

That simple habit can make a world of difference in the level of stress and anxiety you feel. Lorraine, age 42, was a teacher, opera composer, and singer who suffered anxiety about performing her own compositions on stage. Lorraine had a very busy life, teaching every day, private tutoring, correcting papers at night, and working on a major music composition that had to be finalized in two months. She continually told me she was burnt out. When she admitted she was sleeping only six hours per night, I advised her to get a full eight hours for two weeks straight—no matter what. After that "sleep experiment," Lorraine reported that she had more energy and enthusiasm for everything. "I'm getting so much done!" she said. "I have two hours less of awake time, but I get so much more done now when I am awake."

A highly creative teacher and musician, Lorraine expressed her feelings in a poem about her relationship with time:

Fighting with Time

I pick a fight with time each day, but time always wins.

No matter how I punch away, he deftly moves and grins.

No matter what clever plan I aim to break his chin,

His fists too strong, his legs too swift.

Time always does me in.

No matter what strength I fly,

Nor with what speed I run,

Time never stops to give me breath,

Or let me have my fun.

Oh, time, I cry, Can you not pause a moment, once you see?

But time does not listen.

He knocks the wind from me.

TUNE IN: Take the next two minutes. That's 120 seconds. Focus on your rhythmic breathing. Pace your inhale–exhale to at least 8 to 12 seconds. If you can extend this by a few seconds, it means you are getting better at it and taking more oxygen into your system. After your breathing exercise, focus on your skin temperature and resistance (perspiration) and match those sensations with your feelings and thoughts.

You Are What You Eat: Food and Emotional States

Doesn't it make sense that what you put in your body would directly impact chemistry? Doesn't it make sense to invest in creating a strong and healthy physiological foundation for anxiety control? Wouldn't you like to do all you can to create productive energy? Developing a healthy eating plan and taking responsibility for what you consume every day is a stress management essential—the first line of defense, before trying medication or natural supplements.

Annemarie Colbin, Ph.D., is author of the best-selling *Food and Healing* and founder of the Natural Gourmet Institute for Food and Health in New York City. Dr. Colbin served as a consultant for my Comprehensive Self-Therapy Audio Program entitled "Beyond Shyness: How to Conquer Social and Performance Anxieties."

Her theories about food and emotions are right in line with what I believe. For example, she sees the consumption of sugar as revealing an emotional need. "Sugar," she writes, "is closely related to feelings of alienation, despair, and depression." In my consultation with her, she put it even more simply: "Sugar is love." In my personal and professional life, I have seen so many parents who invest in loving their children with sugar. This can become a huge habit as we grow into adulthood and continue to associate sugar with love. And to complicate things, she noted, "Sugar is just about in everything."

Ensuring the right kind of food intake is a matter of balance. Indeed, Colbin's formula for mental health and anxiety management through eating is based on her belief that: "In the body balance happens with movement between opposites."

Just for a moment, imagine your body chemistry as a seesaw. When your food consumption is balanced, the seesaw is level. This is achieved by eating the right combination of "expansive" and "contractive" foods. The center foods are grains and beans and are the pivot point.

To determine whether you need "expansive" or "contractive" foods, you must determine whether your condition is expansive or contractive (spaced out or uptight). You can then choose foods to counterbalance that condition.

Expansive

Drugs (recreational)

Alcohol

Sugar

Coffee

Fruit

Land vegetables

Sea vegetables

Root vegetables

Beans

Grains

Fish

Fowl

Meat

Eggs

Salt

Contractive

Annemarie Colbin, Ph.D.

"There are no studies that show actual physiological data to support this model," Dr. Corbin says. "It is based on how foods feel to the eater. The foods correlate to *psychological* feeling."

From most expansive down to most contractive:

Confused
Spacey
Unable to concentrate
Chatty
Active
Open
Clear
Concentrated
Narrow-minded
Mentally rigid
Arrogant
Fanatical

Anxiety can be seen as a lack of focus and the inability to get grounded, therefore expansive; if anxiety leads to paralysis or extreme avoidance, it is contractive. To help restore balance, consume foods from the opposite side of the equation. For example, if the problem is rigidity, sweet fruits and warm drinks would have a relaxing effect; if the problem is a scattered condition, ingest salty and dry foods and avoid sweets.

The same general nutritional guidelines we all know so well are as critical for brain health as they are for the health of the rest of our bodies. Dr. Colbin's principles are simple: No refined sugar or artificial sweeteners. Only good quality, high-fiber carbohydrates. Plenty of protein. And balanced meals: Make sure that in each meal you have some protein, some whole grain carbohydrate, some fat (butter or olive oil are best), and some vegetables, especially leafy greens either cooked or raw.

Smoking and Stress

People who smoke often reach for their cigarettes for stress relief. Apart from the obvious facts about smoking and the very serious health effects, you should know that smoking causes brain chemistry to undergo dramatic chemical changes. The resulting mood swings interfere with the ability to manage anxiety. Thus a smoker who hopes to alleviate stress is actually perpetuating it.

Self-Medicating with Alcohol

Ross, a 33-year-old horse farm manager, contacted me because of debilitating depression related to his workplace anxiety. He was at "an all-time low," he said, because he had learned that the breeding operation where he lived and worked had been sold. Although he had met several major players in the racing world, he had made no effort to establish business contacts. He was simply too uncomfortable talking to others, even just small talk. "I prefer the barn. I prefer the land. I went into this business to communicate with horses—not people!" He told me that his marriage had ended because, as his ex-wife said, he "never talked." Now, she was taking him to court for more child support—which he couldn't afford without a new job.

Ross confided that he was self-medicating with alcohol and prescription painkillers first prescribed to him when he broke his shoulder in the show ring. When I suggested augmenting therapy with a 12-Step program, he said, "Been there, done that. My problem isn't drinking, my problem is the reason I am drinking." Ross was willing to work extremely hard to beat his anxiety "habit"—and he was sure his dependence on drinking and drugging would diminish as he progressed. By the end of our work together, he had reduced his drinking by 80 percent and seldom even took aspirin. When he controlled his drinking, not only did his anxiety decrease but his ability to handle conflict increased dramatically. I have heard countless such reports.

In his first job out of college, Rick landed an investor relations position with a hip, young dot-com company. The casual work culture embraced a "work hard, play hard" ethic that meant lots of late nights, but also lots of after-hours and weekend parties. Rick did fine with the working-late part. But he was extremely nervous about the socializing. Most of Rick's colleagues brought dates to these events; Rick never did. In his initial session with me, he was both angry and despairing. "Jonathan, you have to help me! I feel like killing myself. I can't socialize. I can't get girls." Imagine how surprised I was just six weeks later when Rick told me he had received the holiday party award for "most social colleague." Strange, I thought. How was that possible? "Six-pack therapy," he said.

Despite its short-term anxiety-reducing effect, alcohol is a depressant and has a down side. This does not necessarily mean it will make you depressed (although with excessive drinking, clinical depression is often a byproduct). But it will sap (or depress) the energy you need for high performance and anxiety management. Never forget that a High Performance Mind requires all five mind states to function. Ongoing use of alcohol to take the edge off is the enemy of self-confidence and sustained proactive thinking and behavior. Drinking to dull your anxiety is defensive positioning! I am not referring to alcoholism—but to how you use alcohol, not how much alcohol you use or how often you consume it. Again, everybody has different chemistry, and I don't contend that "no alcohol allowed" is the only way to be healthy. But a strong caution is definitely warranted here.

A Medical Perspective on Alcohol

Seth Mandel, M.D., a psychiatrist well versed in anxiety treatment and someone to whom I refer patients, offers this medical perspective on alcohol: "Despite the popular belief that alcohol is a social lubricant, the pharmacologic benefits of alcohol in humans have not been definitely proven. It is possible that the expectations of increased confidence and tension reduction accompanying alcohol intake may alone be able to override the fear of social situations."

Alcohol use might actually maintain or worsen social or performance anxiety for several reasons. Alcohol could block the experience of a sufficient fear response needed to adapt to such situations. The individual may also come to believe that the only reason he coped effectively with a given social event was because he drank. Increased anxiety can also occur following drinking due to physiological withdrawal and/or worries about social performance when under the influence of alcohol.

Lower doses of alcohol produce a feeling of stimulation, whereas higher doses produce sedation. The use of alcohol to cope with anxiety, while seemingly temporarily effective, is associated with an increased likelihood of additional mental health problems such as depression and possibly even suicidal ideation or suicide attempts. Alcohol can be dangerous medicine for those with social and performance anxiety.

My Perspective on Alcohol

Here is my perspective on alcohol, based on 59 years of life and more than 30 years as a therapist. Moderate consumption of alcohol can enhance healthy NC behavior. It can even be therapeutic for "taking the edge off" occasionally. Make sure you have a realistic definition of "moderate." (My own definition is fewer than two units of alcohol [unit = one 4-oz. glass of wine, one 12-oz. beer, or one shot of hard alcohol] not more than four times a week.) Other health professionals, including Dr. Amen, say that more than one time a week is too much if you want to maintain optimal brain health. Saving your drinking allowance up for several drinks on a particular night is usually considered a "binge," which will only create distress for the brain. Alcohol is extremely insidious in that it can often entrap the drinker into dependence for mood control.

Is alcohol an issue for you? Use your Adult mind state to assess the quantity of your drinking. Some researchers claim that anything more than two units of alcohol (unit = one 4-oz. glass of wine, one 12-oz. beer, or one shot of hard alcohol) more than four times a week is more than "moderate" intake. But others, including Dr. Amen, who coined the phrase "the hardware of the soul" that we use in this chapter's title, disagree.

However much you may drink, stop to think about the times when you were consuming alcohol. Were you comfortable and relaxed? Were you hyper vigilant and in need of numbness or taking the edge off? Attach to your use of alcohol and, in doing so, attach to the situations that prompt your desire to drink.

In Consideration of Marijuana

I have studied marijuana extensively. I have seen some smokers use it to facilitate creative and positive energy. I have seen it help with pain and depression. I have seen it used to enhance recreational pursuits. I have seen positive things. But I have also seen unhealthy things. It depends on the chemistry of the user and the specific pot.

For example, at 22, Landon felt so inferior to the more experienced 20-something peers at his new job in the film industry that he quit. His parents sent him money to tide him over under the condition that he get professional help for his anxiety and depression. His physician prescribed medical marijuana. Landon was surprised to learn there were 70 brands to choose from. Some pot would bring him up and some would bring him down—but he wouldn't know which until he filled his prescription each time. The active ingredients acted on different parts of the brain.

A star baseball pitcher in high school, Tyler was one of the best players in his southern state and received a full scholarship worth $40,000 a year at a well-known university. In high school, he would usually pitch the entire game. His college team had five high-quality pitchers. Whenever Tyler was pitching, as soon as he let a man get on base, his coach would get another pitcher up in the bullpen. This practice threatened Tyler's confidence, and his negative critical script kicked into overtime. To cope with the stress of performance on the baseball field, he discovered marijuana. Smoking pot did help lessen the actual anxiety, but it also depleted his motivation and drive. Baseball held no appeal for him anymore. He dropped out of college and gave up his scholarship. Now, compare this to the thinking of Kirk Rueter, the major league pitcher we introduced you to earlier. Natural ability is not enough to attain or maintain a high level of athletic performance. It requires a High Performance Mind.

Chemical Imbalance

If you seek medical treatment to discuss whether you have a chemical imbalance, ask questions of the medical professional—ideally a psychiatrist or psychotherapist rather than a general practitioner, internist, or "family practice" physician. That person should consider various questions to determine what kind of imbalance is present; for example:

- Do I have autonomic hypersensitivity?
- Do I not have enough serotonin?
- Do I have allergies?
- Do I have a medical condition that would impact anxiety?

Natural Pharmacology for Anxiety Treatment

St. John's Wort. Cava Cava. Valerian Root. Camu Camu. Hops. Chamomile. California Poppy. All have been used to treat anxiety symptoms. There are many more—both individual substances and combination products. You can find them in natural food stores and online. Some offer stress relief, but also cause side effects including headaches, stomach discomfort, agitation, and oversedation. Natural pharmacology—nutritional supplements, herbal capsules, sprays, tinctures, and tonics—does not *cure* social and performance anxiety. Those products are *tools* to provide symptom relief only. Resolving anxiety lies not in masking those symptoms but in resolving emotions and thinking that cause the anxiety. You must go deeper and do the real work.

All told, the best approach is to rely on medicinal substances as little as possible, which is why the nutritional strategy of healing through eating makes a lot of sense. Eating is natural and structural. Do it right, and it may be the only nutritional supplement you need!

There are two natural dietary supplements that I think are worth considering (with your health care provider's approval, of course),

B-Complex Vitamins. Nutritional experts believe that the B-complex vitamins are especially important in warding off anxiety and depression. Among other things, they can reduce high levels of lactic acid in the blood, which are associated with anxiety and panic.

Inositol. I have recommended Inositol to more than 100 clients with performance anxiety who wanted to try a natural compound before going to prescription medicine. In the 1960s, Carl Pfeiffer, a pioneering physician and researcher, noticed that the brain waves of patients who took Inositol resembled those of patients taking Librium, a potent tranquilizer. Other studies are confirming Inositol's positive effects. Finding the right dosage for you may take some experimenting, starting with less then adding more to increase effectiveness as necessary. It may take several weeks before you attain maximum effectiveness. Inositol should not be mixed with prescription medication for anxiety or depression.

My Take on Pharmaceuticals

In my clinical practice, my philosophy has been to try to do therapy without medicine. I urge my clients to take responsibility for solving the problem as much as is possible. But when clients seems stuck, I may refer them to a psychiatrist for evaluation. I probably recommend medication for about 30 percent of my clients—but typically only for a limited amount of time as a way of facilitating deeper work and getting them "unstuck." When I raise the topic of medication, my clients sometimes ask me, "What about side effects?" And we discuss them. But I always counter with another question: "What about the side effects of being stuck with workplace anxiety? Diseased self-esteem? Poor performance reviews? Job loss?"

When I refer a client to a psychiatrist for medicine, it is with the understanding that that medicine is a *tool* to facilitate productive therapy, with the end result being that the person goes off the pharmaceuticals when a confident level of success has been achieved and sustained. That is our stated intention at the outset, and the prescribing psychiatrist must concur.

Christine, a 35-year-old woman working in middle management in a Boston corporation, contacted me to help her with anxiety about attending weekly managers' meetings. She and her partner, Jenny, were attending Toastmasters, which is a wonderful world-wide self-help program for public speaking. She told me that she was taking a beta blocker before her work meetings and before her Toast-masters engagements. Here is another unhealthy and unproductive use of medicine—after all, Toastmasters is a self-help organization intended to help members become more comfortable speaking in public.

Taking beta blockers regularly only allows you to detach from the adrenaline you fear. If you never feel that adrenaline, you have no laboratory. Avoidance is not an answer. If, however, you use them only occasionally, they can be a productive part of your recovery. Use medicine only to slow the rush so you can learn to handle it. Your goal is to anticipate the adrenaline as a good thing—as the fuel you need to succeed in stressful situations. If you can't feel it, you can't learn to access it as energy.

Of course, it's your decision, not mine. You will work with a prescribing physician and that person will no doubt weigh in on the pros and cons.

Better Living through Chemistry?

I recommended an SSRI to treat an assistant district attorney in Texas for her courtroom-specific performance anxiety and related obsessing, She found a psychiatrist who immediately prescribed an anti-anxiety medication, which had a sedating effect. Sedation not only prevented her from participating in treatment effectively, but it also severely compromised her work performance—exactly the opposite of what she was seeking! Eventually, she was prescribed an (SSRI, a type of antidepressant) with positive results. There are many such stories.

We live in an age of specialization; if you seek an evaluation for possible pharmaceutical treatment for social and performance anxiety, go to a psychiatrist or psychopharmacologist rather than a general practitioner. If you are seeing a therapist and you feel stuck, let your therapist know. You can discuss possible reasons why and raise the topic of medication as a potential part of your treatment.

A non-MD therapist can usually recommend a psychiatrist if prescription medication seems warranted. In any event, remember that your highest commitment is to progress and a cure—so don't languish with a practitioner whose treatment style is keeping you stuck.

I will recommend medication only when a person is invested in psychotherapy at the same time. I believe that when medicine is prescribed without concurrent counseling for social and performance anxiety, it is clinically criminal. When you hear medicine horror stories, you can bet that most of the time it was because the use of medication was not closely supervised. Medicine is *not* a cure for social and performance anxiety. It is a tool! It can have wonderful results when used correctly.

In this day and age, however, the pharmaceutical industry—and our own impatience as a culture—lead us to think there is a pill for everything. Every day, I get e-mails from people accessing www.socialanxiety.com, asking "What medicine do you recommend for social anxiety?" I do not bother to respond to these, because it would require quite a lot of information (as you will see), and those who are asking this as their first line of questioning are looking for a quick fix. The program outlined in this book is the quickest fix I know. Anyone wanting an insta-cure should be searching for a magician rather than a therapist.

A Physician's Perspective

The following is a Question and Answer section with Seth Mandel, MD, my psychiatrist colleague. Dr. Mandel is very experienced with prescribing medication to aid in the treatment of anxiety disorders. Medicating for anxiety is complicated, so careful evaluation and support are critical.

Question: What determines whether a workplace anxiety sufferer is a good candidate for medication?

Answer: For management of social and performance anxiety, I rely on criteria outlined in the *Diagnostic and Statistical Manual of Mental Disorders, Fourth Edition, Text Revision* (DSM-IV-TR). Medication is generally deemed appropriate only if the avoidance, anxious anticipation, or distress in the feared social or performance situation(s) interferes significantly with the person's normal routine, occupational (academic) functioning, or social activities or relationships, or there is marked distress about having the phobia.

Question: What medications are typically prescribed for people who suffer workplace anxiety?

Answer: Social Anxiety Disorder is responsive to treatment with a variety of medications. The primary medications for this disorder are antidepressants, most commonly Selective Serotonin-Reuptake Inhibitors (SSRIs) including fluvoxamine (Luvox, Luvox CR); sertraline (Zoloft); paroxetine (Paxil Paxil CR); citalopram (Celexa); escitalopram (Lexapro); and fluoxetine (Prozac); and the Serotonin-Norepinephrine Reuptake Inhibitor (SNRI) venlafaxine (Effexor XR), with the best evidence existing for escitalopram, fluvoxamine, fluvoxamine CR, paroxetine, sertraline, and venlafaxine extended release). Older classes of antidepressants, including the irreversible Monoamine Oxidase Inhibitors (MAOIs), such as phenelzine sulfate (Nardil), are also very effective. Less studied, but possibly effective agents [medications] include the SNRI duloxetine (Cymbalta) and the unique antidepressant mirtazapine (Remeron).

Benzodiazepines (sedatives or anxiolytics) can also be used for the treatment of social anxiety. Clonazepam (Klonopin) is an effective treatment for social anxiety. Alprazolam (Xanax) or lorazepam (Ativan) can also be used, but there is less scientific evidence behind this practice. [*Author's Note*: Klonopin and Xanax can be addictive, so proceed with caution, especially if there is a history of alcohol or other substance abuse.]

Anticonvulsants or antiepileptics are another class of drugs that has been used to treat social phobia. These medications include gabapentin (Neurontin) and Topiramate (Topamax).

B-adrenergic blockers may be effective in managing performance situations. Propranolol and Atenolol are two such medications. Atenolol is more selective for the heart and may not cross the blood-brain barrier easily, thereby limiting any central nervous system effects such as fatigue or depression.

Limited evidence suggests that augmentation of an SSRI with buspirone (BuSpar) may help to produce beneficial effects for patients with generalized Social Anxiety Disorder. The potential role of dopamine in underlying this disorder has led some researchers to investigate the use of atypical antipsychotics. Olanzapine (Zyprexa) and quetiapine (Seroquel) are two such medications.

Question: If you determine that prescription medications might help, how do you determine which medications to prescribe?

Answer: SSRIs and Serotonin Norepinephrine Reuptake Inhibitors (SNRIs) are recognized as the first-line treatments for generalized Social Anxiety Disorder based on their efficacy, safety, and tolerability. They have been shown to be effective in numerous scientific studies. Social Anxiety Disorder may also be associated with other anxiety disorders such as Panic Disorder, Obsessive-Compulsive Disorder, and Generalized Anxiety Disorder as well as mood disorders such as Dysthymic Disorder and Major Depressive disorder. These disorders are all responsive to treatment with SSRIs and SNRIs, lending further support to their use as the initial choice in the treatment of Social Anxiety Disorder.

Dose-equivalent head-to-head antidepressant studies have not suggested a difference in efficacy thus far. Medications are therefore often chosen on the basis of their side effect profile and potential utility in treating other possibly unrelated conditions. SNRIs also have usefulness in treating some pain conditions, including neuropathic pain, fibromyalgia, and other chronic pain conditions, and also in treating attention-deficit/hyperactivity disorder (ADHD).

For patients whose anxiety is linked to a limited number of particular situations and is marked by symptoms such as increased heart rate and tremor, beta blockers may be effective taken approximately 30 minutes before an event. Despite widespread use, evidence supporting these medications (as an ongoing treatment) for performance anxiety is relatively weak.

Benzodiazepines [commonly called "tranquilizers"] taken on an as-needed basis may be useful in patients who have occasional bouts of moderate anxiety. Benzodiazepines work rapidly, whereas antidepressants can take weeks to obtain a full effect. They may be preferable to maintenance antidepressants for certain patients who have strong feelings about taking medication on a daily basis.

Benzodiazepines are not effective for mood disorders on their own and thus would require the use of a second medication in patients suffering from both conditions; like Klonopin and Xanax, they can be highly addictive and should be used with caution.

A combination of drugs may be prescribed to maximize therapeutic effects. SSRI treatment has been augmented by the addition of benzodiazepines, anticonvulsants, atypical antipsychotics such as risperidone or aripiprazole, or buspirone. Some patients with social anxiety do not experience any therapeutic benefit with SSRI or SNRI therapy; and the medications may be poorly tolerated. In these cases, it may be advisable to try an anticonvulsant or even an atypical antipsychotic such as quetiapine (Seroquel) or olanzapine (Zyprexa) as one drug only as opposed to a combination of medicines (it is more the norm to try an SSRI along with a benzodiazapene).

Question: How does a person weigh potential payoffs against possible side effects?

Answer. The use of any medication always involves an informed discussion between the psychiatrist and patient. There are risks and benefits to taking any medication, and the decision to take medication comes down to whether the potential payoffs outweigh any possible side effects from the medication.

As with all medications, side effects vary. Read about them and discuss them with your prescribing physician before choosing whether to begin pharmaceutical treatment.

I told you this would be complicated. The moral of the story is, use your NP and A. Clearly, prescribing medications to treat anxiety and depression is a high-level skill that is, in my opinion, best left to psychiatric specialists rather than general practitioners and internists, who usually do not have advanced and specialized training in these particular substances.

Healthy Brain Action Plan

Take a moment to acknowledge yourself for an important accomplishment: Getting through this chapter. This was a lot to take in, and it no doubt gives you a lot to consider. If I've done my job, I have persuaded you that the care and feeding of the hardware of your soul is important and worthwhile. Pause now to center yourself.

TUNE IN: Take a long, slow, deep breath in, then out—for a total of 8 to 12 seconds. Oxygen in 1...2...3...4.... Carbon dioxide out 4...3...2...1....Concentrate on your rhythmic breathing for 30 seconds.

Now, using your Nurturing Parent and Adult mind states, write down three to six actions you will take for a healthy brain. For each one, give yourself a deadline by which you will take these actions. The brain likes definites—"By when?" is a good thing to think about.

Action I Will Take for a Healthy Brain   **By When?**

1. _____   _____

   _____

2. _____   _____

   _____

3. _____   _____

   _____

4. _____   _____

   _____

5. _____   _____

   _____

6. _____   _____

   _____

Speak Up: How to Control Your Public Speaking Anxiety

W hat's not to like about public speaking? How about practically everything? If you are nervous at work, chances are that speaking in public, not just giving speeches or presentations, but being the only one talking in any workplace situation—a meeting, a conference call, a Skype conversation, or around the coffee pot—is stressful for you. Here are just some of the feelings workplace anxiety sufferers have articulated:

"When I'm the only one talking, I feel exposed."

"As soon as I'm through talking, I obsess over whether I've said too much."

"There's nowhere to hide."

"Everyone expects me to say something smart."

"If I make eye contact, I'm afraid my mind will go blank. It's happened before!"

"I'll freak if they see me being nervous!"

There's no denying it, having an audience—even of one or two people—can cause crippling fear and a pervasive sense of nervousness at work. Once your internal critical script starts to run amok, you feel as if you are on the path to embarrassment and shame. You feel you are putting your very identity on the line—that your worth as a person rises or falls with your ability to be perfect. The stakes may indeed be high—your career success is certainly tied to performance. But how well you speak is *not* an indication of your self-worth. You must separate these dynamics from performance if you want to convert your adrenaline into energy.

That said, you must also use your Adult to accept the reality that public speaking—speaking up in public situations such as sales calls, conference calls, meetings, presentations, and, when necessary, speeches—is a critical skill. Indeed, Warren Buffett has called public speaking "the No. 1 business skill."

Does that scare you? Do not detach from the fact that public speaking matters to your career and your life. *Attach.* Right now, take a moment to balance your mind states. What message can you draw from each of the following mind states? You really need to *attach* to this exercise. *Focus.*

Nurturing Parent: _____

Critical Parent: _____

Adult: _____

Adapted Child: _____

Natural Child: _____

This chapter is designed to set you up with a laboratory where you can experiment with speaking in public. The techniques you have begun to master, combined with an enhanced understanding of the issues that come into play when it is your turn to speak, will transform who you are at the podium, at the head of the conference table, and next to the speaker phone.

The Number One Business Skill . . .
and the Number One Fear!

It would be funny if it weren't so horrifying: Public speaking is the Number One fear—an even greater fear than *death*. That's right. A vast number of people would rather die than speak in public! From a clinical perspective, I can tell you there is a lot of truth to this. For example, Harold was an engineer in a manufacturing plant. He received a promotion that required him to address a group of colleagues about plant operations—the very next day. He called me, sounding very wired, saying, "I think I might get in an accident on my way to work tomorrow." That's how much he wanted to avoid the group.

One of my clients recognized anxiety in a high-powered billionaire who was giving a keynote speech. All eyes were on the presenter, an entrepreneur who had developed many companies. Suddenly, the man had to stop talking and sit down; it appeared there was something medically wrong. As EMTs escorted him from the room, his colleague took over. An hour or so later, the presenter returned and apologized, saying he had been thinking about a dear friend who had just died." But my client recognized the other man's episode for what it was: a panic attack—the same thing that my client himself, the go-to guy for his hedge fund's presentations, also experienced when he found himself in monologue situations. The moral of the story is that you are not alone.

Why Is "Speaking Up" So Important?

As we define it, "public speaking" is akin to "speaking up"—not just giving a speech, but also chiming in at a meeting or asking a question in a class or during a conference call. Any time you are speaking to two or more people and all eyes are on you, you are engaging in public speaking.

Public speaking matters, and not just because your livelihood may depend on it. Public speaking allows you to communicate, to express yourself, to educate, to learn, to persuade, to impress, to enhance your profile among your colleagues and professional peers, and to invest in your self-esteem. Speaking in public allows you to learn. If you want to ask a question or are confused about a concept but keep silent out of fear, you are choosing to pay a high price: You are *choosing* to remain less effective and less knowledgeable. And if you can step outside yourself for a second, consider this: You are also limiting the contribution you can make to the effectiveness and knowledge of others who themselves may wish to ask that same question. After all, how many times have all of us sat in an audience and listened to someone else raise a point that we were wondering about. "I'm so glad she asked that question!" we think. Take a chance. Be that person—and make a difference in your own life and the lives of others.

Picture Yourself . . .

There's a popular saying that describes the line between suffering from anxiety and using stress management techniques to transform it: *If you always do what you've always done, you'll always get what you've always gotten.*

Here's another way of putting it: *The definition of insanity is doing the same thing over and over and expecting a different result.* As you well know, even if you feel like you're going to die when a panic attack hits, your anxiety is unlikely to strike you down like lightning. You could go on as you have been all along. But your productivity, your effectiveness, and your reputation at work will not improve. "You'll always get what you've always gotten."

As you prepare to imagine a life in which you are no longer nervous at work, take in a long slow deep breath then slowly exhale 4 . . . 3 . . . 2 . . . 1 . . ., pacing the inhale–exhale to 8 to 12 seconds. For the next 60 seconds, focus on your rhythmic breathing—that's about six inhale–exhales. Then, see if you can extend the inhale–exhale to 12 to 14 seconds.

Now, envision your life as it will be when you use your new stress-management skills to conquer your public speaking anxiety. Wrap your mind around the scenarios that have immobilized you in the past. Now picture yourself in those situations—minus your fear but with the addition of your stress management skills. Really picture it: The room, the furnishings, the faces of the people who are listening to you. How will you feel? What will you do? What will that make possible?

_____

_____

_____

Now, return your thinking to the way things have been in the past. Tell yourself, if things continue that way, if I do not use the skills I have learned to control my public speaking anxiety, this will be the result:

_____

_____

_____

Before responding to the next question, pause for a moment. Take in another deep breath 1 ... 2 ... 3 ... 4 ... and exhale slowly 4 ... 3 ... 2 ... 1 .... Pace your inhale-exhale to 14 seconds if you can.

You first took a look at your motivation for mastering your workplace anxiety in Chapter 2. Now, let's get specific: What is your motivation for learning to face your public speaking anxiety?

The Role of Anger in Public Speaking Anxiety

What emotions do you feel when you are speaking up and your anxiety kicks in? Panic? Frustration? Fear? Embarrassment? Shame? Anger? It may not have occurred to you, but anger is a major part of the problem. When adrenaline shows up, you are furious. "Why, why, *why* do I have to feel this way? What is wrong with me? How did I get myself into this?" Often, people turn that anger outward so they can detach from the feelings of self-loathing. They hate their bosses for assigning them to make presentations, and despise them even more for ambushing themselves with spontaneous speaking requests. They hate their colleagues for causing the anxiety simply by being there. If someone tries to help and fails, the anger is turned on the helper. I received a phone call from a middle manager who mentioned he had played semi-pro basketball. He wanted help with his phobia of conference calls. "I will pay you four times the amount of your fee if you help me," he said, "but nothing per session."

"I hope you don't mind if I pass the ball on this one," I said. This guy was obviously angry. I felt sure he had no inkling of the connection between anger and public speaking anxiety, so I just asked him what prompted his attempt to make a deal. It turned out he had participated in a number of public speaking programs and "none had worked." Rather than blaming himself—rather than *attaching* to his response to adrenaline during conference calls and learning to accept it—this man held others responsible for his suffering. That's a shame. My theory about those other programs' failures was that they probably did not teach adrenaline acceptance. If adrenaline acceptance is not learned, anger will appear at the first sign of adrenaline—which, as you know by now, will worsen the problem. Unrealistic expectations, excessive CP, create anger. This is why it's essential to counter the excessive critical script with Adult logic and Nurturing Parent encouragement.

Even so, nonacceptance of adrenaline is a surface issue. Here is an example of a deeper one. Nora, age 48, worked as a manager in a national call center. She was often required to present at regional meetings. While she had substantial anxiety in these scenarios, Nora was good at what she did. She received feedback from her supervisor that her performance was good, and she kept getting raises. Nevertheless, Nora's critical script beat her up with the fact that she did not have a college education.

Even worse, going deeper, she had been living with her partner for over 15 years. She wanted to get married. He always avoided talking about it. He had gone so far as promising to put her in his will but never would show it to her. The few times that Nora pursued a discussion with him about this, he was selectively mute. He simply wouldn't discuss it. Nora was furious, but never resolved the underlying issue. In fact, she was an expert at detaching from such issues.

But detachment does not mean those issues didn't exist. Instead, they lurked under the surface as unresolved conflicts. These issues attacked her self-esteem. They made her feel both powerless and furious at herself for taking no action. She repressed that anger, but it surfaced in the form of physical anxiety symptoms during her presentations (recall Sarnow's mind-body pain connection theory).

Become an Exceptional Presenter

On February 9, 2010, I Googled the term "public speaking" and saw there were 57,100,000 listings. Obviously Warren Buffett was right.

Unfortunately, although there are millions of resources for how to speak publicly, there are very, very few that offer help for those who are afraid to do so. I have sympathy for all the people who have tried to find self-help and never had the chance to get beneath the basic "here's how to give a speech" sort of advice. In working through this program, you have learned the stress management techniques that will allow you to move on and learn the how-to's of public speaking. I discovered just one short paragraph in one of those resources that refers to "channeling your nervousness." In *The Exceptional Presenter*, author Timothy Koegel uses an acronym—OPEN UP—that is easy to remember and implement. According to Koegel, the exceptional presenter is someone who is

Organized

Passionate

Engaging

Natural

And who must:

Understand the audience

Practice

The Monologue

The most common reference to monologue is probably to the first few minutes of Jay Leno or David Letterman's talk shows, when they crack jokes and talk about that night's guests. For our purposes, a monologue is any situation in which you are talking and no one else is. True, it may be a speech or presentation. But it could also be a large meeting, a conference call, or a webcam conversation. When all eyes (or ears) are on you, you're in a monologue situation. You have the floor. Everyone is looking at you, listening to what you have to say. You may believe they are expecting you to be perfect. "I am worried that I am going to be noticeably nervous." "Are they looking at me?" "Can they tell?" "Is my voice quivering?" "Am I speaking too softly?" "Am I making sense?" "I am going to be exposed." "They're going to see who I really am." or "They're not going to see who I am."

One client asked me if I memorize my presentations. This was a good question. At this point in my career, there is an extensive script in my mind that I can pull out at any given time for any audience. Give me an anxiety-related concept and I've got a story, believe me. My ease with presentations is the result of extensive experience and practice. If I were giving a speech on an unfamiliar subject, I would prepare and make notes, but I would not memorize because I would want to preserve the Natural Child mind state's passion and overall confidence.

Use mind state balance to get into High Performance Mind mode before you enter the room or approach the podium. Your audience wants to hear what you have to say. If someone asks a question or is confused by something you've said, interpret it as interest in your topic. For some nervous speakers, a request to "speak louder" feels like criticism. It's not; it's because your audience wants to hear you clearly. Take a deep breath, then let your NP and A work together to improve your performance there and then. Your audience will respect that.

Preparation Tips to Try

- Organize the content in your mind—rather than memorize—with key notes on paper (if needed).
- With your main points established, break the monologue into pieces. Remind yourself to breathe by writing "PAUSE" or "BREATHE" in your notes. Do a brief inhale-exhale. Let go of self-consciousness. This pause serves your listeners, too—they need mental pauses to absorb your message.
- Practice—but don't over-rehearse!

Presentation Tips to Try

- Identify with the piece and let its meaning guide you. Attach to it. Care about what you have to say. Engage your Natural Child to put some passion into it.

- If there is a question-and-answer segment, prompt yourself to be calm as you endure the long silence that may occur before the first audience member pipes up. Take a breath, smile, look approachable. Your audience, too, may need to muster up the courage or energy to speak up.
- Be yourself!

Controlling the Critical Script

If you have ever closely observed a good public speaker, you will see that even the best make mistakes—saying the wrong word, pronouncing something incorrectly, or maybe even stuttering. The effective speaker does not focus on the mistake. He or she just moves on to the next word or concept. I see this all the time. Once I was doing a radio show with a substantial audience in New York City. One of the interviewers had a substantial stuttering challenge. During this 40-minute interview, she stuttered at least five times but proceeded confidently into her next words. Don't let your minor human mistakes faze you!

Selective Mutism and Public Speaking

Remember Alice, the human resources professional who for one solid year never said a word in her weekly meetings with 20 of her colleagues? Her silence at meetings was selective. She said she "had nothing to say" and "did not want to sound stupid." She was censoring herself. This was extreme CP. Her A and NC were absent in interactive scenarios where her role required spontaneity. Her mute moments were characterized by obsessive overanalyzing, which turned into paralyzed speech. Yes, she had public speaking anxiety, but the dynamics of selective mutism were the specific cause of the problem.

Zach, age 28, was a parks department policeman, whose selective mutism was triggered by interaction with his supervisor. For example, Zach was in the coffee room at the office when the road supervisor came in to ask him for an update. "What's been happening the last couple of days?" he asked. "Not much" was all Zach said. Then the supervisor asked the same question of Zach's associate, who holds the same position as Zach. He gave a long, informative answer, detailing situations that he and Zach had taken care of together. How ridiculous Zach felt that he hadn't communicated! He spent the rest of the day obsessing about his gaffe. He was sure his supervisor would think there was something wrong with him—that he was uptight, unobservant, or even incompetent. And he may well have been right.

Just as you have established your hierarchy of adrenaline challenges, it is necessary for you to do the same with verbal expression challenges if this issue applies to you. One step at a time—utilizing the same principles as the Five-Step Technique as you experiment (NC) with your verbal skills. In establishing this challenge hierarchy, you will discover which situations are relatively easy for you to handle and which are a major challenge.

An Example of a Challenge Hierarchy

Ed was a 40-year-old chiropractor who had developed a successful practice. One day, seemingly out of nowhere, he had a panic attack during his weekly community educational seminar. His wife researched options for help, acting as his administrative assistant, and made the initial call to me. This was approximately two months after the initial attack, a point at which Ed was certain the problem was worsening. Here was Ed's Challenge Hierarchy, which he compiled three weeks into treatment:

1 = lowest
10 = highest

10 = Giving his Ph.D. dissertation in front of a group of 50 colleagues and professors. (This was scheduled approximately six months after his first panic attack.) It was that underlying anticipation that was draining him.

8 = Being his brother's best man and giving a toast at a wedding.

7 = Speaking at Toastmasters.

6 = Being in a group social event without drinking.
5 = The weekly community education seminar he conducted.

In Ed's case number 5 was the starting point and was built into his calendar on a weekly basis. He could not escape it. Ed was a quick learner and applied the Five-Step Technique quickly and productively. During treatment it was discovered that the anticipatory worry about the upcoming dissertation presentation was pervasive and worrying him on both a conscious and unconscious level.

Take some time now to establish your own Challenge Hierarchy. If you like, you can begin by listing all the situations you can think of that make you nervous at work. Don't censor yourself. Just note whatever comes to mind. Once you have made the list, rate each item on a scale of 1 to 10.

Natural Child Development

One client, an enterprising 20-year-old who had just sold a recreation-related Web site for enough money to support himself for a few years, expressed to me that he was mute in many situations: social gatherings, business meetings, and some family events. Dating was a real challenge because he would only go out with women who approached him first. He was quite creative, and his Natural Child mind state was evident in his having developed and sold his Web site at such a young age. He used that same mind state to come up with his own public speaking "laboratory," an improvisational theater workshop. This did take courage (NP) and was a big risk, if not adventure (NC again). The experience had a wonderfully positive influence on the development of his spontaneous verbal skills (NC).

Amy surprised herself several years ago by taking the courageous step of confronting her phobia of singing in front of other people—engaging both her NP and her NC. Without telling any of her friends, she signed up for a class called "Singing for Shy Voices," which was targeted specifically to people like her who "couldn't even sing Happy Birthday in a crowd." She says now, "I did not know anyone in the class—which made me far less self-conscious than if I had." At the third class, the 10 students stood in a circle, each taking a turn singing one line or the other of a two-line folk song. But when

Amy's turn came, she had a full-blown panic attack. She burst into tears and headed outside to pace in the cold winter air. "I was outside for half an hour, crying and trying to catch my breath. Eventually, I was able to calm myself with a nurturing thought that this was my laboratory. I went back in, still crying. But I shared my feelings. A few of them observed something I had been completely unaware of: Before I panicked, I sang my line with perfect pitch and pacing!"

Internal Awareness Exercise

This 12-minute exercise is designed to serve as your personal relaxation retreat. Set aside uninterrupted time to complete it. Sit in a comfortable chair. Make sure there are no obvious distractions such as the television or phone. Get out of range of hearing computer noises. The goal is to have a focused, solitary experience.

What is the temperature of your hands now? 78 degrees? 85 degrees? 94 degrees? What do you think? Identify your specific emotions at this moment. Identify your specific thoughts at this moment. Allow yourself to feel comfortable with this attachment.

Survey your body, and identify any muscle groups that feel tense. Focus on each area for a few moments, and replace the tension with the sensations of looseness. Take your time.

The goal now is to take at least 12 minutes to focus on your Quieting Response. Start by slowing yourself down with your breathing, consciously maintaining the 8-to-14-second pace and then evolve into an unforced even rhythm at your own pace. Can you feel the oxygen upon inhale? Can you feel the tension release upon exhale?

When you are comfortable, close your eyes and use your hand-warming suggestions and technique; continue to do so for 12 minutes. Then open your eyes and do a deep inhale and exhale.

Exactly what is the temperature of your hands now? Exactly what are you experiencing emotionally? Exactly what are your thoughts?

Types of Intelligence

A brilliant engineer who had gone to one of the world's top universities, Raj worked for a well-known corporation. Despite his potential, he was stuck in a low-level management position. A native of India, Raj hardly interacted with his peers because he believed his accent made him difficult to understand. He censored himself verbally to the point of developing social phobia, becoming one of millions of children and adults who suffer from selective mutism. In reality, his accent was not hard to understand; during my telephone sessions with him, there was only about 5 percent that I had to ask him to repeat. Raj was highly analytical. His intellectual intelligence was impressive. At the same time, his social avoidance and emotional repression were characteristic of delayed social and emotional intelligence.

Raj was passed over for promotions for eight years despite his highly respected expertise. He worked hard to overcome his selective mutism. At first, he came across as combative, but then he got under control through these Quieting Response exercises. Raj recently managed to answer a question in a seminar with 100 people. He had been the focus of attention and had handled it well.

Toastmasters and Your Hierarchy of Challenges

Toastmasters is an international self-help program for public speaking. I have referred hundreds of people to this program as an adjunct to therapy. When a client is working Toastmasters, I teach the concept that giving a good speech is a secondary goal to befriending adrenaline. That's why I considered Christine's decision to take beta blockers before her Toastmasters meetings unproductive—like wearing a life jacket at swim team practice. Toastmasters is a place to experiment with adrenaline management and the Five-Step technique. In Toastmasters people give formal speeches as well as "the topic of the day," which allows for spontaneous two-minute presentations—think-on-your-feet exercises such as "Talk about restaurants in your city."

At this point you, too, want to be actively implementing your Five-Step Technique, working your way up from lowest to highest on your hierarchy of challenges. Again, the idea is to use your life as a laboratory: Take on an easy challenge for practice, and then work your way up. For most people with public speaking anxiety,

Toastmasters is a solid six, seven, or higher. For some people, though, it's much lower precisely because the group is designed to serve as a laboratory and therefore has a more sympathetic and receptive audience. If and when you're ready, consider joining Toastmasters. It has been a great asset to many of my clients.

An Advanced Toastmasters Technique

Remember Victor, the economist who very much wanted to give presentations, yet felt too nervous to pursue the opportunities presented to him? He was working Toastmasters for about a year before he started working with me. At a certain point in therapy, when I was convinced he was ready for a higher level of risk-taking, I suggested he do the 40-Second Embarrassment Control Exercise. Instead of launching directly into his speech, he was to stand in front of the group for 40 seconds with his eyes closed in a kind of meditative posture, feeling his adrenaline and doing the Five-Step Adrenaline Control Technique. Of course this paradoxical approach would itself require embarrassment control. What in the world would the audience think he was doing—standing there for a minute or two breathing in and out in silence? He used his Natural Child mind state to experiment with being different! It was a reach for him—but it was also a triumph. He was quite successful. Only a low percentage of my clients have the courage to pull this off. But work up the courage some time when, realistically (Adult) you know your job is not on the line. You will have the adrenaline—take advantage of the learning opportunity in a relatively benign scenario that offers a tremendous growth opportunity in real time.

Amy has given group presentations, taught nonfiction writing to adults and children, and served as discussion panelist or moderator numerous times—and she has learned to see the public speaking-related stress as a normal, natural, and very valuable part of the experience.

I definitely feel the adrenaline wave that occurs as I am about to begin. The truth is, it feels kind of good! Ahead of time, I plan what I will say, and I may even make notes to have with me if I think I need them. But what truly makes a difference in how I feel—and how well I speak—are the techniques in this program. I breathe, but my audience doesn't see the breathing exercises. They see someone who moderates her voice and paces her speech, someone who is prepared, yet natural, someone who is actually having fun up there at the front of the room.

Public Speaking Empowerment Exercise

Do the following exercise as often as you want. It is especially useful when preparing for public speaking. Before you begin, take a moment to realize how well-trained you are at self-regulation: If you have been diligent and precise in practicing the 35 or so exercises in this book, *your mind will have begun to develop an autonomic internal Quieting Response to the word "warm," even if your hand is not actually warm.*

If, however, you've merely skimmed the exercises, or picked and chosen the ones you felt like doing and ignored the others, then I can't confidently say this next exercise will work for you. If you believe you should be able to be productive with this exercise right now without having been diligent, then you have done a wonderful job of detaching and investing in excessive AC.

This exercise is effective as a regular practice and also before a public speaking event. You can do it anytime you have at least four or five minutes for yourself. Note: As with the other exercises in this book, you must perform this exercise precisely as it is written here—be mindful of both the instructions and the timing.

1. Do one to two solid minutes of diaphragmatic breathing—pacing each inhale—exhale to 8 to 12 seconds. Focus on deep, steady breaths, rhythmic, natural, and unforced.
2. Make a fist with your right hand and hold it for about 15 seconds. Then let go and focus on the looseness for 15 seconds.
3. Make a fist with your left hand and hold it for approximately 15 seconds. Then let go and focus on the looseness for 15 seconds.
4. Say to yourself three times, "My right hand is warm"—pace your statement to between 12 and 15 seconds.

5. Say to yourself three times, "My left hand is warm"—pace your statement to between 12 and 15 seconds.

6. Say to yourself three times, "I feel the blood flowing into my right hand"—pace your statement to between 14 and 18 seconds.

7. Say to yourself three times, "I feel the blood flowing into my left hand"—pace your statement to between 14 and 18 seconds.

8. Focus only on the rhythm of your diaphragmatic breathing for 30 seconds.

9. Close your eyes and, for 30 seconds, visualize in your mind's eye: You are speaking in front of the group, accepting the adrenaline, using its energy for productive, effective speaking. *You are Organized, Passionate, Engaging, and Natural. You Understand your audience and you have Practiced.*

10. Open your eyes. Take a deep breath.

You are ready to go!

CHAPTER
9

You Don't Need Nerves of Steel: You Just Need an Attitude Adjustment

O ccasionally I half-seriously joke with some clients by asking them, "Would you like to know how to cure performance and social anxiety in one hour?" Want to know the answer? Here it is: Ship yourself off to a war zone. When the tanks are coming after you or you have to sidestep roadside bombs and see people being killed all around you, it's likely that you will put certain feelings like embarrassment, shame, and fear of looking stupid in a more appropriate perspective as you focus on survival. You would feel fear on the front lines. You would feel anxiety. But not because you're afraid the guy next to you will notice if you're nervous.

By now you know that eliminating anxiety is not the answer. Nor is ignoring it and wishing it will go away. We all need our anxiety. We need our stress. Without it, we cannot achieve our personal best. Do you need nerves of steel? No. Must you shift your relationship with adrenaline from one of avoidance to one of welcome? Absolutely.

Not that I am suggesting this is simple. I do not mean to diminish the severity of your anxiety at work. I know how excruciating it can be—I have heard about it thousands of times. Remember David, the Israeli army officer who said he "would rather go door to door in a combat zone than publicly speak"? I recall another client who was working as a construction manager in Iraq; he said basically the same thing. I suppose that Carol, the ovarian cancer survivor who said "I'd rather be back in chemotherapy," is in the same category.

Objective research would demonstrate that I have worked directly clinically with more anxiety sufferers than any other therapist. I challenge anyone to refute this, and I challenge anyone to come forth with more actual documentation of success (as exemplified by both this book and the interviews at www.socialanxiety.com).

Think of your life before this program: Worrying constantly, even obsessively, about what the workday will hold, whether you will go blank when your supervisor asks you a question you aren't prepared for, what colleagues you have let down by missing a deadline. Most people who are nervous at work wait to get help until their *survival* is on the line: Their nerves are frazzled, they are burning out, their careers are in jeopardy, their relationships at work and at home may be deteriorating, or they have lost their jobs. Unfortunately, the same embarrassment and shame that they feel at work prevents them from acknowledging their problem. The CP-AC twin towers cast a dark shadow, and such people's internal critical script is too loud to ignore. Unless they are objective about it, they cannot take effective action. I wish that weren't the case, but it is reality. All that wasted time, those months and years in which they were depleting their most valuable asset—when they could have been turning that adrenaline into energy to fuel their success. The earlier a person gets help, the less potential there is for the anxiety to work its way into the personality and affect your mind states balance.

Your Positive History

At this point, your notes should tell quite a fascinating and uplifting story. Your journey is something to be proud of. You are building a positive history for yourself to which you can return for encouragement (NP) and ideas (NC) and to remind yourself that you set a goal and completed it (AC). If you have followed the instructions and worked this program for 21 days straight, now would be a good time to refer back to your diagnostic exercises. Compare where you were with where you are today. Acknowledge yourself for how far you've come.

If you have followed this program precisely, you can count these significant achievements among your successes:

1. You are creating your map for change through a series of self-diagnostics.
2. You are investing in mind states balance, creating profound structural change.
3. You are learning how to attain and maintain a healthy brain.
4. You are learning the Five-Step Adrenaline Control Technique, which allows you to make adrenaline your friend and the source of power.
5. You are beginning to understand the positive impact of paradoxical thinking and behavior.
6. You have begun to grasp why you should *attach* vs. *detach* to thoughts, feelings, and physical cues.
7. You are perfecting the process of channeling anger into productive energy.
8. You are doing the deeper work of resolving the emotional conflict that drives anxiety.
9. You are practicing more than 35 exercises that comprise a systematic Quieting Response that is the most direct way to control anxiety.
10. You are discovering the true meaning of success.

Now that you have reached the end of this program, you are familiar with the mind states and how each of them can play a positive role in your F.A.T.E. (Feelings+Actions+Thoughts+Emotions). Think back to the mind states, which you have now internalized. Each of us requires all five of these mind states. You can't simply suppress one or allow another to skyrocket. The key is balance. Take a moment to review the Unbalanced Mind States graph that you first saw in Chapter 3 (repeated here in Figure 9.1).

As you look at the graph, recall how it feels when CP and AC dominate the other mind states. Imagine this graph as a dynamic

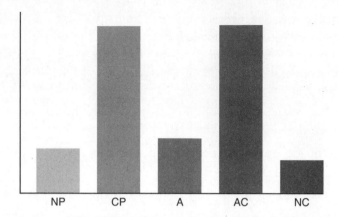

Figure 9.1　Unbalanced Mind States—the Twin Towers Anxiety Graph

illustration. Picture the Nurturing Parent, Adult, and Natural Child mind states growing. Imagine the CP and AC towers retreating as the other mind states grow.

Now, review the Balanced Mind States graph (repeated here in Figure 9.2).

Focus on this graph for a moment. Really take it in. Move left to right, attaching to each mind state on its own and in relation to the others. Associate it with balance and power. Raising NP, AC, and NC will naturally result in lowering the twin towers, so there is no need to attempt to lower CP and AC. They will retreat as your other mind states advance.

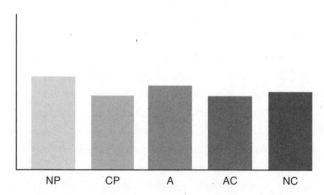

Figure 9.2　Balanced Mind States

Get Back on the Horse

The graph of success shows ups and downs. But the trend line is up, up, up. You have all the tools you need to follow that trend. Will the graph still look jagged? Of course. We all have our better and worse moments, the times when, for whatever reason, we revert to our default. But this program is not about your default. It is about identifying tools, becoming skilled at using them, and taking your toolbox with you wherever you go. I see Amy as a success in this regard. She still responds to stressors with anxiety, detachment, and avoidance. Those things are her default. But she now routinely opens her toolbox and selects the right instrument for converting her adrenaline into energy, for attaching to the facts of the matter, and for confronting rather than avoiding. If she falls off the horse, she gets right back on. Here is Amy's description of what she does:

Anxiety shows up. The first thing I do is the Awareness Exercise. What is the temperature of my hands? What are my thoughts and feelings? I attach to those feelings and let myself feel them rather than pushing them down. I then let my mind states "speak" to the issue that is upsetting me, and I extract an empowering message from each. Once I achieve balance, I "tune in" again with the Awareness Exercise. The entire process I've described to you takes me maybe five minutes max.

Managing my integrity as a health practice requires that I use mind states balance to first, see where I fell off the integrity wagon, and next, restore my integrity by being in communication, and recommitting to meet the deadline, complete the task, or learn the skill I was lacking.

Your Mind States Toolbox

The strategies in this book exist in service to mind states balance. If you have worked this program to the letter—practicing and perfecting each technique right down to the number of seconds I specify—you should be seeing a difference in your anxiety level at work. Your mind states should be balancing; if they start to shift, you now know how to recognize that shift and what to do to adjust the dynamic. Keep using these strategies—your skill will continue to increase over the years. I plan to count you among the thousands of success stories this program has produced. Please take my confidence in you as a compliment, and pause to access your Nurturing Parent, Adult, and Natural Child mind states as you reflect on the techniques you have learned, among them:

Hand Temperature Awareness Exercise, page 14

Five-Step Adrenaline Control Technique, page 26

Diaphragmatic Breathing, page 27

Tuning In: Feelings List, page 29

Heaviness Exercise, page 107

Problem-Solving Technique, page 108

Imagery Exercise, page 123

The Five-Minute Integrated Biofeedback Exercise, page 133

The Stress Reinterpretation Exercise, page 156

The Quieting Response Exercise, page 159

The Embarrassment Challenge Exercise, page 168

Daily Attachment Exercise, page 178

Nurturing Attachment Exercise, page 179

Embarrassment-Logic Exercise, page 184

You Didn't Ignore It

Most of my clients begin therapy with me by asserting that if they ignore their anxiety problem, it will disappear. Taylor, age 35, was his firm's top investment professional. He made a very good living. But he suffered anxiety in anticipation of meeting with potential clients. His anxiety caused him to stammer, which lasted into a meeting's first 10 minutes before he could get it under control. This went on for years, yet Taylor checked 5 = "strongly agree" with the statement "If I ignore my anxiety, it will go away," on my treatment history form. Sadly this belief, which derives from the excessive Critical Parent mind state, makes the problem worse.

Of course, the learning curve for resolution of social and performance anxiety is different from person to person. When new clients ask "How long will this take?" my answer is, "How fast can you run?" Meaning how fast can you learn? The primary variables include severity and length of the problem, the level of motivation, ability to integrate new concepts, expressive ability, and readiness to face fear. And practice—as often as possible.

How thoroughly did you work this program? Have you invested in mind state balancing? How has this work affected your F.A.T.E.?

Feelings:

_____

_____

Actions:

_____

_____

Thoughts:

_____

_____

Emotions:

_____

_____

What is the primary positive difference you are seeing in yourself?

_____

_____

_____

What will you do to maintain and develop this difference?

_____

_____

_____

Resolving workplace anxiety requires resolving excessive shame, embarrassment, and humiliation. To do so, you must identify and attach to those emotions rather than ignoring or suppressing them. You have been using the Feelings List on page 29 in Chapter 1 to identify your emotions. Naming them brings them to the forefront, where you can attach to them and confront them head on. When emotions are out of control, anxiety wins. As for a "resolution"—I do not use this word easily. "Resolution" requires you to maintain mind states balance. People who operate with a High Performance Mind are constantly balancing their mind states for optimal productivity and well-being. They are in control of their emotions and their actions. They are in control of their F.A.T.E. They have made mind states balance a way of life.

Embrace your emotions. They are real and important and crucial to your self-expression. Unless you have the skills to move forward *despite* the emotions you are feeling, your nervousness at work will continue. What is courage? Action in the face of fear. Here's a metaphor: Amy once saw a little Chihuahua out in his front yard barking furiously at a huge Rottweiler across the street. He was acting as fierce as possible, snarling and barking through the fence boards. Amy peered over and saw that he was peeing down his back legs the whole time—no doubt from the heightened anxiety and fear of confronting the big dog. Action in the face of fear.

Competitive Advantage

The need for increased productivity and performance within an increasingly technological and competitive world is going to continually increase. Do you define success as happiness? You should. A recent study found that "Therapy is 32 times more cost-effective at increasing happiness than money." Believe me, I have worked with countless wealthy individuals who have been tormented by anxiety.

"Governments pursue economic growth in the belief that it will raise the well being of its citizens," states the report entitled "Money or Mental Health: The Cost of Alleviating Psychological Distress with Monetary Compensation versus Psychological Therapy." However, the research suggests that more money only leads to tiny increases in happiness and is an inefficient way to increase the happiness of a population. The research suggests that if policy makers were concerned about improving well-being they would be better off increasing the access and availability of mental health care as opposed to increasing economic growth.

Thousands of patients have told me how hard it was for them to find productive, effective help for workplace anxiety. Psychiatrists see avoidant personalities as indelible, and they scarcely know how to address selective mutism. This is the state of traditional therapy today and it personifies anxiety treatment in general. You are lucky and skilled because you have worked through this book. You have learned what is necessary to resolve your nervousness at work so that you can develop the confidence to succeed. Amy describes her own newfound freedom as follows:

For me, the difference between my life before working this program and after is not perfection—that is not possible. Ultimately, the difference is attachment: to my fears, my disappointments, my limitations, my strengths, my weaknesses, my anxiety symptoms, my adrenaline, and ultimately, myself. Being nervous at work is not "just the way I am." It is not out of my control. But I must attach to it.

A High Performance Mind is a mind in balance. A mind in balance knows that we all have stress and always will—that we need it.

I use the hand-warming technique daily. I keep Jonathan's Biocard on my desk, and I check it often. I also do the Breathing Exercise whenever I happen to check the clock. It takes only seconds, and it has changed my physical comfort more than pain relievers had. I use the imagery exercise before any meeting I dread. I used the Problem-Solving Technique just a few days ago when I lost track of exactly where we were in the book revision process.

Triumph over anxiety is a major accomplishment—for me, and for you. The cage door is open. You are ready to fly. You can now be all that you are, all you know yourself to be. Will there be setbacks? Yes. Will you feel that familiar flow of adrenaline and sometimes react with fear? Probably. But now, you know what to do about it. Use these strategies every day. Notice or generate situations in which to practice. Make a note of your results. When you find yourself reverting to your "old ways," determine what stopped you from using your new toolkit. Walk yourself through a mind states assessment. I actually count it out on five fingers, thumb to pinkie—Nurturing Parent, Critical Parent, Adult, Adapted Child, and Natural Child—to be sure I take each "voice" into consideration.

What are you hearing from your internal critical script? What should you replace it with? Go through each mind state again and correct—dialing Nurturing Parent, Adult, and Natural Child up; Critical Parent and Adapted Child will then start to recede. All mind states are essential. Do not attempt to shut one down completely or turn another one all the way up. Return once again to the Unbalanced Mind States graph, Figure 9.1. Imprint the image in your memory. If possible, animate it in your mind's eye: Picture it shifting from imbalanced to balanced: NP, A, and NC grow as CP and AC shrink somewhat. The Balanced Mind States graph, Figure 9.2, is the result.

With balanced mind states, you can operate with a High Performance Mind. And with a High Performance Mind, anything is possible. You can pursue your destiny, which by rights includes contentment, fulfillment, well-being, and full self-expression. Accept that you have the tools to abandon your fear of nervousness and get on to other things. Conquering anxiety is not the same as eliminating it. We all need our anxiety. As famed life coach Tony Robbins says, "Frustration is good. It gets you to the next level." If you stay stuck, if you detach from the feeling of paralysis, you will never progress. This is why you have been training yourself to convert your adrenaline to energy. It is okay to have anxiety. It is not okay to let the anxiety control you. You don't need to avoid. You are free now. Free to be yourself.

> *Our deepest fear is not that we are inadequate. Our deepest fear is that we are powerful beyond measure. It is our light, not our darkness, that most frightens us. We ask ourselves, Who am I to be brilliant, gorgeous, talented, fabulous? Actually, who are you not to be? Your playing small does not serve the world. There is nothing enlightened about shrinking so that other people won't feel insecure around you. We are all meant to shine, as children do. And as we let our own light shine, we unconsciously give other people permission to do the same. As we are liberated from our own fear, our presence automatically liberates others.*
> —Marianne Williamson, A Return to Love

You want a High Performance Mind? Invest in the belief that anxiety is excitement in need of an attitude adjustment.

What is the temperature of your hands?

BIBLIOGRAPHY

Chapter 1   The Real Story of Anxiety at Work

Arden, Paul, *Whatever You Think, Think the Opposite*. New York: Portfolio/ Penguin Group, 2006. "Famous People With Social Anxiety Disorder." About.com (http://socialanxietydisorder.about.com/od/celebrities withsad/Famous_People_With_Social_Anxiety_Disorder.htm [accessed March 12, 2010]).

King, Peter, "Tip: Job Loss Worries Can Be Bad for Your Health," *New York Newsday*, February 20, 2010.

Rehm, Diane. *Finding My Voice*. New York: Alfred A. Knopf, 1999.

Strobel, Charles. *Quieting Response Training*. Manchester, UK: BMA Publications, 1978.

Weeks, Linton. "Diane Rehm Finds a Voice of Her Own." *Washington Post*, August 23, 1999.

Chapter 2   Diagnose Yourself and Create Your Map for Change

Berent, Jonathan, with Amy Lemley, Beyond Shyness: *How to Conquer Social Anxieties* (New York: Simon & Schuster, 1992).

Cappacio, John T. "Loneliness Can Kill You." *Forbes*, August 24, 2009.

Dockery, Alfred Michael. "Happiness, Life Satisfaction, and the Role of Work: Evidence from Two Australian Surveys." Working Paper, Curtin Business School, Perth, Australia, 2003.

Geranios, Nicholas. "Internet Addiction Center Opens in U.S." Associated Press, September 4, 2009.

McKay, Matthew, and Patrick Fanning. *Self-Esteem: A Proven Program of Cognitive Techniques for Assessing, Improving, and Maintaining Your Self-Esteem*. Oakland, CA: New Harbinger Publications, 2000.

Chapter 4 Balancing Your Mind States for a High Performance Mind

Berk, Lee S., "The Laughter-Immune Connection: New Discoveries." *Humor and Health Journal* 5, no. 5, September/October 1996.

Chapter 5 The Positive Power of Stress: Make It Work for You

Crowley, Katherine, and Kathi Elster. *Working for You Isn't Working for Me.* New York: Penguin Group, 2009.

Friedman, Meyer, and R. H. Rosenman, *Type A Behavior.* New York: Alfred A. Knopf, 1974.

Holmes, Thomas H., and Richard H. Rahe. "Social Readjustment Rating Scale." *Journal of Psychosomatic Research* 11 (August 1967): 213–18.

Sills, Judith. "It's Scary at the Office." *Newsday*, December 18, 2009.

Tanner, David. *Total Creativity in Business and Industry.* Self-published, 1998.

Chapter 6 Going Deeper

Rauch, Estelle. "The Psychology of Uncertainty: The Job Search." *Newsletter of the New York Society for Clinical and Social Work—Nassau Chapter.* December 2009.

Sarnow, John E. *Healing Back Pain: The Mind-Body Connection.* New York: Warner Books, 1991.

Shapiro, T. Rees. "Psychotherapist Jerilyn Ross Dies at Age 63." *Washington Post*, January 8, 2010.

Chapter 7 The Healthy Brain: "The Hardware of the Soul"

Amen, Daniel. *Healing the Hardware of the Soul: How Making the Brain Connection Can Optimize Your Life, Love, and Spiritual Growth.* New York: Free Press, 2002.

Colbin, Annemarie. *Food and Healing: How What You Eat Determines Your Health, Your Well-Being, and the Quality of Your Life.* New York: Ballantine Books, 1986.

Greenfield, Susan. *The Human Brain: A Guided Tour*. New York: Basic Books, 1997.

Reynolds, Gretchen. "Phys Ed: Why Exercise Makes You Less Anxious." *New York Times*, November 18, 2009.

Diagnostic and Statistical Manual of Mental Disorders, Fourth Edition, Text Revision (DSM-IV-TR). Washington, DC: American Psychiatric Association, 2000.

Chapter 8   Speak Up: How to Control Your Public Speaking Anxiety

Koegel, Timothy J. *The Exceptional Presenter: A Proven Formula to Open Up and Own the Room*. Austin, TX: Greenleaf Book Group, 2007.

Chapter 9   You Don't Need Nerves of Steel: You Just Need an Attitude Adjustment

Boyce, C., et al., "Money or Mental Health: The Cost of Alleviating Psychological Distress with Monetary Compensation versus Psychological Therapy." *Health Economics Policy and Law*, 2009, 1 DOI: 10.1017S1744133109990326.

Williamson, Marianne. *A Return to Love: Reflections on the Principles of "A Course in Miracles."* New York: HarperCollins, 1992.

INDEX